Family Reunion Handbook

A Complete Guide for Reunion Planners

Second Edition
Completely Revised

Thomas Ninkovich

REUNION RESEARCH • SAN FRANCISCO • CALIFORNIA

98 99 00 01 02 03 04 06 : 9 8 7 6 5 4 3 2 1

Published by:

Reunion Research
3145 Geary Blvd. #14
San Francisco, CA 94118

Distributed by:

Betterway Books, an imprint of F&W Publications
1507 Dana Ave.
Cincinnati, OH 45207

Printed in Canada

Library of Congress Cataloging-in-Publication Data:

Ninkovich, Thomas.

Family reunion handbook : a complete guide for reunion planners/ Thomas Ninkovich. — 2nd ed., Completely rev.

p. cm.

Rev. ed. of: Family reunion handbook / Barbara E. Brown. 1st ed. c1992.

Includes bibliographical references and index.
ISBN 0-9610470-6-2

1. Family reunions—United States—Planning. 2. Family reunions —Canada—Planning. I. Brown, Barbara E., Family reunion handbook. II. Title.

GT2423.N56   1998   98-8245
                                                      CIP

IN MEMORY OF

Alex Haley

who showed us why.

"…of all the nostalgias that haunt the human heart, the greatest of them all is an everlasting longing to bring what is youngest home to what is oldest."

—*Laurens van der Post*

"…the effect of order within the family is to create an influence that brings order into the world."

—*I Ching*

Contents

OLD ECHOES from a FAMILY REUNION

Around the festive board, old faces missed
Replace themselves with new ones: likeness-kissed—
The sweetness of a certain curve of cheek;
The tone of voice when one is heard to speak;
The grave regard of granite-colored eyes
Repeat the portraits on the wall; surprise
The senses with a spurt of memory
That answers every questing enquiry,
As potent as the scent of a pressed rose!
How does a child reflect an aunt's repose,
Who never knew her mentor, long at rest,
But read her yellowed diary, frightened lest
The pages crumble in her smooth young hand?
A boy who knew not his ancestral land
Still bears the stamp of mountains and fjords;
The music's in his bones—the primal chords.
All that we have become, we owe the old
Who went before—their warmth would pierce the cold
Of this year's end and grey December day,
Where past has more than present words to say.

—Jane Carpenter

Foreword

No other institution in our society has more influence on the lives of all its members than the family. As the provider of nurture and socialization, it is the basis of individual well-being. It remains the unique source of identity, and emotional satisfactions that meet basic human needs.

As society changes, the ways in which we relate and convey the family functions also change. The family reunion can be a vehicle for carrying out the extended family functions that many of us experienced when families lived closer together and in the same neighborhoods. Family reunions offer a potential structure for enhancing and maintaining the vitality and viability of the extended family concept.

Reunions have several benefits. Through the activities that are planned, reunions transmit values, foster greater communication between family members, provide a great deal of education, and recognize the talents and role models within the family. A most important factor is the confirmation of identity and sense of belonging that occurs. Families grow and develop as the extended family members play out traditional roles which have been diminished in a mobile society.

Families may not usually gather with these benefits in mind. But a well planned reunion inadvertently makes them happen. Thus the family reunion is to be encouraged and can help us strengthen our extended family.

—Ione Dugger Vargus, Ph.D.
   Professor Emeritus and
   Chair, Family Reunion Institute,
   Temple University, Philadelphia, PA.

Introduction to the First Edition

More and more people are finding family reunions assuming an important role in their lives. As well as being joyous events, reunions can be rewarding in ways that modern day society seems to have lost.

For untold years, everything available to a person was to be found within a few miles and among a few people. We still long for this simple and effective type of social structure. It's no accident that family reunions awaken strong feelings of need and potential fulfillment. They provide a means of harkening back to times gone by, when aunts and uncles and grandparents were part of the fabric of everyday life, dispensing lore and psychology as required. This kind of contact is still needed, but the ways of providing it have slowly disappeared. The extended family is gone. The nuclear family is less common; a child is lucky to have two parents these days. Aunts, uncles, and grandparents are visited infrequently, if at all. The family reunion is a way of recapturing some of the warmth and nurturing of older times.

Family reunions can also provide an historical "anchor," a sense of historical continuance, especially when several generations—ranging from great-grandparents to little babies—are present. In essence, a family reunion can make one feel less alone in a society seemingly characterized by a lack of familial cohesiveness. Ronald Eddy Austin singled this out as one of the rewards of his reunion: "(It) gives you a sense of your place in history…a sense of belonging to a larger extended family, which in turn, is part of the world family." Elizabeth Jones echoed this feeling when describing her family's reunion: "(It) made me think about where we all come from and where we are going."

We encourage you to begin—to start planning your family reunion. The rewards are great. You'll know just how great when that long-lost favorite cousin walks through the door or when your kids ask expectantly when the next reunion is going to be.

—Tom Ninkovich
Miramonte, California, 1992

Introduction to the Second Edition

I've researched reunions for many years now because I'm trying to figure out *why* they are so powerful. As I talk to more and more reunion planners, the answer has slowly changed for me over the years. With this second edition of this book, published 6 years after the first, I submit this revised introduction:

We all have a story—the personal story of our lives—which, of course, is intricately intertwined with our family story. Most of this story is imbedded somewhere in the misty past where truths and untruths and dreams mingle. Some of us try to find out as much as possible about this story, others try just as hard to not learn more than they already know, others try to alter it to fit their needs. Some will tell their story at the drop of a hat, others are very secretive about it. But one thing's for sure: our story is always changing. If we try at all, we can always find out new things about our past.

And with every new thing we find, we become a slightly different person—hopefully for the better. And therein lies the secret and the power of the past, and of reunions. Each new segment of our story, as we carefully pick it up, wipe it on our sleeves, and put it in place, can help us better understand ourselves, where we've been and where we're headed. Such knowledge can only lead to a better society and a better understanding of the world we live in.

I submit that our story is the most valuable thing we own. One thing for sure: it will far outlive us. One of the strongest needs a person has is to tell this story, especially as one gets older. But before a story can be told it must first be learned. After all, we can't know our story until we know where we came from. To know where we came from we must talk with, or at least "rub elbows" with, those who came before. We must learn their story to more fully understand our own.

And of course, this story exudes from all of us at all moments, whether we wish it to or not. In fact, most people don't actually "tell" their story, they show it. But both the "told" story and the "observed" one are important. One polishes the other and a combination of the two is a closer rendering of the truth.

A reunion is like a small showcase of your family story. It's all laid out there in front of you for you to read and interpret and contribute to as you wish. Reunions are rare opportunities. I encourage each of you to pay close attention when planning one and when attending one. Future generations will be very grateful.

—Tom Ninkovich
    Auberry, California, 1998

Chapter   1

Early Decisions
First Things First

Chapter Highlights
▸*Types of Reunions.* ▸*When to Circle the Calendar.*
▸*How Often?* ▸*How Long?* ▸*Reunion Size.* ▸*Where?*
▸*Site-Choosing Check List.* ▸*Banquet Room Check List.*
▸*Negotiating/Contracts.*

Types of Reunions

Reunions, like family members, come in all shapes and sizes. The first task of those planning a reunion is to decide what kind to have. It can be a huge, joyous gathering or a small, low-key event. It can last for several hours or several days. It can be held on the same weekend every year or once every five years. It can be in Grandma's back yard, at a dude ranch, or in a hotel. Some reunions return to the same spot each time. Others move around.

You can start with a small, simple reunion and work up to a big, expensive one in future years. Or, more realistically, a big, expensive reunion can be a once-in-a-lifetime event that could be announced years in advance so that everyone has time to plan and save.

One of the points this book emphasizes is that different types of reunions add variety and create interest. This is especially helpful if your annual reunion has reached the "boring" stage, as some occasionally do. Fortunately, boring reunions can be changed to interesting ones without throwing money at them, as we shall see. But no matter what kind of reunion you choose to have, the focus is on bringing the family together to celebrate its roots and for people to get to know each other better.

Your first consideration is the family members themselves—their ages, agility, disabilities, where they live, their financial resources, and who is to be included. If everyone is to be included from young to very old, disabled, rich and poor, out-of-towners and locals—then the most popular type of reunion is a picnic or barbecue in a city or state park. That's because such a reunion tends to be the cheapest and easiest to plan. However, other options are possible that don't involve too much more expenditure of time and money—and offer variety and interest as well.

If you would like something other than the usual picnic or barbecue, consider your family's background and interests. Ask yourself, what is unique about your family? Do family members have interests in common? If they do, plan your reunion to include one or more of these interests. For example, if your family likes outdoor activity, plan a reunion at a guest ranch or have a camping/RV reunion. Or plan a reunion around the most popular family sport; it may be on the water, the ski slopes, or the baseball diamond.

If the family interests are more intellectual, a reunion near a Shakespeare festival, a group of art galleries, the Smithsonian or at an archaeological dig could be a great experience. Another family might want a catered event in a fancy resort with evening entertainment. If the family is interested in exploring its roots, it could meet near the old family homestead, tour the hometown area, travel to the family homeland, do genealogical research, or restore the family cemetery or the old family home. Another family might be ecology-minded and want a reunion focused on helping the environment in some way, such as building or restoring a trail, helping students catalog insects, or studying glaciers.

We found many families around the country creating reunions based on shared interests. The Hudson Family patterned their reunion after a country fair. This creative family displayed its crafts, art, and collections, including the work of the children. They held classes during the event to stimulate interest in each individual craft or art. Relatives demonstrated, among other crafts, rattlesnake skin tanning and wood-root clock making. These classes created an appreciation for the talents of family members and passed on skills that might have been lost. Food booths and games added fun, challenge, and excitement to the festive fair atmosphere.

Another family visited the community where the great-grandparents were buried, took pictures in the cemetery, and looked up family obituaries on microfilm in the local library to add to the family genealogical information.

Since the widely-scattered Eymann family grew up with camping in their blood, it seemed only natural for them to gather for a campout reunion. The first one was held on a cattle ranch in the Sierra foothills of California. The family arranged their tents and RVs around a central campfire, covered-wagon style. Ranging in age from three to 80, the Eymann's hiked, panned for gold, and exchanged news as they cooked family favorites on their camp stoves. The most treasured times were spent around evening campfires where everyone sang favorite songs and listened to both true and "tall" tales of the family's past.

As mentioned before, many families have a picnic reunion

in a nearby park. This type of reunion, too, can be made interesting and fun by planning special events. The Kuhlmann Family met one year in Faust County Park, Missouri. Their picnic was catered by friends, leaving family members free to enjoy each other's company. The young people played ball, some older folks played cards, but most enjoyed just visiting and getting acquainted.

Other possibilities:

➤ join a tour (historical, sight-seeing, religious)
➤ stay at a guest ranch
➤ lose weight at a spa
➤ go on a cattle drive, pan for gold, join a wagon train
➤ experience the wilderness by rafting down a river, backpacking, or camping out
➤ live in a Native American village
➤ rent a houseboat on a lake
➤ watch whales
➤ take a riverboat cruise
➤ go on a bicycle trip
➤ enroll in a summer class at an Elderhostel or at the Smithsonian
➤ visit a national, state, or historical park
➤ bareboat in the Caribbean or in the San Juan Islands
➤ take a cruise to Alaska, Mexico, Hawaii, or up the St. Lawrence River
➤ go windjamming
➤ join an archaeological dig
➤ gather at a church retreat
➤ attend a YMCA family camp
➤ take a train ride, coast-to-coast
➤ attend the Olympics or World's Fair
➤ meet at Ellis Island, Salt Lake City, or other genealogy mecca
➡ For more ideas, see Chapter 13 and "Real Reunions."

When to Circle the Calendar

Certain decisions about the reunion must be made at least 8 months to a year ahead—in some cases, as much as 2 years ahead. *The most important decision is to set the date* so that family members can put it on their calendars before planning vacations. The year-end holidays can be a good time to communicate about a reunion planned for the following summer. Sending an announcement in your annual holiday cards can save on a separate mailer. However, this means the committee must meet before then to determine the date, location, and type of reunion. Elaborate plans such as renting a popular resort may require two or three years of advance planning time. Even some small, local facilities may need to be reserved a year in advance. Start early!

Most family reunions are held between June and September because the weather is better, travel is easier, school is out, and summer is the traditional time for vacations. However, some organizers are starting to take advantage of the "value" or "off" seasons in different parts of the country, which include April-May and October-November. These are the times of low tourism when accommodations and airline rates tend to be lower. A little-known fact is that, in many areas, Memorial Day, the Fourth of July, and Labor Day are also "off" seasons. Accommodations that are normally full with business trade can be relatively empty during the holidays. Holiday weekends in these areas are perfect for multi-day reunions. Good examples are Chicago, Washington DC, and New York City.

Except in ski areas, the most extensive "off" season of all takes place between December and February. However, weather and travel conditions (especially for driving) can be discouraging. For much of this time, school is still in session, and areas with good weather, like Miami and Phoenix, are having booming business and rates are actually at their highest.

Thanksgiving or year-end holidays can be a good time for some small family reunions close to home. However, this rarely works for large groups because most people are focusing on their own nuclear family at this time of year rather than on their large extended family.

A reunion date can also be chosen because of a family milestone or special day, such as:

➤ a silver or golden wedding anniversary
➤ a grandparent's or elder's birthday
➤ an ancestor's birthday or date of immigration
➤ a christening or baptism
➤ a wedding or graduation
➤ the anniversary of the date the ancestors opened their first business or bought their first farm
➤ a retirement party
➤ a special ethnic or religious holiday

Many families set a particular reunion date they can count on from year to year, such as the "second Saturday in August." The reunion may not be held every year, but when it *is* held everyone knows when it will be.

By the way, it's important to set a date for your reunion and stick to it. There will always be conflicts for someone, but changing the date will only create conflicts for others. If there are certain family members who must be included, contact them before setting the date.

How Often Should Reunions Occur?

A successful first-time family reunion is actually very easy to pull off. You don't have to concern yourself with nonstop activities and programs because just being together will inspire activity and communication. All you need is a comfortable place where people can talk and children can play. These first-time reunions often turn out so well that family members ask for reunions every year. The first two or three are fine, but then interest and attendance dwindles and the reunion "blahs" begin.

The most often-heard complaint from experienced reunion planners is that annual reunions quickly become boring; the original "spark" is no longer there. There are two ways to deal with this: One is to put some years between your reunions, so that the old "yearning" comes back. The other is to show folks a really good time, especially the kids. Of course, a combination of the two is even better.

Annual reunions require the effort of a "primary mover" with lots of enthusiasm. If you lack this enthusiasm year after year, you should seriously consider putting 3 to 5 years between your reunions. It will do wonders for the "reunion morale" of your group, and you may find your own interest returning as well.

How Long Should They Last?

Family reunions vary in length from an afternoon to 3 or more days. A general rule is that the farther people must travel, the longer the reunion should last. An afternoon may not be long enough to justify the time and expense of a long trip.

The average length of a small reunion is one very full day. Larger reunions last two and three days. Four days may be a bit too long. You don't want it too short, but too long is worse. Your next reunion will benefit if you "leave them wanting more."

Reunion Size

If you've not had reunions before, one of the tricky aspects is estimating how many will attend. This number affects the size of the facility you will need and the cost per person. An early survey could be mailed out stating the projected date, list of possible sites, possible costs, and requesting a response by a certain date. The response should indicate who and how many hope to attend. With this information, the committee can rent a facility and determine actual costs per person.

Another consideration is how many family members to invite. If your family is small, there's no problem—invite them all. If it's large with many branches, the question is where to draw the line. Every family is different and only you can decide. However, if in doubt, start small and expand later. A reunion for 20 people is a lot different than a reunion for 200. Most people will tell you that the small "first time" reunions are the best anyway.

Then if your group has the interest and resources for a larger reunion next time, go for it. But always choose a group size that you feel comfortable managing. Having too many people to coordinate may greatly diminish your interest in organizing the next reunion. And remember, it's difficult to reduce the size of your reunion by leaving out family branches that have been previously included.

Some years you could hold mini-reunions. For example, one year all the younger cousins could hire a pack station to take them into the Rockies for a week of fly fishing and hiking. Another year the older generation might travel to visit the family homeland. Yet another year the whole clan may get together and share the adventures from these mini-reunions, showing slides and videos, and sharing stories. Such a reunion could be held near those who, because of age or disability, couldn't participate in the more active reunions. In this way, the elderly or disabled can share vicariously in the adventures of their clan. Everyone is included and family ties are strengthened.

Where, Oh Where?

Site selection is one of the most important early decisions because it's going to affect other decisions. Budgetwise, you won't even know what to charge until you settle on a site. And you certainly can't send out invitations until you know where the reunion is going to be.

Many separate factors are involved in choosing a site, such as the time of year, the length of the reunion, and how easy it is to get there. But the most important factor of all is the *type* of reunion which, in turn, should be based on the interests of your group, as mentioned before. If it's a rafting trip, you need to pick the river. If it's a picnic in the park, the best location may be determined by its proximity to the greatest number of family members. If it's a cruise, you must pick the destination.

Some groups opt for the convenience of a full-service hotel located near a large metropolitan airport. The sales manager will gladly explain the attractions and conveniences of the particular hotel and area. Most hotels offer special group rates, and many can take care of some of the details for you, such as kid's programs, signs, photography, music, decorations, tours, etc.

You could rent meeting and banquet rooms that are located near, but completely separate from, your accommodations. For example, you could book a motel, then use a nearby community center or park for meals and program, and hire a caterer to serve the meals. This arrangement can certainly save money on sleeping rooms (motels with meeting facilities tend to be more expensive), and possibly on the meeting/banquet rooms, too. Do your homework; make some comparisons.

Of course, many large restaurants have banquet rooms. And, depending on your group's size, this may be ideal if the restaurant is near good accommodations and there is space nearby (especially outdoors) for the kids to play. This can also work well if your group has few children.

Some colleges and private schools rent out dormitory rooms in the summer, and allow access to their cafeteria and sports facilities. Dude ranches and resorts often have group plans. State, county and city parks are perhaps the most popular places of all. And county fair grounds are becoming popular, too. ➡See Chapter 13, "Real Reunions," and "Resources" for more ideas.

Of course, a reunion is easier to plan if it's near your home. However, don't let this fact prevent you from eventually ranging farther afield. There are many interesting opportunities awaiting your family out there. Remember, when you *do* choose a distant location, having a family member or "helper" who lives somewhere near the chosen site is always a great advantage.

Some families enjoy taking their turn hosting a reunion in their hometown or state. This can add interest to the reunion and everyone learns more about the host family and host area. However, if the host family lives "off the beaten track" or at a great distance from the rest of the family, such an arrangement could be expensive for those who must travel. But an "out of the way" reunion could be held occasionally.

To attain the best attendance at a first-time reunion, it's important to pick a location that is centrally located to those invited. Still, you probably won't be able to please everyone. Family members might pitch-in to help finance the trip for older family members on fixed incomes or others who could not afford the trip otherwise.

If you would like to host a reunion but feel that your hometown isn't very interesting, check with your Chamber of Commerce to see what they list as attractions in your area; locals are often unaware of this information. Touring a local gallery, park, or factory, though familiar to you, might be great fun for others.

Your Site-Choosing Check List

Photocopy this list to use as a guide when picking a site. You can add other items that pertain to your individual situation. If you have a particular interest in children's activities, also see the site selection list in Chapter 8.

➤ Facilities in suburban or rural areas surrounding a large city are usually cheaper than those located in downtown areas. Get a map of the area and write or call the Chambers of Commerce in some of the smaller outlying towns to find out what accommodations and facilities are available.

➤ Find out if convenient, inexpensive transportation exists between the airport or train station and where people will be staying. Is there access to public transportation? Is there a commercial shuttle service?

➤ Ask each facility manager you contact for the names and phone numbers of other family reunions or similar events that have recently used the facility. Call these people for their opinions and suggestions; while you're at it, get referrals from them for suppliers you may need, such as photographers, musicians, florists, etc.

➤ If a member of your group lives in the area, have her check each potential facility in person. Provide her with this list.

➤ Find out when the facility's "off" season occurs (the time when rates are lowest).

➤ Ask if a deposit is required. When it is due? The refunding policy. Does the deposit cover "cancellation" only or does it also include "breakage and damage"?

➤ Always ask what "freebies" are available. Every facility has its own rules in this regard. The most common "freebie" at a hotel is a free sleeping room for so many paid rooms (the usual ratios are 1–40 or 1–50).

➤ Watch for extra costs. A general meeting room, doughnuts and coffee, audio-visual equipment, extra tables and chairs, etc., can range from being free to costing much more than they are worth. Discuss every detail with the manager. With a little persuasion, some of the above items may be tossed in free.

➤ Are tables and chairs available for registration? Tables and bulletin boards for memorabilia? Are there moveable chalk boards or placards for announcements and signs? Is there a charge for these?

➤ What is the "smoking/nonsmoking" policy? Are "no
smoking" sleeping rooms available?
➤ If needed, is there wheelchair access?
➤ Are there nearby RV and camper accommodations?
➤ Is there ample parking? Is it free? Is there a public lot
nearby? Handicapped parking?
➤ Always have the facility prepare a contract with all details
covered. Then you can be assured that you both agree.
➤ Ask the facility for a map of the surrounding area, including the airport and train station, and written driving
directions to the site (for your mailers).

Your Banquet Room Check List

If you intend to rent a banquet room, here are some specific
things to watch for:

➤ How many people can the room accommodate? Are there
different rooms to choose from? Ask for a floor plan of
the room showing how they intend to set it up (tables,
chairs, etc.).
➤ What are the "hours of access" to the room? When is
closing time?
➤ What is the timetable for guaranteeing the "meal count"
(usually 48 hours before the event for the minimum
count, 24 hours for the final count)? What about people
who show up unannounced? What is the "overset" (percentage over the final meal count that can be served—
usually 5%)?
➤ Can the room be decorated? What time can you start?
What are the limitations? Can you use masking tape or
thumb tacks? Who removes the decorations?
➤ Can you attend a function to see the facility "in action"?
Can you sample the food? (Offer to be discreet when
you observe and offer to pay for the food.)
➤ Can you bring your own wine for a toast? Are wine glasses
available? (Don't forget a corkscrew and ice bucket.)

➤ Is there a public address system? Who sets it up? Is there a stage? A lectern or podium? What is the cost?

➤ Is there a slide or movie projector and screen? Extra bulbs? Extension cords? Table for projector? VCR and monitor? Duct tape to secure extension cords to the floor?

Call or write the Convention and Visitors Bureau or Chamber of Commerce in any given area for a list of facilities and other services. It's handy to have a telephone book of your chosen city. Get both white and yellow pages, if they are separated (as with most large cities). Ask a hotel or the Convention Bureau if they can send these to you. Otherwise, ➠see "Resources" for a source of any phone book in the country. For those with computers, CD-ROMs of all white and yellow pages in the country are available. Or search them for free at the library.

Negotiating and Contracts

Most people don't even realize they can negotiate terms and rates with hotels and resorts. In fact, not doing so is equivalent to paying the sticker price for a new car. Most reunion planners, especially first-timers, *do* pay more than necessary, or fail to get some extras that could be theirs for the asking.

Negotiating. It's true that large groups have more bargaining power than small groups when it comes to negotiating. That's the nature of the game. But don't think you are too small to negotiate successfully. Negotiating will work to some extent regardless of your size.

Proper negotiating allows both parties to win and to look good. It's important to be well prepared. This involves:

➤ Identifying the needs and desires of your group.
➤ Knowing the economic value of your reunion.
➤ Understanding the hotel/resort's position.
➤ Knowing what is negotiable.
➤ Comparing rates with other facilities.

Of course, you should always negotiate a "group room rate." But you should also ask for some complimentary items. If you don't ask, they won't be offered. While you may not get something for free, you may get some things at a reduced rate. The list below will give you an idea of what may be available.

But remember, getting one or more of these items depends on how the hotel views the economic value of your business. If this is your first reunion, or if your reunion is very small, don't expect to get all or even most of these items.

Some negotiable items:

> ➤ A complimentary welcoming reception.
> ➤ One free sleeping room for every 40 or 50 sold is standard, but maybe you can do better.
> ➤ Free storage for supplies shipped in advance.
> ➤ Free recreational activities.
> ➤ Complimentary suite for your hospitality room.
> ➤ Suite for the price of a regular room.
> ➤ Meeting room.
> ➤ Audio/visual equipment.
> ➤ Free parking.
> ➤ Early check-in, late check-out.
> ➤ Use of hotel limo or bus.
> ➤ Signs for your registration area.
> ➤ Free meal or sleeping room to use as door or raffle prize.
> ➤ Flowers and table decorations.

Contracts. When finished negotiating, ask for a written contract from the sales manager. This is a very important document and, once signed, is legally binding on both parties.

A good contract or letter of agreement is a road map spelling out the responsibilities of both parties, and ensures that they will meet their obligations. It does not have to be in fancy legalese, but don't use unclear words such as "may" or "a reasonable amount." Once you sign it, return it by certified mail.

One word of caution: Most contracts are written up by the hotel and therefore benefit the hotel. Some of the small points that were verbally agreed upon during negotiations may not be included. Read it all very carefully before signing. Do not take anything for granted, and do not be pushed into signing quickly. Everything that you agreed to should be listed, no matter how small. If items must be added to the contract, spell them out very carefully and ask the hotel to do the rewriting. Small items can be written in by hand, and should be initialed and dated.

The following list is a guide for checking your contract:

➤ Accommodations: types of rooms and beds, total number of rooms reserved, check-in/check-out dates and times, complimentary rooms, extended stays/early arrivals, suites, reservation cut-off dates.
➤ Finances: deposits (how much and when?), master billing accounts (when due?), billing arrangements, authorized signatures, taxes, built-in gratuity.
➤ Transportation.
➤ Meeting space.
➤ Food and beverage (common: 50% due 30 days prior, balance due 7 days prior).
➤ Equipment, signs, services.
➤ Parking.
➤ Renovation/construction inconvenience.
➤ Change of ownership/management agreements.
➤ Termination/cancellation agreements (individual room cancellation charges, if any, should not be borne by the group; there should not be an event cancellation charge other than loss of deposit).
➤ Procedure if facility is over-booked.
➤ Extras agreed upon during negotiations.

Chapter 2

Getting Organized
Committees/Meetings

Chapter Highlights
▸*Beginnings.* ▸*Committees.* ▸*Meetings.*
▸*Tips for Committee Leaders.* ▸*Seed Money.* ▸*That Special Idea.*
▸*Areas of Responsibility.*

Beginnings

The first family reunion is usually organized by the person or family who originally has the idea. Someone starts wondering about a cousin they used to spend summers with as a kid or wishing their children knew more about their roots. So they call that cousin and discover that he or she, too, has been thinking about the rest of the clan. One of them says "Let's get together" and the first step towards a family reunion has been taken.

At least one enthusiastic person who can get things done is the key to successful reunion organization. This person usually has the time, energy, creativity, and organizational abilities to do the necessary planning and arranging. However, if this doesn't describe you, don't worry; maybe you are just the catalyst. Many reunions would not happen at all if it were not for someone getting the idea started. Show this book to others in your family; maybe your spark will take flame.

Committees

If your group stays small, one person may be all you need for leadership. However, in some families, especially if reunion interest increases, other forms of leadership may evolve in order to handle all the work.

Most reunion planning eventually becomes a team effort; in other words, committees are formed to share the work. The committee members may all be from one family branch or from different branches. Branches can take turns being in charge from year to year. Heads of sub-committees can be chosen and each head has helpers or teams of helpers who do different tasks. In fact, the more family members who can be involved, the more interest will be generated for attending the reunion.

In large families with lots of branches, teams can be organized to handle special concerns within their own families, such as dietary needs and mobility problems. Each team has a liaison on the main committee. Different family branches can be in charge of specific details, such as lodging, food, events, child-care, cleanup, etc.

Larger families and family associations often have a Reunion Committee headed by a Reunion Chairperson. These committees may also have a Site Coordinator who is chosen because she lives near the reunion site. It's this person's job to be the liaison between the Reunion Committee and the local suppliers (the people and businesses providing goods and services for the reunion). If subsequent reunions are held in different locations, then the Site Coordinator changes accordingly. In many cases, the person is picked first, and then the site is chosen near where that person lives.

Meetings

With family reunions, it can be difficult for a committee to meet, given the fact that members are likely to be scattered around the country. Your meetings may have to take place through phone calls and letters unless some of you live within driving distance of each other. (A conference call system, called "3-way calling," is available on most residential private lines with touch-tone dialing.) E-mail is also a possibility. It may help to schedule a meeting of the committee at the reunion site a day or two before the reunion begins. Formal family associations tend to schedule board and committee meetings before, during, or after their reunions, depending on their needs and preferences.

Your first meeting (by phone, letter, e-mail or in person) should cover picking a date, determining the type of reunion, and possibly choosing a location. Give each person something to research. One person or family could check into the availability and cost of facilities. Another person could survey family members to get ideas on the kind of reunion that would interest them. Someone else could see if there are certain dates to avoid, such as family weddings or graduations. Or perhaps organizing a reunion around a wedding or graduation would work best.

Tips for Committee Leaders

Suppose you are a committee chairperson; volunteers have been found, jobs and authority have been delegated, and things are getting done. At this point, your job *begins*! Once assignments have been agreed upon, you must follow up. After all, the main role of a committee leader is to see that all the little details get done. Make sure people are doing what they said they would do, and within the time-frame agreed upon. Whatever you do, don't neglect your job or expect that people will maintain a high level of enthusiasm and commitment over the many months it takes to produce a successful reunion. You must provide leadership, and that may include keeping people motivated.

In the initial flush of excitement, some people may take on more than they can handle. Some have a hard time saying no. Several weeks down the line they may find themselves with a crucial job and no time to do it. However, someone has to do it. If you are keeping track of your volunteers, catch the over-committed ones before it's too late and reassign some of their work to others.

Don't be tempted to take on their tasks yourself unless it is absolutely necessary. You want to make it to the reunion without becoming terminally stressed out. Since you can't do everything, keep everyone on track doing "their thing."

It's important that the people assigned to certain tasks understand why, when, and how their tasks are to be accomplished. Since people can forget, give each volunteer a check list of duties. Creating this list and going over it is time well spent. Understanding and accomplishment go hand in hand. (See next page for a list of the various responsibilities.)

Seed Money

(See "Collecting Money" on p. 27 for more information.)

While you are getting the ball rolling, who is paying for phone calls, photocopying, postage, envelopes, etc.? At first *you* may have to cover expenses, but eventually the costs must be shared among your family members. Start asking for donations or dues right away and keep accurate records. Make requests through your mailers or a few strategic phone calls. A good way to convince people of your trustworthiness is to send out a financial report. Also, ask the most interested people to pay their reunion fees ahead of time. By the time the reunion gets close, there should be enough seed money for mailing, phone calls, office supplies, and a deposit to hold the facility.

If, for some reason, the reunion never gets off the ground, people should still be reimbursed from these funds before returning the remainder. However, unless you clearly state otherwise from the beginning, this should be a break-even situation; no one should profit from it or charge for labor.

That Special Idea

Occasionally someone will come up with a really great idea, but can't convince others on the committee to go along with it. Committees are notoriously conservative because they must compromise; this can really take the "spark" out of an excellent idea. If someone in your group is really committed to an idea, but can't get others to see her viewpoint, perhaps that person should be allowed to do the project by herself, or with the help of a few people of her own choosing. This approach could work well if the project covers only a particular part of the reunion, such as decorations, a newsletter, or a portion of the program, and if it doesn't cost too much.

Areas of Responsibility

Here is a list of various responsibilities that can be delegated. They can be assigned to individuals or subcommittees. Some can be combined; some may not pertain to your reunion.

To do before the reunion (or year-round, if you are an ongoing group):

➤ Locating family members
➤ Registration by mail
➤ Maintaining the mailing list
➤ Budgeting/finances
➤ Bookkeeping/bank account
➤ Fund-raising

➤ Writing newsletters and mailers
➤ Mailing
➤ Handling information: answering questions, receiving
   information on missing family members, receiving
   donations, etc.
➤ Keeping historical data: scrapbooks, old movies, videos,
   mementos, family history, genealogy, oral history, etc.
➤ Conducting surveys/compiling statistics

To do at the reunion:

➤ Food/beverage: organizing meals, refreshments
➤ Music: band/DJ/tapes
➤ Program
➤ Extra events: tours, church service, memorial service,
   sports events, etc.
➤ Public address system, audio-visual equipment
➤ Decorations
➤ Photography
➤ Memory book
➤ Video
➤ Children's activities
➤ Adult activities
➤ Registration desk
➤ Name tags/badges/signs
➤ Door prizes
➤ Housing/RV arrangements
➤ Parking
➤ Selection and presentation of gifts, scholarships, or special
   awards
➤ Family store/merchandise
➤ Fund-raising
➤ Set-up/clean-up

Chapter 3

Money and Finances

Chapter Highlights

▸*Who's in Charge?* ▸*The Budget.* ▸*Raising Money.*
▸*Take-Home Gifts.* ▸*Tickets.* ▸*Bank Accounts.* ▸*Bookkeeping.*
▸*Saving Money.* ▸*Keep a Financial History.*

Who's in Charge of Finances?

If your reunion is small, perhaps you can do everything and handle the money, too. However, as your reunion gets larger, you may need help. The two basic financial areas are "money management" and "bookkeeping." If you can find a family member with both these abilities—great! If not, or if one person simply doesn't have the time to do both, then divide up these responsibilities. Since all well-managed households have such people, you shouldn't have to look too far to find them. In family associations, this structure may evolve into a Finance Committee with the treasurer as chairperson.

The Budget

Some reunion planners assume that the finances will take care of itself. However, creating a budget, collecting funds, and using these funds appropriately are important parts of a successful reunion and must be attended to.

When creating a budget, here are two important tips:

1. Be as thorough as possible. Anything you leave out or miscalculate can cause a shortfall. These oversights can come back to "haunt" you in some embarrassing ways, such as asking reunion members to kick in more money at the last minute.

2. Miscalculations can be made, especially by those with little or no experience. A "fudge" factor of about 10% will help offset such mistakes. This factor can be adjusted with experience.

Sources of income. Sources of income for your reunion will normally come from the following:

➤ Registration fees and/or dues
➤ Ticket sales for meals and tours
➤ Donations
➤ Advertising in, or subscriptions to, your family newsletter
➤ Fund-raisers
➤ Sale of merchandise, family histories, group photos, memory books, videos, etc.

Figuring expenses. When preparing a budget, figuring expenses is of great importance. Remember, though, that some expenses are paid for directly by the attendees. For example, the reunion fund should not pay for:

➤ Hotel rooms or travel (exception: honored guests)
➤ Tours or cruises (in most cases)
➤ Meals not included in the program

It's easy to overlook an item in calculating the total cost of a reunion. Below is a list of basic items you can use as a guide.

List of possible reunion expenses:

➤ reimbursing out-of-pocket costs incurred up to the time a reunion fund is created (phone calls, mailings, expense of finding people, deposits, stationery, office supplies, etc.)

➤ food and beverage

➤ discrepancies in meal counts at prepaid meals, discrepancies in tour counts, etc. (If your count is off by more than the agreed upon amount, you are responsible.)

➤ coffee/refreshment breaks, snacks

➤ wine or after dinner drinks for toasts

➤ music/entertainment

➤ photography/videography

➤ decorations (room, table, banners, flags, flowers, etc.)

➤ cost of mailers (calculated from number of mailings, how many pieces in each mailing, how much postage per piece, printing or copying costs, envelopes, rubber stamps, etc.)

➤ printing of programs, invitations, etc.

➤ signs/placards

➤ shipping (of items too large or awkward to transport any other way)

➤ awards/door prizes

➤ name tags

➤ fund-raising items (for auction or raffle)

➤ mementos (personalized take-home gifts)

➤ long-distance phone calls

➤ flowers or wreaths for memorial service

➤ taxes

➤ rentals (movie/slide projectors, camcorders, PA system, extra tables or chairs, podium, stage, bulletin board, punch bowls, coffee makers, utensils, canopy for shade, tents, playpens, sports equipment, wheelchairs, etc.)

➤ honored guest's rooms, meals, transportation

➤ public gift or scholarship fund

➤ funds for next reunion or on-going expenses
➤ cleanup

Expenses at hotels:

➤ hospitality suites
➤ meeting rooms
➤ tips
➤ local room–use tax
➤ rentals

Setting the rates. When figuring income, one of the questions to address is the relationship between adult and children's rates. Children's rates can be diverse; different ages pay different rates. In many public places, children twelve and older are charged adult fees. Sometimes children under a certain age are free. If you set different fees for different age children, make sure your adult rates are high enough to cover discrepancies in the costs. You may want to skip charging for children entirely and divide the costs among the adults. This is fair unless you have families with large numbers of children.

Be sure to find out from rental facilities if they are 1.) charging you by-the-person, and 2.) what age groups they include. If you assume, for example, they won't charge for babies, and they do charge, it could be a problem.

You could offer large families a price break to make the reunion more affordable for them. You might also consider a price break for the older members on fixed incomes. This can be facilitated by spreading the costs to other family members. All this calculating can be tricky; that's why you need someone with a good grasp of figures.

Be sensitive to the financial resources of the various families you want to include. *Do not plan an event that is so expensive that members cannot attend or will have to go into debt to do so.* This will not only encourage resentment, but will reduce the number attending. There is a place for fancy or expensive reunions, but they should occur only occasionally, and be announced far in advance so that people can plan accordingly. ⇒See the beginning of Chapter 13.

Collecting money is an issue that causes problems for many reunions. Three problems are most common: 1.) not making costs clear from the beginning, 2.) not collecting enough to cover expenses, and 3.) family members not paying their share.

The exact amount each family will be charged should be explained in your mailers six months or more before the event. This gives people time to cover their share. If done right, it will also give you working capital for your mailers and setup expenses, and deposits required by facilities and caterers. You can request half (or a percentage) be paid immediately and the rest at the reunion. Or you can ask for the total ahead of time. Set a deadline for when fees are needed and, if necessary, send out friendly reminders. It's always easier to collect before the reunion than afterward. ⇒Also see "Seed Money" on page 20.

And be sure to outline the finances in the mailer or newsletter so that people can see how you arrived at the costs. Not having organized a reunion themselves, many people are totally unrealistic about what it should cost. By explaining how you arrived at the price, family members will be more understanding and willing to pay.

Work out some type of *refunding policy* ahead of time. If a family cannot come because of a last minute emergency (for example, a child had an appendectomy the night before the reunion), you should refund some of the fee, but not the entire amount. Retain enough to cover their share of mailing costs and any other costs or deposits that will not be refunded to you if people do not show up (for example: meal costs). Be sure to make the refunding policy clear in all your mailers.

Raising Money

Making a profit. Most one-time or first-time reunion organizers are satisfied, and consider it a job well-done, if the bank balance is zero when the whole thing is over. This is an accurate assumption because it means that it was a well-managed reunion and the attendees got the most for their money.

While breaking even is a reunion's primary financial goal, some families with on-going reunions may start aiming for a little profit. However, this isn't "profit" in the ordinary sense of the word, *i.e.*, no one is taking any of this money home. It can go toward starting the next reunion, locating more people, funding recognition awards or scholarships, memorial funds and donations to service groups, printing a family history, arranging transportation for someone who could not be at the reunion otherwise, or any number of worthy causes. Also, until you get very good at reunion finances, it could serve as your "fudge" factor.

If your group is interested in making a profit, you will need to look at some aspects of the reunion differently. With a profit-making plan, many reunion components can be for sale. Tours, photos, memory books, videos, merchandise, family histories, even the banquet meals can be bought at one price and sold to family members at another. However, there can be some risk involved. For instance, if you rent a tour bus for $300, and five people sign up for the tour at $20 per person, you've lost money.

Good financial planning is absolutely essential if you want to go this route. It's also important to explain that no one individual is making a profit—only the group is making a profit.

Some reunion organizers will not consider money-making ventures or fund-raisers, feeling they involve too much time and effort for the amount of return. However, if handled properly, they can add fun and excitement to your reunion and money to your coffers, while taking only a short time to organize. There's really no reason why every reunion shouldn't stage some type of fund-raiser—unless you are allergic to extra money, a complaint we have yet to hear!

The family store. Many companies produce special mementos that can be sold at a family store: coffee mugs, steins, wine glasses, ash trays, paperweights, playing cards, pennants, T-shirts, caps, bumperstickers, coasters, decals, tote bags, embroidered patches, badges, pens and pencils, etc. T-shirts and baseball caps are especially popular with family reunions. Decide which of these items would interest your family and contact several suppliers to get the best prices.

Occasionally, a family store is the brain child of one person or family unit that uses it to reduce their own reunion costs. However, it is more often run by the committee or family association to benefit everyone. Prices range from $1 to around $20 per item, sometimes more for items such as jackets and family crest rings. Items can be sold at the reunion and by mail.

If merchandise that's offered on speculation doesn't sell, money is lost. One way to minimize losses is to not print the year or reunion location on family store items. Then they can be sold any year. Dated items are best used for planned fund-raising, awards, or gifts.

Other items to offer for sale can be Aunt Eleanor's family history, Cousin Barbara's latest book, a family cookbook, Grandma's wonderful raspberry jam, cousin Judy's dolls and quilts, snacks, or even donated clothing that your kids grew out of. (This is a nice place to sell or trade garments you would like to "keep in the family" that were knit by a special aunt or sewn just for your children by Grandma.)

Next to this area you can sell tickets for a pastry sale or cake walk with each family donating their favorite goodies. At a large reunion, children could set up their own flea market table to trade or sell clothes, books, and toys.

Planned fund-raisers. (For emergency fund-raisers, see the next section.) The secret to planned fund-raising is simple—don't gamble. A sure-fire method is to build the fund-raising cost right into the registration fee, automatically selling an item to each person who attends the reunion. There will be few complaints if the item is of high quality, reasonably priced, and you explain that part of the price of each ticket is going to a worthy cause— the reunion itself. Also, this method sells more merchandise which may put you in a lower cost-per-item category when you place your initial order (higher volume = lower cost). And it solves the problem of how many units to order. Choose items that aren't too exotic, too much of a novelty, or that appeal only to a few people. Keep in mind that the most desirable product you are selling is the reunion ticket. A few dollars added to it won't be met with much resistance. Common items for planned fund-raisers are group photos, memory books, cookbooks, and T-shirts.

A few words about artwork for your personalized or imprinted items: Unless you have a professional artist in your group, let the supplier do the designing. They deal with such requests daily and their charges are usually quite reasonable (sometimes free). You should, however, send examples, photocopies, or sketches of what you envision (if anything), as well as the basic color scheme that you would like to use.

Be sure to allow enough time for ordering and delivery. Sometimes it takes 2 or 3 weeks just to get a company's brochure, and delivery can take 8 weeks or more. To save time, request the brochure by phone and ask that it be sent immediately.

The best way to establish "quality control" on your items is to ask for samples of the things you are interested in before you place an order, even if you have to pay for them. The photo and description in the brochure may not exactly represent the product. In the interest of time, make this request by phone.

Be sure to get the name of the person you talk to regarding an order so any follow-up questions can be directed to this person. About a week after you send in your order, call again to make sure it's being processed. If you ask to see proofs of artwork and they are acceptable, phone or fax (rather than mail) your approval. Ten dollars in phone calls can save you weeks of time. Many companies have toll free numbers, even if not listed in their brochures—ask!

Emergency fund-raisers. Even with a 10% "fudge factor," you may still come up short due to unforeseen expenses or insufficient income. If there is enough time before the reunion, send an appeal in the mail. Explain exactly how much you are short and what that translates to per person or per family; often you will get back even more than you asked for.

If the time-frame is too tight to use the mail, present the problem at the reunion. But remember that reunions are famous for last minute, unannounced arrivals. If six extra people show up, at (say) $20 each, that's $120, which may make the difference. However, it's important to go to the reunion knowing *exactly* where you stand financially and be ready to conduct a fund-raiser, if necessary.

One solution is to create a donation jar with accompanying sign, showing expenses and how much you are short per person. Put the jar in an obvious place, announce its presence at a group meeting, and have someone circulate it occasionally. Kids often enjoy this responsibility.

The Duncan family had this problem and solved it by requesting donations for an auction. Aunt Mary brought her famous canned peaches, Cousin Edith a handmade baby quilt, Uncle Bill an heirloom rifle he could part with, and Uncle Phil one of his oil paintings. These items went on the auction block, bringing in funds far beyond their actual value. Plus everyone had great fun at this extra reunion event.

Raffles are the most common fund-raisers in emergency situations; they are quick, easy, and offer some entertainment. The concept is simple: offer something of value and sell tickets for a price that seems trivial ($1 each, or 6 for $5).

Raffle items should be useful and something that everyone would want. Stay away from unusual, exotic items and anything that comes in a size. A sign like this one will help advertise the raffle. Be sure to indicate how much money is needed and when the drawing will be held. Display the sign and the item(s) to be raffled in a prominent place.

A *silent auction* is actually another form of raffle. Place the items on a table, and a coffee can with slotted plastic lid next to each item. To avoid mix ups, number the item and the can with the same number. Leave the items out for several hours to allow people to place pre-bought tickets in the cans of their choice. The winning tickets are drawn from each can during the program or after the main meal.

Rolls of numbered theater-type tickets can be bought at stationery or office supply stores. Double rolls are preferable and have two tickets side-by-side with the same number: one for the drawing pot and the other for the purchaser to keep. Avoid the type of tickets that require the purchaser to fill in name, address, phone number, etc. This is too time consuming at an exciting event such as a reunion and will discourage people from buying a long string of tickets. ➠See "Resources."

Other fund-raising ideas. Actually, anything that is bought low and sold high can generate income. Imprinted items are the most popular, but you could also consider enlarged photographs (poster size) of your last reunion or of an old family photo, or a special family calendar. Such a calendar lists family birthdays, anniversaries, and special dates. ➡See "Resources."

Family cookbooks are popular with some reunions and you don't have to create them yourself. There are cookbook printers who will do everything for you except collect the recipes. These spiral-bound books contain recipes contributed by family members and are sold to friends and "back home" communities, as well as family members. They cost between $2 and $5 each to produce, depending upon size and quantity printed. The amount of profit is based on "anything the market can handle" above cost—usually around $5 per book. To sell more books, include as many recipes as possible, and be sure to credit all contributors. Everyone loves to see their names in print! Most cookbook

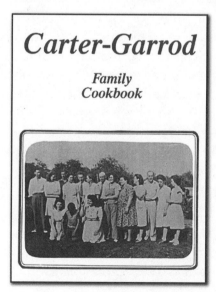 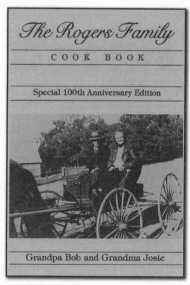

Cookbooks are very popular fundraisers at family reunions. Above are shown two custom covers.

printers have "how-to" instructions available and a free kit showing different styles of covers, dividers, and formats to choose from. ➡️See "Resources."

Another popular fund-raising idea is to stage your own *lottery*. Lottery "scratcher" tickets are available from various companies. These are printed with your own messages and prizes or in a cheaper "generic" form. ➡️See "Resources."

Planned raffles are similar to emergency raffles, except that the prizes can be more elaborate. At family reunions, the grand prize can be a refund of registration fees, free transportation, a free copy of the family history, or free registration for the next reunion. A good bottle of wine makes a nice prize.

People feel like they are getting more for their money if there are several drawings for prizes instead of just one. For details on how to run a raffle, see p. 32.

Underwriter certificates. Here's an innovative idea submitted by Crockett A. Harrison, a member of the board of the Bartholomew-Stovall Tricentennial. From a mailing list of around 600 people, nearly 200 bought close to 300 certificates for a total of $6000. Some people bought as many as five. Mr. Harrison explains, "In spite of our hedged promise [read certificate], we paid every note in full plus a dividend of $2 per note. This amounted to a rate of about 10% for the average time that the notes were outstanding. Most notes were endorsed over to our research fund. I insisted on the dividend and priced everything so to have the money to pay for it."

UNDERWRITER'S CERTIFICATE FOR
BARTHOLOMEW-STOVALL TRICENTENNIAL

THIS CERTIFIES THAT _____ HAS ADVANCED $20 TO HELP DEFRAY THE EXPENSES OF PLANNING AND ORGANIZING THE BARTHOLOMEW-STOVALL TRICENTENNIAL. THIS AMOUNT, OR AS MUCH OF IT AS FUNDS REMAINING IN THE TREASURY WILL PERMIT, WILL BE REPAID AFTER ALL OBLIGATIONS HAVE BEEN SATISFIED.

CERTIFICATE NO. _____

DATE _____   TREASURER _____

Take-Home Gifts

Take-home gifts are given to those attending as a goodwill gesture. They can be some of the same type of items found in the family store, but the expense is planned and the gift is a surprise. The price is usually covered by the registration fee and items are not marked up. A gift of good quality will be appreciated and valued as a reunion remembrance. Some items may become keepsakes and handed down within the family, generation after generation.

Take-home gifts should be of high quality. A cheap looking item will draw complaints ("waste of money"), while a high quality item will receive compliments. Most reunions choose items that range in price from $3 to $10. Some possibilities are paperweights, wine glasses, cups or mugs, coasters, key rings, etc. ➠See "Resources."

The Matter of Tickets

At some point you will be collecting registration fees by mail. It may seem to be good business practice to indicate that a financial transaction has taken place by sending out receipts or tickets. However, tickets cost money to print or buy; addressing and mailing envelopes to send them takes more time and money.

An easier method is to indicate on all correspondence:

"NO TICKETS WILL BE SENT—RECEIPT OF YOUR
CHECK RESERVES YOUR SPACE"

For this method, you must have a list of those who preregistered, plus the bookkeeping records, available at the registration desk.

Another common method is to state on all correspondence:

"YOUR CANCELLED CHECK SERVES AS YOUR TICKET"

However we can't fully recommend this method for the following reasons: 1.) Most people will forget to bring their cancelled check, 2.) Some people won't have their checks because some checking accounts are set up so that cancelled checks are not returned except by request, and 3.) A late payment may result in the cancelled check not being returned in time.

Bank Accounts

It's important to set up a reunion checking account. This step eliminates having your personal finances mixed with reunion finances. Your monthly statement is a legal and permanent record of your transactions and anyone who might question your finances can see the results in black and white (and sometimes red). Instead of having checks made out to you, they should be made out to the name of your family group. Many banks have a policy allowing free checking accounts for temporary events such as one-time reunions, but you will need to ask the bank manager about this. To get the best rate, phone several banks to check their policies.

Some families require two signatures on the reunion checking account. However, getting the other signature on each check can be time consuming and awkward. For instance, what if the other person goes on vacation just when you must pay the printer? A more realistic approach is to have two or three people able to make withdrawals with just one signature required. Of course, with a formal organization the treasurer will sign checks.

When the reunion is over, and you are sure all the checks have cleared the bank, you can put any leftover money into a savings account to gain interest until the next reunion. This is a good time to have two signatures required for withdrawal.

When dealing with banks, the sticky part comes—if you are an informal group—with interest-bearing accounts (checking or savings). Technically, the federal government requires that someone be responsible for paying taxes on the earned interest. This means the bank may ask for a social security number and the person with that number must treat the interest from the account as part of her personal income. Obviously, some people may be reluctant to do this. With a checking account, you can get around this problem by opening an account that is non-interest bearing. With a savings account some banks will allow you to register the account as owned by a nonprofit group (your reunion committee) even though technically you are not nonprofit. The banks are simply trying to stay on the good side of the federal auditors and such an arrangement will usually appease them as long as there is not a huge sum involved.

It's best to deal with a bank where you or someone in your group is well known. If someone in your family works in a bank, so much the better. Keep in mind that a bank manager *does* have the authority to set up the accounts in the manner described above. If you find yourself dealing with a "new accounts" clerk who seems reluctant, ask to speak with the manager. If that doesn't work, try another bank.

Bookkeeping

The actual business bookkeeping (bank deposits, bank balance, bills due and paid, etc.) should be done on a double-entry spreadsheet. But exact bookkeeping instructions are beyond the scope of this book. If you don't know how to keep double entry books, find someone who does. This is especially important for family associations. If necessary, hire a bookkeeper or at the very least, hire a professional to set up the books. This is the most time consuming and technical part, and once it's done, it should be fairly obvious how to continue.

Using the Family's Talents and Resources to Save $$$

Donations, volunteers, and special projects can help reduce reunion costs. Let members know of your needs and make suggestions concerning how they can help. Does someone own a printing company that might donate paper or printing? Will a cousin with a large home garden or farm donate fruits or vegetables for meals? Are there children who would lick stamps and put address labels on the envelopes?

Put an "items needed" and "help wanted" list in every mailer along with a request to return it by a certain date. This "check-what-you-can-do" system gets results and allows people to volunteer who otherwise might feel too pressured if asked directly.

You might plan a special fund-raising activity before the reunion to cover extra costs. If the family teenagers would like to have music and dancing at the reunion, encourage them to organize a car wash to raise funds for a disk jockey. Another popular way to raise money is to have a bake sale. Look around your community for the types of activities local groups do to raise money. Fund-raising has an added benefit: Involving people at this stage of planning will result in more interest in the reunion.

Keep a Financial History

The process for planning a first reunion is the same as for a 20th except that you should have been saving your financial information from year to year for comparison. Your financial history should list estimated expenses, actual expenses, and the difference between them. After the reunion, review the numbers and jot down thoughts that come to mind. Keep a notebook listing all of your assumptions, considerations, calculations, suggestions, and mistakes. This helps you (or someone else) prepare for future reunions and hopefully eliminate hidden costs and surprises. Take the time to do it right; write it so someone else can make sense of it.

A financial history is absolutely necessary to get the best possible group rates from hotels and resorts—and the larger your group, the more important this is (see "Negotiating and Contracts" in Chapter 1). Hotels and resorts will not give their best rates based on speculation. You must "prove" your past reunion attendance for them to seriously listen to you.

Chapter 4

Keeping Records

Chapter Highlights

▶*Keep It Simple.* ▶*Types of Information.* ▶*Filing Systems.*
▶*Example of a Record Keeping System.* ▶*Coding/Earmarking.*
▶*Lists.* ▶*Other Important Information.* ▶*Other Useful Tips.*
▶*Using Computers.*

Keep It Simple

Regardless of the size of your group, you will need to create a system to keep information on family members. This chapter has more material than you will need on record keeping. Your job is to evaluate the possibilities, use the information that pertains to your situation, and disregard the rest. You should create the *simplest* system that will give you what you need. For example, some families are so small they know where everyone is. Such a group would have no need to record information on finding, re-finding, and tracing people. It would only need a system to record addresses and financial transactions.

For the sake of clarity, let's discuss some of the terminology in this chapter. Organizing and updating information is referred to as *record keeping*. A *record* is the information pertaining to one individual plus her immediate family. A *file* is a group of records. A *list* is accumulated information derived from these files, usually in printed form.

Types of Information

Two types of information are most useful: *personal* and *financial*.

Personal Information. Here is a list of personal information that can be collected for your records:

> ➤ Name and address (mailing list).
> ➤ Phone number.
> ➤ Biographical information.
> ➤ Replies to surveys.
> ➤ All information that led to finding a person or family.
> ➤ Information that can lead to "re-finding" a person or family.
> ➤ Information furnished to help find others.
> ➤ Skills, services volunteered, goods donated or available.
> ➤ Special dietary or personal needs.
> ➤ Financial information.

Financial Information. A financial file on each family should be maintained separately from the bookkeeping records of the reunion. For a one-time reunion (or a first-time reunion), this financial information could simply go on the bottom of the record as in Figure 1E. However, groups that have reunions regularly should have a separate "financial file." This could be a separate card file arranged by last name. Or you could add a "financial card" (use a special color) behind the name card in your regular file. The financial file contains information on all ongoing financial transactions such as:

➤ Registration fees paid/owed.
➤ Dues paid/owed.
➤ Donations.
➤ Merchandise bought/ordered.

The information in this file should include check numbers, the dates they were deposited, and the items paid for. This is important because, in most cases, this record of deposit is the only verification available at the reunion.

Filing Systems

There are three common ways the files can be kept:

1. **On file cards** (one name or family per card). 4 x 6 cards are better than 3 x 5s because they hold more information. If more room is needed, add cards behind the first (use a different color for additional cards).

2. **In a 3-ring binder** (one name or family per sheet of paper). This is the best way (other than using a computer) for reunion groups that intend to put a lot of time and effort into finding extended family members. Some "finds" may take several years and a lot of searching. In such cases, an 8.5 x 11 binder system is more efficient than a card system because it will hold more information. Add sheets as necessary.

3. **On computer disk.** Computers are amazingly efficient and time saving, but to go this route you should have someone with experience or who is willing to put in the time and effort that computers require. See "Using Computers," p. 51.

Example of a Record Keeping System

Records are usually filed by last name—one record per family or per individual if a person (adult) is single. As children leave home or become adults, they are given their own records.

Refer to the flow chart on p. 43. All names that have no

address or an "improbable" address, start off in the *"Where RU?"* *file*. Your intention is to eventually make this file as small as possible. An "improbable" address is an old address that you wouldn't bother wasting a stamp on. You should not discard this address, however; it can still prove useful if you have time to visit the neighbors and ask questions or use the "city directory" method to find them (see p. 166).

Once you have a mailing address, the record goes into the *mailing file* which is divided into verified and unverified addresses. The verified addresses can further be divided into those attending the reunion and those not attending. The important thing to remember is these *sub-files* do not necessarily have to be physically separated from each other as long as they are marked or coded so that you can easily tell the status of each record at a glance (see "Coding/Earmarking," below).

On the other hand, if your group is small and/or you have a good memory, you might want to separate out some sub-files. The problem with separating the files comes when you want to check on the status of a particular family or individual and you can't remember exactly where the record is. With separated files, in order to find the record, you may have to go through all the files. The general rules are:

➤ The fewer the sub-files (that are physically separated from each other), the easier it will be to find a particular record.
➤ The larger the group, the more you should try to keep your files consolidated.

See "status list," below, for a tip on how to maintain large separated files.

All records in the mailing file have addresses you intend to mail to; therefore, the mailing labels are derived directly from this file. Remember, there are two types of addresses in this file,

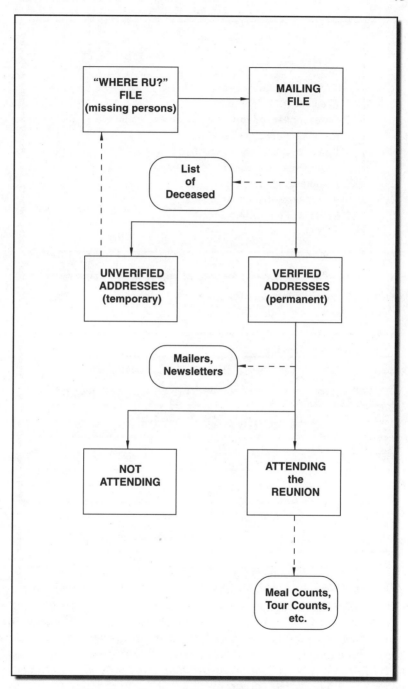

A flowchart for the example described on p. 42.

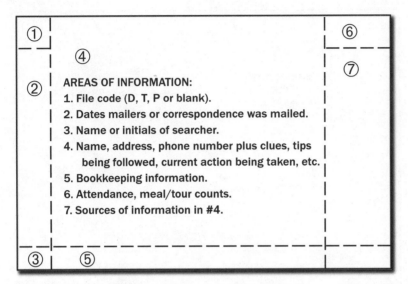

① ② ③ ④ ⑤ ⑥ ⑦

AREAS OF INFORMATION:
1. File code (D, T, P or blank).
2. Dates mailers or correspondence was mailed.
3. Name or initials of searcher.
4. Name, address, phone number plus clues, tips
   being followed, current action being taken, etc.
5. Bookkeeping information.
6. Attendance, meal/tour counts.
7. Sources of information in #4.

FIGURE 1A. Possible areas for codes and information on a file card.

PHYLLIS JONES
— MOVED TO PORTLAND, ORE. OUT OF HIGH SCHOOL. 〉 NELLIE (209) 555-1234
— MARRIED A SCHOOLMATE SENIOR YEAR AT SMITH COLLEGE 〉 UNCLE AL (503) 555-3456
4-15 — SENT LETTER TO SMITH COLLEGE ALUMNI ASSN, TO BE FORWARDED

PAM

FIGURE 1B. First of all, the card itself is of a certain color designating a particular branch of the family. Information is accumulated gradually. Two people (names on right) recall that Phyllis moved to Portland to go to school and that she married while in college. A letter to be forwarded to her (see p. 158) was sent to the alumni association of the school. The searcher's name is in the lower left corner.

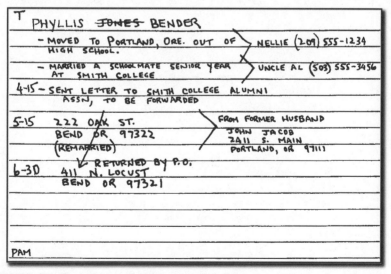

FIGURE 1C. Phyllis' former husband received the letter and sent along an address. She is now remarried. All names are recorded. A mailer is sent to this address on 5-15. A "T" (for Temporary address) is put in the upper left corner.

FIGURE 1D. The address furnished by her former husband turns out to be old, but because "Return Service Requested" was written on the envelope, the Post Office returned the mailer with the updated address. The mailer was then sent to the new address on 6-31.

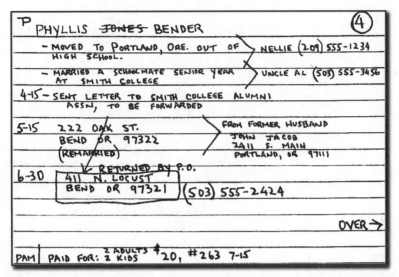

P PHYLLIS ~~JONES~~ BENDER   ④

- MOVED TO PORTLAND, ORE. OUT OF ＞ NELLIE (209) 555-1234
  HIGH SCHOOL.
- MARRIED A SCHOOLMATE SENIOR YEAR ＞ UNCLE AL (503) 555-3456
  AT SMITH COLLEGE
4-15 - SENT LETTER TO SMITH COLLEGE ALUMNI
        ASS'N, TO BE FORWARDED

5-15   222 OAK ST.   FROM FORMER HUSBAND
       BEND OR 97322   JOHN JACOB
       (REMARRIED)   2411 S. MAIN
                               PORTLAND, OR 97111

6-30   ↙ RETURNED BY P.O.
       411 N. LOCUST
       BEND OR 97321 (503) 555-2424

                                          OVER →

PAM | PAID FOR: 2 ADULTS $20, #263 7-15
                2 KIDS

FIGURE 1E. Phyllis responds and sends the $20 fee for herself, her hus-
band, and 2 children. A box is drawn around her verified address and the T
is changed to a P (for Permanent address). The date of deposit and check
number are recorded on the bottom of the card. A circled "4" in the upper
right corner indicates that 4 people from her family will be attending.

HUSBAND : RALPH
OCCUPATION: ELECTRICIAN
HER OCCUPATION : PART-TIME CLERK
CHILDREN : KIM 14, ALICE 12
HOBBIES : CAMPING

- PHONED 7-2
- WILL HELP WITH REGISTRATION
- WILL BRING HER GRANDMOTHER'S DIARY
- SAYS HER COUSIN MARGIE JONES IS
  MARRIED AND LIVING IN NEWPORT, RI.
  WILL TRY TO GET HER ADDRESS.

FIGURE 1F. (Back of card) On 7-2 she calls to offer her help with registration and has some information about her cousin, Margie Jones. The biographical information came from a survey sent with the mailer.

verified and unverified. An address is unverified until you know for sure that it is accurate. (Just because a mailer doesn't come back by return mail, doesn't necessarily mean the addressee received it.) Unverified addresses plus the "Where RU?" file make up the missing person list.

Coding/Earmarking

Coding means marking a record or list by writing on it. Colored ink or pencil can be used for indicating different categories of information. For example, use red ink for bookkeeping information and green for mailing information. The "position" of the code can be informative, too (see Figure 1A).

The upper left corner of a card can contain a code indicating which sub-file the record is in. No code (blank) means the record is still in the "Where RU?" file. A "D" indicates a deceased person; a "T" (for Temporary) is used for an unverified address ; a "P" (for Permanent) is a verified address. Note that a *T* easily becomes a *P* without having to erase. A box is drawn around a verified address (use colored ink).

The mailing date in the left side margin indicates when a mailing was sent, and appears next to the address that the mailer was sent to. If two mailers are sent, both dates should be recorded. If a "lost" person is "found" just before the reunion and, as a result, both mailers are sent together, the date is underlined twice.

The bottom left corner contains the searcher's initials. This way you always know who is (or was) in charge of finding the person. If a different searcher is assigned, put the new searcher's initials above the first.

Earmarking is a way of marking a record without writing on it. It can be done with paper clips or colored self-stick dots. There are also plastic clips made for file cards called "file card signals." These work somewhat like a paper clip, but stick up above the card. A similar item is Post-It Tape Flags that come in bright colors, can be written on, and are removable.

The position of the marker on the card could also have a meaning. For example, a paper clip on the left top of a card could mean one thing and on the right top could mean another. The same goes for color coding. Most clips, including the metal ones, are available in colors. Possible reasons for earmarking: owes money, paid for family photo but can't attend, volunteered to work during reunion, candidate for an award, has special presentation or skit for the program, etc.

Both coding and earmarking save a lot of time; however, you must figure out *beforehand* what they are going to mean. Making up meanings as you go along can create confusion. Keep a list of the meanings of your codes to remind yourself and others who might inherit or use the files.

Lists

A "list" is accumulated information that is derived from these files, usually in printed form. For example:

- ➤ Missing person or missing family list (a printout of the "Where RU?" file).
- ➤ Those attending the reunion.
- ➤ Those not yet arrived.
- ➤ Meal counts, tour counts, etc.
- ➤ Survey and statistical information.
- ➤ Those owing money.
- ➤ Award candidates.
- ➤ Those who volunteered for jobs.
- ➤ Deceased list.

If you have a large group (and, therefore, large files), a *status list* can be useful because it allows you to keep your files separated and still be able to quickly find the status of a particular record. The status list is simply a list of your group in alphabetical order. Next to each name put the file code (see previous section).

It is often helpful if a list and its corresponding records are linked by a note, code or earmark. For example, as you add a name to the list of people attending the reunion, be sure a code appears on that person's record. In this case, a circled number in the upper right hand corner would do. The number within the circle indicates the number of people attending from that family (adding up these numbers from all cards gives you the attendance count). Then if the attendance list is lost, it can easily be re-created by checking all records for a circled number in the upper right corner.

You could put other coded information in this list, thereby eliminating the need to create other lists. For example, "$X" means "owes money" (write it in red); "$GP" means "can't attend, but paid for group photo"; etc. Again, always be sure an equivalent code or earmark appears on the individual records so if the list is lost, it can be re-created.

Other Important Information

Other categories of information that can be contained in, or derived from these files are:

1. **Information for tracing people**. When you collect information, write down everything: sources talked to, databases checked, letters written, dead-ends followed, phone calls made, etc. Date each entry. You are leaving a "trace"—a running record or log of all the steps taken to find a person. If someone else takes over the search, they won't have to reinvent the wheel. Also, if the person disappears again, a "re-find" will be much easier, and dead-ends can be avoided.

Some family organizations intentionally collect information for the purpose of more easily "re-finding" a person. Social security number, driver's license number, service number, birthdate,

and next of kin (or "someone who will always know where you
are") all fall under this category.

2. **Clues for finding people**. Indicate on the back of each
record any names, tips, or other information that a person has
provided for finding other people. Sometimes it's handy to know
the source of information in order to know who to contact for
more leads or to verify the original information.

3. **Biographical information**. If using cards to collect data,
put this information on the back or on a separate card (different
color) filed behind the first. The amount of biographical information you collect can vary (see "The Survey," p. 78). Names
and birthdates are minimum family data to record. File cards
are limited in the amount of information they can hold, therefore, more information should be kept in a separate file, such as
a 3-ring binder.

4. **Helpful notes on each family**. Keep notes about each family, such as services and donations they have offered, skills they
have that may come in handy, items that could be borrowed,
homes available for accommodations, special transportation
needed for elderly and/or handicapped, special requests, dietary
needs, etc.

5. **Missing Person List** ("Where RU?" file). If it's not too
long, this list should be updated and sent out with each mailing
or newsletter.

Other Useful Tips

➤ *The less you copy and recopy information, the better.* Stick with
   the original record; lightly cross out the old info and add
   the new. Don't erase—the old information may prove
   useful if all other leads die out. (Old information is
   especially useful to future reunions because if a family
   member "disappears" again, the old sources will be the
   most likely to help relocate the person.) If the front and

back of the card become full, add a second card behind
the first, paper clipping the two cards together.

➤ *Be sure to save all information.* It's best if one person is in
charge of the records, preferably someone who will not
be moving often. Give copies of the address and phone
number list to two or three other people for safe-keep-
ing. Announce who is in charge of the address list in
your mailings and at the reunion so that people can send
change-of-address announcements to that person. Also,
have copies of the address list available at the reunion
along with scratch paper so people can copy the addresses of family members they would like to stay in
touch with. A profitable alternative is to offer a family
directory for sale (see page 146).

➤ As your file grows and contains more and more information (especially financial information), it becomes more
valuable. Take good care of it. Don't loan it—not even a
portion of it. All of the information, even just a name
with no address, is valuable. If someone wants to try
their luck at finding some people, don't give them the
records, not even the ones that contain names only.
Give them a list of the names instead or a separate
copied group of records, but never the original set. If
your information is on computer, insist that the operator
maintain a backup copy.

➤ Address labels, file card trays (metal or plastic and in three
sizes), and file cards (lined, plain, and in colors), 3-ring
binders and paper are available from Quill Corporation
and others. ➡See "Resources."

Using Computers

Most reunion records are kept on file cards or in 3-ring binders. However, the personal computer is changing these somewhat time consuming methods. If you have access to a home
computer with a printer, by all means use it. However, unless

you have experience or the time to experiment, this may not be the best option. Be sure the operator has "hands on" experience with both the computer and the software. If you are converting your system to computer, maintain parallel paper files until you are sure the computer system is working properly. And *always* have a "back up" system to protect your information. *Always!*

It's best to keep two backup disks (or tapes)—one near your computer and the other with a friend or relative. This is in case a fire or other calamity destroys your computer and all its disks. A Zip Drive (or other removable cartridge drive) is a cheap and handy way to store backup information.

A computer can streamline the whole process of creating, updating, and maintaining your filing system. You will be able to insert each new address alphabetically with a keystroke. Biographical information, a missing person list, a list of those attending the reunion, printed address labels, or a meal count can be run off at any time. You are only limited by the software and the experience and ability of the operator.

FileMaker Pro is a good program to use for maintaining reunion records. It's available for both IBM compatibles and the Mac. If properly configured, it can derive almost any information you wish to see (how many for dinner on Saturday night, how many vegetarian meals, a list of the number of residents by state, who can't attend but wants to buy a group photo, etc.). You can even store photos in it.

➥For information on using computers to find people, see p. 161. For information on using the Internet, see Chapter 14.

Chapter 5

Family Communications
Flyers, Newsletters, Round Robins, Surveys

Chapter Highlights
▸*Reunion Announcements.* ▸*Frequency.*
▸*Fancy Flyer/Simple Newsletter.* ▸*Developing a Newsletter.*
▸*Contents.* ▸*Be Encouraging.* ▸*Design and Layout.* ▸*Clip Art.*
▸*Using Photos.* ▸*Include Some Entertainment.* ▸*Tools of the Trade.*
▸*Using Computer Printers.* ▸*Round Robin Letters.* ▸*Surveys.*

Reunion Announcements

Reunion announcements are an important and necessary part of any reunion. They may be in the form of postcards, flyers or newsletters. But rest assured: most of the impressions—good, bad, or indifferent—that will be formed concerning the upcoming reunion, will come from these announcements that are sent out. Some people think that reunion announcements are tossed into the trash like junk mail. This is a myth! If they end up in the trash, it's only after serious consideration. And even then, they may be fished out again.

If your announcements are carelessly worded, have missing
or incorrect information or appear sloppy, they may convey the
impression that the reunion will turn out the same way. This
gives the reader a good reason to say "no thanks." The time
spent to produce high quality, thoughtfully worded announce-

```
What:      Davis Family Reunion

When:      As usual, the 2nd Saturday in July: This year
           July 10.

Where:     At Aunt Ann's & Uncle Jake's, 444 Oak St,
           Pineville. (209) 555-3333.

Time:      2pm to 9 pm.

Bring:     Potluck dish of your choice and drinks for 5
           people. Old photos of your family. Eating
           utensils will be provided.

Take:      Route 12 into Pineville, at 2nd light (Fern
           St) turn left, 2 blocks to Oak, turn right,
           2nd house on right.
```

The simplest type of reunion announcement.

*A fancier postcard. Nice concept; however, "ghosting" a photo behind the
type makes it hard to read.*

An example of a family reunion invitation from the 1890s.

ments is well worth the effort. It will not only help your reunion succeed socially by encouraging greater attendance, but economically as well, since greater attendance means more income.

Reunion announcements come in two basic forms: the flyer (or letter) and the newsletter. A *flyer* is comprised usually of one sheet of paper (occasionally a postcard) and proclaims the bare essentials of the reunion such as time, place and what to bring plus, perhaps, words of encouragement.

More influential, however, is the *newsletter* which serves as a family newspaper, containing articles, recipes, photos, puzzles, etc. It can create a "thread" that ties people together and keeps them interested in the "goings-on" of the family and in the developing reunion plans. The value of a family newsletter was summed up nicely by Doris Rodriquez in a recent article in *Ancestry Magazine*. Doris explains "…the family newsletter not only bridges the gap between today and our past, but it also inspires excellence and achievement in future generations by increasing our awareness of who we are and what we hope to achieve." A newsletter, of course, need not be limited to simply announcing a reunion. In fact, most family newsletters are published on an on-going basis and have no connection to a reunion except to promote it before it occurs and report on it afterward. Many families have a newsletter and no reunion.

Frequency of Reunion Announcements

Whether you send flyers or newsletters or both, one announcement per reunion is not enough. Family members who are really hard to sell need to hear about the reunion once or twice more. Three announcements is about right. More than that is belaboring the point. The first should come out 9–12 months before the reunion (earlier is okay, too), the second 4–6 months before, and the last 4–6 weeks before.

Fancy Flyer/Simple Newsletter

A flyer can be a simple invitation stating only the basics such as "what, where, when, what to bring, and how to get there." Or it may be in letter form such as in Figure 2A. Another approach is to spruce up a common, average flyer to resemble a small newsletter (Figure 2B). *The wording in Figures 2A and 2B is exactly the same and the same typewriter was used.* The difference is the use of some clip art, some transfer lettering, and a photocopy reduction of the text. Creating this type of mini-newsletter can serve as a transitional or exploratory step to see if you would like to dive into a full-fledged newsletter.

Developing a Newsletter

First, get samples of other newsletters. These can help tremendously by providing examples of format, content, clip art and layout. Each year *Genealogical Helper* prints a list of family newsletters in one of its issues. The *Directory of Family Associations* lists family associations and includes a notation if a newsletter is produced by the association. These publications are in most libraries or ➠see "Resources." Write to some of the newsletters asking for samples. Be sure to include a donation to cover costs and postage. You can also submit your own publication to either of these sources.

Next, get *Creating Family Newsletters* by Elaine Floyd, a wonderful book that not only tells you what to do but also explains the subtle nuances of content and design. ➠See "Resources."

Choose a name for your newsletter. The editor can choose it or the family can have a contest, voting on the final choice with a prize of a free subscription for the winner. Names for newsletters range from the sedate—*Thomas S. Markay Association Bulletin*—to something lighter, such as *Chapman Chatter, Butcher's Block, Bell's Chime,* or *Grin and Barrett.* Most names, however, tell it like it is—*Stone Newsletter, Schneider News, Hay's Paper.*

January 20xx

Dear Family:

Thanks to Aunt Lou's efforts, it looks like there's enough interest in a family reunion to go ahead and schedule one. You may recall that she sent out a survey last Fall asking us if we'd like to have a reunion. She's also made a LOT of phone calls since then, and the consensus is that this summer is a good time for our first family reunion in over 30 years. Over 60 people have signed up.

So we rented the pavilion in Roeding Park in Fresno for August 18 and 19 (Saturday and Sunday). There's lots of shade, room for the kids to play, BBQ grills, tables, softball field, and a zoo next door. The petting zoo is available Sunday PM.

In order to pay our expenses, we've decided to charge $15 per household to attend the reunion. This covers mailing, phone calls and deposits. We need your money the sooner the better. Please don't wait until the reunion to pay. Make checks out to: Carson Family Reunion.

FOOD. There will be a catered BBQ Sunday noon. This will cost $7 per adult and $4 for kids under 12. The meal Saturday night will be potluck, which I will coordinate by phone. Lisa (209) 555-4444.

FIGURE 2A. This is part of a typical reunion mailer. Now see Figure 2B.

Reunion News

SPECIAL REUNION EDITION
January, 20xx

LET'S GET
TOGETHER
Aug. 18-19

Thanks to Aunt Lou's efforts, it looks like
there's enough interest in a family reunion
to go ahead and schedule one. You may recall
that she sent out a survey last Fall asking us
if we'd like to have a reunion. She's also
made a LOT of phone calls since then, and the
consensus is that this summer is a good time
for our first family reunion in over 30 years.
Over 60 people have signed up.

So we rented the pavilion in Roeding Park in
Fresno for Aug. 18-19 (Sat & Sun). There's
lots of shade, room for the kids to play, BBQ
grills, tables, softball field, and a zoo next
door. The petting zoo is available Sunday PM.

IF YOU HAVE ANY QUESTIONS ABOUT THE
REUNION, CALL OR WRITE: Lisa Carson
Smith, 1234 Eucalyptus St., Fresno, CA
92711, (209) 555-4444.

Carson
Family
Reunion

HELP!

IN ORDER TO PAY OUR EXPENSES, we've decided to
charge $15 per household to attend the reunion.
This covers mailing, phone calls and deposits.
We need your money the sooner the better.
Please don't wait until the reunion to pay.
Make checks out to: "Carson Family Reunion"
and send to our treasurer: Lou Carson, 123 Oak
St., Albany, NY 13456.

*   *   *   *   *   *   *   *   *

FOOD. There will be a catered BBQ Sunday
noon. This will cost $7 per adult and $4
for kids under 12. To attend this meal,
fill out the enclosed form. The meal Saturday
night will be potluck, which I will coordinate
by phone. Lisa: (209) 555-4444.

FIGURE 2B. This is the same mailer as Fig. 2A but put into a newsletter format. The same typewriter and exactly the same wording was used in both. The difference is some clip art, some transfer lettering, and a photocopy reduction.

It doesn't take a lot of extra effort to make a newsletter entertaining. It could contain recipes, articles about family events, photos, columns, contests, family sayings, favorite proverbs, family historic dates, quizzes and puzzles, brain teasers, trivia, clipart, cartoons, birthdays, jokes, etc. Such a friendly approach generates interest and allows the newsletter to become a vehicle for creating stronger family bonds.

You might solicit material from various family members in the form of letters, articles, or responses to a questionnaire. A questionnaire can ask about recent family events: births, graduations, awards, promotions, achievements, deaths, travel, new addresses, marriages, etc. Ask for photographs, old newspaper clippings, children's art work, poems or stories—anything that would convey interesting information about your family.

Various family members might be assigned as columnists, guest editors, or in charge of particular sections such as a children's corner, a recipe or old photo section, or a puzzle page. You, as editor, may want to write more formal articles in the style of an editorial, a column, an interview or biographical sketches on relatives living or deceased. New findings in genealogy charts or records might be included.

A visit to your library can result in filler material that will embellish your newsletters for many issues to come—items such as trivia, inspiring quotes, sayings and proverbs, clip art, puzzles, word games and riddles. In fact, such material can be found around the house in magazines and newspapers, if you learn to keep an eye out for it. ➠See "Resources" for helpful books.

Contents of Reunion Announcements

The following list is for your reference to jog your memory. There may be other items to include which will pertain specifically to your reunion, such as food and sports equipment to bring.

Essential

- ➤ time, date and location of the reunion.
- ➤ return address and phone number.
- ➤ registration fees/registration form.
- ➤ payment procedure.
- ➤ cancellation policy and refunding rules.
- ➤ how to get there (general driving instructions).
- ➤ what to bring (if anything).

Optional

- ➤ list of committee members with phone numbers.
- ➤ short history of decisions made and those in progress.
- ➤ ask for comments and suggestions; ideas for the program; award categories, and prizes; volunteers; information on "missing" families or family members; memorabilia: old photos, movies, videos, scrapbooks, Bibles, photo albums, old letters, family trees, genealogies, newspaper clippings, etc.
- ➤ advance registration incentives.
- ➤ a survey.
- ➤ give name, address, and phone number of person in charge of mailing list.
- ➤ names and phone numbers of places and people with available accommodations, such as family members, bed and breakfasts, hotels, motels, and RV campsites in the area.
- ➤ give approximate date of the next announcement.
- ➤ include jokes, cartoons, interesting trivia, and historical family data.
- ➤ pet policy.

The last announcement before the reunion could include:

- ➤ updated information, last minute news, changes or additions to original plans.

➤ encouragement for borderliners and procrastinators. (A list
  of those planning to attend will often entice others.)
➤ a reunion schedule or description of program/events.
➤ a hand-drawn or simplified map showing family homes,
  reunion location, airports, train stations, and main
  highways.
➤ driving instructions to the reunion location.
➤ phone numbers of car rental companies.
➤ bus, taxi or shuttle prices.
➤ type of weather to expect.
➤ what to wear.
➤ another reminder to bring old photos and other memorabilia, to wear family T-shirts, buttons, etc. And to bring
  insect repellent, flashlight, sun lotion, medications,
  aspirin, etc.

➽Books and resources for graphic designers and newsletter
editors can be found in "Resources."

Be Encouraging

The more encouraging the reunion announcement, the more
successful the reunion. Here's a great example of encouragement in print. All the details are included and it exudes enthusiasm. (Source: *A Practical Guide to Planning a Family Reunion* by
E. Wisdom, page 45. Modified by T. Ninkovich.)

Dear Family Members:

There's excitement in the air, feelings of
anxiousness, and feelings of caring and love.
Why? The celebration of the SMITH FAMILY RE-
UNION, scheduled for July 21 and 22, is just a
few months away. Your interest and excitement
makes me happy, too, because it's your partici-
pation that's going to make this a great reunion.

I know the deadline for payment is June 30

but you can start sending in partial payments now so as not to make it hard for you. We don't mind the extra bookkeeping. Also, your early registration and payment will enable me to negotiate with the hotel in a more positive way regarding the Banquet. I know we can depend on you to get your registration fee in to us as soon as you can.

The Program Committee has met and the Reunion activities were approved by our Reunion Committee. The Program Committee has laid out an excellent program that will be enjoyable and remembered for years to come.

The Program Committee would like to inform you of the following:

Our Reunion theme this year is "We Are the Children." Our Family Reunion colors are red and white. We are hoping everyone will wear something red and/or white at the picnic on Saturday. Please familiarize your family with the song entitled "We Are the World" for the Banquet Program.

Are there any musicians, soloists or group singers out there? If you would like to participate in the Program, contact Ann at 615/555-6675.

Nashville and surrounding area family members, our Housing Committee chairperson needs to hear from you about available beds for our out-of-towners. Call Helen at 615/555-6767.

Out-of-town family members, please contact Helen at 615/555-6767 about your needs for sleeping space by July 16. Accommodations will be for Friday, July 20 through Sunday, July 22 only. With prior planning, you will know with whom and where you will be staying.

And for you who will really have vacationing fever, enclosed is a list of hotels in Nashville with their rates, locations and phone numbers. You are to arrange your own accommodations.

Nashville family members, I hope you are talking with your immediate family about the picnic food. Our out-of-town family members are making plans in a big way to come, so let us be ready with plenty of good Southern food to share with them.

On Saturday, July 21, we will kick off our Family Picnic with a Family Meeting which will be held from 10 a.m. to 11 a.m. It is so important that you attend and be on time, for we must make some immediate decisions for our next Reunion.

Immediately after the Family Meeting, there will be time for sharing family photo albums. Please bring an album to share. Also, there will be games and prizes for all.

See the enclosed map for instructions on how to find the picnic area and the banquet hotel.

Let's continue to remain excited and encourage everyone, family and friends, to attend this historical event. If you have any questions, ideas, criticisms, concerns, etc., please don't hesitate to let the Reunion Committee know about them.

I hope I have not forgotten anything. Be certain to keep this letter and refer to it as this will be the last written communication the Reunion Committee will send. Please get your registration fee to Dan or me, contact the Housing Committee, and make plans to attend the Reunion activities. We feel it will be an event you will always remember and cherish.

Sincerely,

Mary Smith Singleton

Reunion Planning Committee

Design and Layout for Newsletters and Flyers

Anything that is put into printed form—flyers, newsletters, surveys, questionnaires—can benefit from application of a few layout and design techniques. Such techniques are not that diffi-

cult to learn, and the tools needed are inexpensive (until you get into computers). *See the next section for a list of tools,* and ➥see "Resources" for a list of helpful books. Also, your local library is a good place for further information—there is no lack of printed material on the subject.

There is no question that computers give the most efficient results when it comes to creating newsletters and flyers. By all means, use a computer if you have access to one. However, this section focuses on the "kitchen table" approach to layout and design—that is, the cheapest way that still gives good results. A typewriter is the most expensive tool needed.

Layout. A flyer or newsletter may be comprised of several separate pieces called "elements" (for example: text, clip art, borders, photos, letterhead, lines, etc.). These elements are usually on separate pieces of paper and are "pasted up" onto planning paper (also called paste-up paper). This is called the "original." "Pasted up" means "attached"—usually with nonpermanent glue or wax. The "original," when finished, is taken to the printer.

Originals should be pasted up on only one side of a sheet of planning paper. Two-sided flyers or newsletters will be "backed" or "double sided" (printed on both sides of one sheet) at the print or copy shop. Always use planning paper for a lay-out guide. This paper is very inexpensive and is available at graphic art supply stores (less than 50¢ per sheet).

The basic rules of paste up are simple: keep things clean and aligned. "Clean" means the original should have no specks or smudges. If these occur, they are easily remedied with white-out or correction tape. Don't use an eraser—more smudges may result. "Clean" also means an original that doesn't produce "shadow lines" in the final printed product. Shadow lines result from edges of elements that stick up too high either because the paper is too thick or they were not glued down tightly. They cast a shadow when their picture is taken in the printing or photocopying process. This shadow shows up as a thin black line. The problem is you won't know if shadow lines will show up until the first piece is printed. That's one reason why it's very important to be there to inspect the first piece of paper that comes off the press or out of the photocopier. Shadow lines are easily corrected with white-out or correction tape. The best way to prevent shadow lines is to be sure the glue or wax is applied to the entire back surface of each element, especially to the edges.

"Proper alignment" means that horizontal lines (such as lines of print) should be level to the page and vertical lines should be straight up and down. Eyeballing for alignment is *not* good enough. To ensure proper alignment, the first step is to make sure the paper and T-square are aligned with each other. To do this, place the T-square in position along a straight edge of the cutting board (preferably the left edge for right-handers). In this position, the long, ruler part of the T-square will be horizontal. Now align the bottom or top edge of the paper with the T-square (or use a horizontal guideline if one is printed on the paper) and tape it down to the cutting board with masking tape on all four corners.

To assure consistent positioning, always use the T-square from the same edge of the cutting board. This is in case the left and right edges of the cutting board are not exactly parallel to each other. The best way to assure accurate vertical positioning is to use the triangle in conjunction with the T-square. Placing the triangle on top of the T-square provides a vertical edge.

When an element is placed exactly where you want it, it's important to burnish it down. This is done best with a flat plastic burnishing tool. Place a buffer sheet (any clean piece of paper) over the work and rub vigorously with the burnisher. Press hard. This assures that all edges are tightly adhered to the paper below and that small elements won't fall off on the way to the printer.

Letterheads. A good looking letterhead really adds a lot to a newsletter. An artist in the family could design it or a typesetter or commercial artist could develop one. Since you can use the original copy of a letterhead over and over again, this would be a one-time expense.

You can create your own letterhead (and headlines) by using "rub-on" or transfer lettering. There are hundreds of styles and many different sizes. Visit a graphic art supply store and check out the possibilities. Bring home catalogs and how-to pamphlets and study them.

When creating a line of type using rub-on or transfer lettering, remember that exact size and positioning on the page is not important at the first stage. Create the line of type somewhere in the middle of a clean, white sheet of paper. Pay close attention to the positioning of the letters in relation to each other but not in relation to position on the page (as long as they don't run off the edge). Then when it's finished, reduce or enlarge it if necessary, cut out this line of type, and position it properly on the original.

The methods of applying rub-on and transfer lettering are not discussed here because detailed instructions come with the manufacturer's catalogs or sometimes as a separate pamphlet.

Rub-on lettering requires a small burnisher for application. Transfer lettering requires a sharp X-acto knife and a headline setter (a special plastic ruler), both available from where you purchase the lettering.

A *reverse* (white becomes black; black becomes white) often looks very nice as headlines and letterheads. Set the type in the normal fashion and then have a reverse PMT made—it should run $4–6. Your printer may provide this service or, at least, know where it can be done. (PMT is a professional term that stands for Photo Mechanical Transfer.)

Reunion News

Reunion News

Keep the original of your letterhead in a safe place and label it with a blue pencil or a Post-It note. Don't use it again and again for each issue of your newsletter. Instead, make several high quality copies to use for this purpose.

The **format** is the framework of your newsletter. It involves such things as paper size, how many columns and what size, position of the letterhead, etc. Many good examples are shown in *Editing Your Newsletter*, a book highly recommended to anyone interested in newsletters. ➡️See "Resources."

Develop a format that appeals to your aesthetic sense, but don't feel that it must be adhered to issue after issue. There's nothing wrong with changing the design of your newsletter as you learn more about typography and graphics. (Note: This goes against the advice given to professional newsletter editors but you're not professional. You get to play as you learn.)

In **creating text** for your newsletter, it's best to use a professional quality typewriter, preferably with a carbon ribbon. If your typewriter uses a fabric ribbon, put in a fresh ribbon and clean out the o's and e's and other letters that may be clogged. You want a crisp, dark print that will reproduce well. If you have a choice of type styles, "Letter Gothic" from IBM (or equivalent) is ideal. Stay away from "script" type faces. They don't reproduce well and are tedious to read.

In its simplest form, a flyer or newsletter can be filled margin-to-margin with type. The only problem with this is that it makes for difficult reading. The longer the line of type, the harder it is for the eye to track back to the beginning of the next line. For this reason, columns have been invented. Figure 2B on page 59 shows a simple 2-column format. Here are instructions for creating a 2-column format with text reduced down to 80%:

(But first, a quick explanation of the term "percentage" as it relates to reductions and enlargements. 100% means the same size. Anything below 100% is a reduction in size; anything above 100% is an enlargement. For example, if an object 10" wide is reduced to 8" wide, the amount of reduction is 80% ($^8/_{10}$). Going from 4" wide to 5" wide is an enlargement of 125% ($^5/_4$).)

```
This is what regular typing looks like.
It's large, takes up a lot of space, and
looks like a business letter. To dress
up your mailers and newsletters, you can
try some of the tricks listed below.

Columnize your format. If the final result will
be printed on 8 1/2" x 11" paper, and you have a
1/2" margin on both sides plus a 1/2" between
columns, then each column will be 3 1/2" wide.
But to get the final result of 3 1/2", your
original should be 4 3/8" (80% of 4 3/8" is
approximately 3 1/2").
```

Note that you do not have to type up the text in side-by-side columns as it will appear in the final result. Using a nonrepro blue pencil, draw 2 vertical blue lines 4 3/8" apart straddling the middle (more or less) of a sheet of typing paper. Stay within these margins as you type. Make more of these typing templates as you need them. When finished, reduce them down to 80% at a copyshop then cut out the text and paste these column-strips into the proper position on the original.

Add some other interesting things if you like such as separators, borders and clip art, all of which you can find at a graphic supply store. You can use a line of asterisks as a separator like this:

*   *   *   *   *

or just draw a short line like this:

_____

or throw in a fancy store-bought one like this:

_____

Another neat trick is to make the first letter of each article a "drop cap" by using some rub-on type or transfer lettering. Make sure you get the right size letters. As a guide, type a couple of lines on your typewriter and take them to the graphic art store. A letter that's a little too big looks better than one that's too small. You can also apply the letter after the copy has been reduced.

YOU CAN BEGIN EACH ARTICLE with about a half line of capitalized type. The capitalized part should include a complete phrase or idea, and not be chopped off just anywhere.

FIGURE 3. Clip art and transfer lettering can help make your mailers and newsletters more interesting. Examples like these and many more are available in clip art books, on computer disk, and for free in newspapers and phone books.

Clip Art and Other Extras

"Clip art" is any line image or drawing that can be used to enhance a printed work. It looks best if it's solid black or white with no shading (small black dots) like those found in screened photos or half tones. See Figure 3 for examples. Clip art comes in books or sheets, available at graphic art stores. You clip them out (hence the name) and paste them onto your original. Dover Books has clip art books on many topics and themes. However, the cheapest source is magazines, newspapers, and telephone yellow pages. If you find something you like, but it's the wrong size, it can be made larger or smaller by using photocopiers that can enlarge or reduce.

When laying out your newsletter, remember to not crowd the pages too much. Professionally this is known as leaving some white space. It's entirely for the benefit of the reader. It helps her relax while reading your wonderful information.

Using Photos

Nice looking photos are a great addition to any newsletter. But too often they come out muddy, faded or almost solid black. That's usually because the photocopy process was used instead of the quick print method. Quick printing is more expensive on quantities under 300–400 but well worth the extra expense if photos are to be reproduced.

Photos must always be screened. Screening breaks the photo into small black and white dots. This can be done photographically for about $8 per photo (or less if several are done at once). The newer methods involve computer scanning and laser output for about the same price, perhaps a little more. If your print shop can't do the screening, they know who can.

It's always best if the original photos are black-and-white but color photos can be used, too, though the results sometimes come out a bit muddy. If in doubt, ask your printer.

It's possible to reduce or enlarge a photo or use only a portion of it (called cropping). A description of the methods is a bit beyond the scope of this book but can be found in *Creating Family Newsletters* (➠see "Resources"). It's easiest to have your printer do it (though it will cost extra).

Include Some Entertainment

It's fun for the reader as well as the editor to include trivia, family sayings, proverbs, quotes, jokes, cartoons, family historic dates, bits of wisdom, recipes, quizzes, puzzles, brain teasers, and items of nostalgic or historic interest (especially if they compare the past with the present). There are many books that can provide you with such information or you can ask family members to contribute. ➠Some books are listed in "Resources"; many more can be found in your local library.

There are mail-order companies that offer "historical print-outs of any date." The time span is usually from 1900 to present; the main purpose is to show people what was happening in the world on the day they were born. The price is certainly right, around $8 per printout on an 8 ½ x 11 sheet. The printout of a significant date will give you enough information for three or four newsletters. Next page shows an example. ➠See "Resources" for a source.

Examples of trivia:

In 19xx:
- The price of gas was ___ per gallon.
- We mailed a letter for ___.
- Bread cost ___ per loaf.
- The ballpoint pen was not yet invented.
- Credit cards did not exist.
- The Zip Code was __ years in the future.
- Life magazine was ___ per copy.

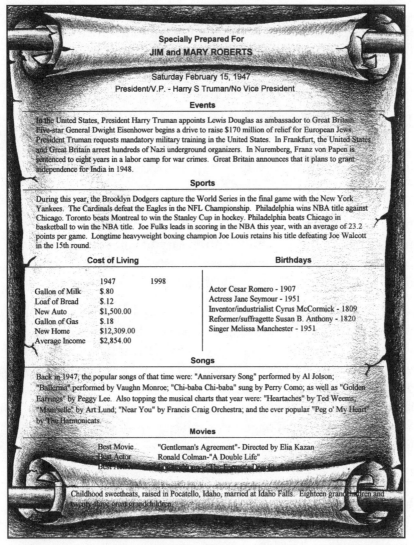

Specially Prepared For

JIM and MARY ROBERTS

Saturday February 15, 1947

President/V.P. - Harry S Truman/No Vice President

Events

In the United States, President Harry Truman appoints Lewis Douglas as ambassador to Great Britain. Five-star General Dwight Eisenhower begins a drive to raise $170 million of relief for European Jews. President Truman requests mandatory military training in the United States. In Frankfurt, the United States and Great Britain arrest hundreds of Nazi underground organizers. In Nuremberg, Franz von Papen is sentenced to eight years in a labor camp for war crimes. Great Britain announces that it plans to grant independence for India in 1948.

Sports

During this year, the Brooklyn Dodgers capture the World Series in the final game with the New York Yankees. The Cardinals defeat the Eagles in the NFL Championship. Philadelphia wins NBA title against Chicago. Toronto beats Montreal to win the Stanley Cup in hockey. Philadelphia beats Chicago in basketball to win the NBA title. Joe Fulks leads in scoring in the NBA this year, with an average of 23.2 points per game. Longtime heavyweight boxing champion Joe Louis retains his title defeating Joe Walcott in the 15th round.

Cost of Living			Birthdays
	1947	1998	
Gallon of Milk	$.80		Actor Cesar Romero - 1907
Loaf of Bread	$.12		Actress Jane Seymour - 1951
New Auto	$1,500.00		Inventor/industrialist Cyrus McCormick - 1809
Gallon of Gas	$.18		Reformer/suffragette Susan B. Anthony - 1820
New Home	$12,309.00		Singer Melissa Manchester - 1951
Average Income	$2,854.00		

Songs

Back in 1947, the popular songs of that time were: "Anniversary Song" performed by Al Jolson; "Ballerina" performed by Vaughn Monroe; "Chi-baba Chi-baba" sung by Perry Como; as well as "Golden Earrings" by Peggy Lee. Also topping the musical charts that year were: "Heartaches" by Ted Weems; "Mam'selle" by Art Lund; "Near You" by Francis Craig Orchestra; and the ever popular "Peg o' My Heart" by The Harmonicats.

Movies

Best Movie　　"Gentleman's Agreement"- Directed by Elia Kazan
Best Actor　　Ronald Colman-"A Double Life"
Best Ho...

Childhood sweethearts, raised in Pocatello, Idaho, married at Idaho Falls. Eighteen grandchildren and twenty-three great grandchildren.

Historical printouts are available by mail (see "Resources"). They can provide good information to use in your mailers, newsletters, or program.

You might use such a page when a couple is celebrating their 50th wedding anniversary to show what it was like when they were married.

Tools of the Trade

Graphic artists use all sorts of fancy equipment, most of which you don't need. Here is a bare-bones list of tools needed to do a good job on your flyers or newsletters. Average prices are given in parentheses below.

➤ *A typewriter.*

➤ *Something to cut on* when you use the razor blade. Your 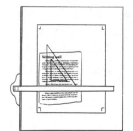 kitchen table or similar hard, flat surface with good lighting is an ideal work area. However, using the table top for razor blade cutting will produce scratches. Instead, use a piece of glass, marble or similar hard surface. Or use a plastic cutting board made for the purpose. These boards are very inexpensive and have milled edges which means the edges are perfectly straight and at exactly 90 degrees to each other. ($11–17)

➤ *Paste-up paper* or planning paper. This is printed with 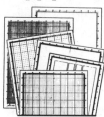 "nonreproducible blue" guide lines and is used to create (paste-up) the originals. It comes in different weights, sizes, and grids, and is useful for aligning the work properly. Small quantities are available from graphic art stores.

➤ *A T-square.* Used for horizontal alignment and with the triangle for vertical alignment. ($2 to $24)

➤ *A triangle* with a right angle, preferably of metal or colored plastic (clear plastic gets lost easily because it's hard to see). Used for vertical alignment and to provide a straight edge for cutting.

➤ *A ruler* for measuring. Or your T-square or triangle may have a ruler.

➤ *A proportion wheel.* Not absolutely necessary but it sure helps when figuring reduction and enlargement percentages. ($4)

➤ *Razor blades* (single edge) or X-acto knife with #11 blades. ($4)

➤ *Scissors* ($4)

➤ *Burnishers.* Two kinds: a flat plastic burnisher ($2) for rubbing down large pieces and a small spoon burnisher ($1) for applying rub-on or transfer lettering.

➤ *A blue pencil* (50¢). Used to make marks or notes on the original that won't show up on the final product. Most copiers and printer's cameras are designed to not "see" light blue. Get a "nonrepro blue" pencil, not a pen. A ballpoint pen will occasionally leave a dark blob of ink on the paper which will show up as a black speck on the final product.

➤ *White-out liquid.* Comes in a small bottle with applicator. Commonly used to cover typing errors and will get rid of "shadow lines."

➤ *Correction or cover-up tape.* Same purpose as white-out. Comes in various widths. The "one-line" width (1/6") is the most useful. ($3)

➤ *Masking tape.* Used to hold down the original while you are working on it. ($1)

➤ *Nonpermanent glue* or spray adhesive, or wax. Used to hold the various pieces down on the original. Professionals use wax because it allows you to pick up a piece and re-set it as many times as you like. The cheapest little hand-held electric waxer is $60—a good investment if you can afford it. However, for flyers or small newsletters, the best bet is to paste-up with either a wax stick (like a lipstick) ($1) or nonpermanent spray adhesive ($14). By the way, rubber cement and cellophane tape are not recommended. They can be very messy to work with if repositioning becomes necessary (and it will).

Using Computer Printers

If you are using a computer to create your newsletters or mailers, here's a word about computer printers:

Newsletters and flyers can be created with dot matrix printers, but laser and ink jet printers produce much better results. The good news is that you don't have to own a laser printer to use one (since they are rather expensive). If your software can "print to disk," you can take your disk (or mail it) to a typesetter or printing service bureau that will output laser printer copy for around $2–5 per page. These pages become the originals from which photocopies or quick-print copies are made. Some computer stores also rent computers by the hour (you work at the store), but you have to know how to use the software or else you will be wasting your time and money. Some of the fancier copy or print shops near universities offer such services.

*   *   *   *   *

Hopefully you have been encouraged here to try your hand at creating a newsletter or at least in sprucing up your flyers. The tools are really quite inexpensive and the techniques not that hard to learn. The books mentioned in "Resources" are all you need to get started. In particular, get Elaine Floyd's book, *Creating Family Newsletters*. It may help to think of newsletter editing and graphics as a new hobby—one that will benefit your family for many generations to come.

Round Robin Letters

The simplest type of family communication with the lowest cost is the round robin letter. It works this way: You write a letter telling about your family, then write out a list of names and addresses of relatives that have agreed ahead of time to participate. Send your letter, the mailing list, and a short letter of instructions to the person on the top of the list. Each person adds her letter and sends them all on to the next person on the list. When it comes back to you, remove your first letter, put in a new one, and send it around again. A good number of participants is 10 or 15.

Round robins can be great fun and a joy to receive. They cut down on your correspondence because you write one letter to many people. They also allow you to be in contact with a greater number of family members. The only cost is your postage each time you send them on. But round robins are successful only if the participants are willing to keep the letters moving. Some families have a rule that you must add your letter within two weeks or send them on without your contribution.

The Family Survey

A survey of your family can provide interesting information. However, there is no use going to the extra trouble unless you know *for sure* that you will compile and use the results. Here are some ways that a survey can be used:

1. *To provide information for awards to be presented during the reunion program.* Decide on the award categories first, then formulate the questions that will provide the answers. Or it may be more appropriate to ask for the following type of response: "If any of you think you may qualify, or you can suggest someone else who qualifies for any of these awards, please let us know: Most Recent Parent/Grandparent, First to Retire, Youngest Grandparent, Traveled the Farthest." Of course, you should still not judge the winner solely by the responses received. Some people will not bother to send back the survey or feel too modest to do so. Just before each winner is announced, ask if anyone can better the record in question. See p. 107–108 for more award categories and suggestions.

2. *To compile biographical information* for a family directory, a newsletter, a genealogy, or a family history. The minimal information to gather: name, address, phone number, spouse's name, and children's names. The next level of detail to gather could

include occupation(s), birth and marriage dates, and hobbies. Beyond that you might request a short biography of a family; a favorite quote, saying, or proverb; favorite books, movies, or music; and pet peeve.

3. (For large groups) *To collect information that can be used later to "re-find"* a person who gets "lost." Ask for birthdate, social security number, military service number, driver's license number, or address of "someone who will always know where you are." When gathering this type of information, always explain your purpose.

4. *To create a chart of "Family Statistics"* to be displayed at the reunion. The chart can also be a part of a directory, a family history, or included in a newsletter. This statistical "family portrait" can include the following:

➤ Total number on mailing list.
➤ Total number present at the reunion.
➤ List of those who live outside of U.S. and/or Canada.
➤ Total number of states represented by group.
➤ List of first-timers attending the reunion.
➤ List of those born, married, died since last reunion.
➤ List of those who have not missed a reunion.

Encourage everyone to fill out and return the survey, even if they can't attend the reunion. Be sure to have survey forms at the registration desk for those who did not send them in.

Chapter 6

Mailing/Postage

Chapter Highlights
▶*First Class vs. Standard Mail.* ▶*Endorsements.*
▶*A Mailing Label System.* ▶*Information on the Envelope.*
▶*Resources.* ▶*Other Mailing Tips.*

First Class vs. Standard Mail

Many reunion planners, especially those in charge of large reunions or who send several mailings per year, wonder if it may be cheaper to use Standard Mail (formerly called Third Class) rather than First Class. The answer is: "probably not." Here's why:

1. Standard Mail (formerly Third Class) must be mailed in batches of 200 or more.

2. A bulk mailing permit costs $85 per year plus an $85 one-time imprint fee (1998 prices). You can send by Standard Mail without the imprint but then you must hand-stick special precancelled stamps or use a meter. (*See next page.)

3. First Class Mail is automatically forwarded (more than once, if necessary), and arrives much more quickly than Standard Mail (which is always last priority).

4. First Class Mail is returned to you if it can't be delivered; Standard Mail is discarded, which means you'll never know if it got there or not unless you put on a special endorsement (see "Endorsements" below).

5. Sending by Standard Mail requires that you sort the batch by zip code, bundle it, put special stickers on each bundle, weigh them, fill out special forms, and deliver everything to the Post Office (and only the Post Office that issued the permit).

In exchange for some of the headaches outlined above, you save around 11¢ per piece of mail (under one ounce) using Standard Mail. It just doesn't seem worth it.

*There are companies that will process Standard Mail for you. They use their own permit and imprint. The return address can be your own address. They can also stuff the envelopes and attach the labels. Of course they charge for these services. Look under "Mailing Services" in the Yellow Pages.

Endorsements

Endorsements (technically known as Ancillary Service Endorsements) can be written or printed on the envelope of any class of mail to request an addressee's new address and to provide instructions to the Post Office on how to handle your mail if it's not deliverable as addressed. The endorsement phrase consists of three words (see next page) printed in one of four places on the envelope: 1. below the return address, 2. above the mailing address, 3. to the left of the postage area, 4. below the postage area.

There are four classes of endorsements, only two of which should be considered by reunion groups—for reasons too complicated to explain here. For more information, ask for Publication 95 (*Quick Service Guide*) from your local Post Office. Or contact their Web site at *www.usps.gov* or bulletin board service at *http://ribbs.usps.gov*.

Address Service Requested (replaces "Address Correction Requested"). If undeliverable, mail is returned with reason for nondelivery. If forwarded, a separate change-of-address notice is sent to you. Free for First Class Mail; a postage charge for Standard Mail (80¢ for returned mail under 1 oz.; 50¢ for change-of-address notice; 1998 prices).

Return Service Requested (replaces "Do Not Forward, Address Correction Requested"). Mail is not forwarded. Mail is returned with new address information or reason for nondelivery. Free for First Class Mail; a postage charge for Standard Mail (80¢ for returned mail under 1 oz.; 1998 price).

a (Noncomputer) Mailing Label System

With small families (under 50 on the mailing list), addressing envelopes by hand is not a big problem. Of course, a computer with a printer can make it a very simple process. But if you have a large group and no computer, you can use the system described below.

Peel-off, self-sticking mailing labels come in blank sheets of 33 (three across the top and 11 down). These sheets are the same size as a sheet of typing paper (8.5 x 11). Your master list is photocopied onto these sheets (you may have to take your own blank labels to the copy shop). To prepare your master list, write or type each new address onto a plain white sheet of paper using a label template (see explanation below). Each label entry can be "generally" alphabetized by assigning a certain letter or letters to each sheet. Depending on the size of your group, you may have (for example) the A's, B's, and C's on one sheet, or perhaps just the A's, or you could assign one letter per row of 11 down. The names within each section do not necessarily have to be in alphabetical order. Just before each general mailing, the master list is photocopied onto the mailing labels which are then peeled off and stuck onto the mailers.

A *label template* usually comes with each package of labels you buy (if you buy typewriter labels and not laser or ink jet labels). The template is a regular size sheet of paper with heavy black lines representing the label edges. When placed behind an ordinary sheet of white paper, the black lines show through to guide the placement of the addressing information onto the plain paper (you can type or write). The template is never written or typed on, itself; it functions only as a guide.

Another use for these labels, by the way, is to paste one with a new address over the old address on the file cards (see Chapter 4). If it turns out that the old information becomes of interest again, the label peels off easily (if you use the ones with nonpermanent adhesive). Also, if you want to create a separate financial file, you could stick the labels onto cards and alphabetize the cards.

For those people who are not "found" until just before the reunion, don't bother photocopying labels—simply hand-address their mailers. If these people missed previous mailings, send them all the prior mailings along with the current one; be sure to enclose a note of explanation to avoid confusion.

If a previous reunion chairperson or committee has left you with no file cards but only a batch of mailing labels or label originals (created using a template), you can easily create a new card file by photocopying onto new labels, sticking these new labels onto cards, and alphabetizing the cards.

Information on the Envelope or Mailing Face

Lots of pertinent information can appear on your envelopes (or "mailing face," if not using envelopes). Most of this information is for the Post Office but some can be for the addressee. It can be printed directly on the paper during the printing (or photocopying) process, written by hand, applied by rubber stamp, or by attaching self-adhesive stickers.

Possibilities for information on the envelope or mailing face:

1. Return address (include phone number).

2. "(approved Post Office endorsement)" (see p. 83).

3. "(family name) FAMILY REUNION INFORMATION ENCLOSED"

4. "FIRST CLASS MAIL"

5. Family crest.

Resources

Preprinted return address labels (gummed or self-stick) are available very cheaply from Walter Drake and Sons (➠see "Resources"). They also provide imprinted envelopes in quantities of 100. It may take three to six weeks for delivery. Order early.

Number 10 (long) envelopes with your return address printed in the upper left hand corner (minimum order is 1000) are available from Quill Corporation (➠see "Resources").

The U.S. Postal Service can provide you with personalized stamped envelopes in quantities as few as 50, and in either regular or business size. Ask your local Post Office to send you a "Personalized Envelope Order Form" which explains the options and prices.

We (Reunion Research) offer special self-adhesive stickers like this one shown at actual size. See p. 248 for more information.

Ordinary rubber stamps can be ordered through office supply stores, and can be used with brightly colored inks for emphasis and decorative effect. In larger towns and cities there are rubber stamp shops that will deliver your stamps the same day you place the order.

Rubber stamps have also reached an art form in the last few years and can be used for creating truly impressive reunion invitations and envelopes. Techniques include brightly colored hand-applied inks, thermography and embossing powders, and special scissors and die cuts for decorative edges and holes, all of which can be done at home. For more on these special types of rubber stamps, see the Yellow Pages under "Rubber Stamps." Look for ads with the phrase "art stamps" in them.

For rubber stamps for genealogists and family reunions, try Rootstamps (➡see "Resources"). They create special stamps like this one and many others.

Other Mailing Tips

We recommend using envelopes to mail in, but you can also fold the paper in thirds or in half, and tape it shut. The maximum size for First Class Mail is 6 ⅛" x 11 ½" after it's folded. If the piece is folded, it must be taped shut to qualify as First Class Mail (don't use staples—your mailers can easily get torn by the sorting machines).

When sending mail to a person in the military overseas, regular domestic rates apply if you use an A.P.O. or F.P.O. address.

Chapter 7

Getting Ready
Services, Supplies & Special Touches

Chapter Highlights
▸*Help from the Commercial Community.* ▸*Being Good Hosts.*
▸*Registration.* ▸*Family Identification.* ▸*Decorations.* ▸*Music.*
▸*In Memoriam.* ▸*Planning for Emergencies.* ▸*Tipping.*

Help from the Commercial Community

As plans for your reunion progress, needs will develop for certain services and supplies. Before you purchase anything or go looking elsewhere, find out what is offered by the Convention Bureau and Chamber of Commerce in the area where your reunion will be held. They all offer something. Some things may be provided free; for others there may be a nominal charge. The larger your reunion, the more value it is to the commercial community, and the more help you can get.

Below is a list of services and supplies that *may* be available. Most Convention Bureaus and Chambers of Commerce offer no more than two or three of these. Some may be available from convention centers and hotels as well.

- Help with site inspection.
- Discounts with airlines.
- Name tags, badges, banners, table decorations, signs.
- Gifts of local merchandise.
- "Shells" (One-page flyers containing local information or ads with space for your reunion program. Printing is usually provided free.)
- Maps, local information brochures, official greeting/ welcome letter from the mayor, and other giveaways to include in your registration packets.
- Cash boxes.
- Copy machines/typewriters to use during registration.
- Photocopying and printing services.
- Parking permits.
- Registration cards.
- Mailing services.
- Secretarial services.
- Shopping programs.
- Sight-seeing trips.
- Phone books.

Being Good Hosts

Hospitality can make the difference between a good reunion and a really great one. Often it's the little things that make you and your committee members gracious hosts. Here are some examples:

- Have "greeters" at the front door pointing the way to the registration area and answering any questions.
- Have enough people staffing the registration table during "rush hour."

> At large reunions, identify the main staff and "people who can answer questions" with special hats, caps, or badges.
> Give first-timers special attention. Make it easy for them to mix.
> Give recognition to old-timers with awards, special name tags, etc.
> Reach out. Help the person who appears lost.
> Provide local gifts (*e.g.*, salt water taffy in Atlantic City, maple syrup in Vermont).
> Serve refreshments and/or play music during registration.
> Use glasses instead of plastic cups.
> Put flowers in the rooms of honored guests.
> Decorate with flowers.
> Provide free or validated parking.

Such thoughtful yet inexpensive considerations will help make this reunion a hit, and will go a long way toward making the next reunion a success as well. When you've made the people feel comfortable, they are more likely to have a good time and will want to attend the next reunion.

Get Ready for Registration

The registration area is the "front door" to your reunion, and its atmosphere and organization will set the tone for the remainder of the event. First impressions are lasting impressions. It's important to have an efficient, painless, practical registration at your reunion.

> Carefully think through the whole process of registration: forms, kits, tickets, name tags, verification, receipts, refunds, etc. Try to anticipate and solve problems that may arise.
> The registration area should be easy to locate, with signs pointing the way. This is especially true if another activity is taking place simultaneously (as often happens in convention centers and large hotels).

➤ Make sure supplies and furniture are ordered well in advance. Items might include tables, chairs, wastebaskets, signs, typewriter, paper, cash boxes, change, marking pens, scotch tape, masking tape, paper clips, scissors, staplers, pens, pencils, etc.

➤ Greeters should be stationed at the entrance area in front of the registration table. Their job is to make everyone feel welcome and comfortable, and to answer questions. Remind them to stay focused on their job and not drift away into private conversations.

➤ Develop a registration "kit" or "packet." This is simply a large envelope full of everything the person or family will need for the event. It can contain local information, tour information, maps, local give-aways, name tags, event tickets, the reunion program, a survey, evaluation questionnaire, family directory, etc. These packets are "stuffed" ahead of time and each envelope has the family's or individual's name on the outside, printed in big letters. For large reunions, arrange them in alphabetical order.

➤ Provide a list of those who have paid and those who owe money. Keep all financial records at the registration table. Each family's financial standing can be written on, or stapled to, the packet.

➤ Provide relief for greeters and those doing the registering. No volunteer should do this job for more than an hour without a break. If the person is being paid (such as hotel staff), she should still be relieved occasionally.

Family Identification

It may happen that some family members will meet for the first time at the registration area. Which Brown are you related to? Is Paul or Earl your father? Keeping clans straight can be made easier by some visual helpers prepared ahead of time.

Families around the country have come up with clever systems of dressing that make family identification easier at the reunion. For instance, the Martinez family wears different colored T-shirts. Uncle Joe and Aunt Maria's clan—adults, children, grandchildren—all wear red T-shirts while Uncle Frank and Aunt Delores' family wear blue T-shirts. A poster displayed in a prominent place shows a family tree indicating the different branches drawn in colors corresponding to the family T-shirt colors. Once the color system is memorized, you know at a glance whose grandchildren are playing on the swings. Family physical characteristics become easier to spot when you can mentally put all the family members together. This adds interest to your reunion and helps people to get to know more about each other.

You can design your own special reunion shirts using colored T-shirts and permanent magic markers, or using the many decorating materials available in fabric or craft stores. Decorating T-shirts during the reunion could be an enjoyable activity for both kids and adults. ➡️See "Resources."

Aside from T-shirts, families might opt for wearing matching baseball caps, jackets, etc. You can be as elaborate or as simple in your identification process as you choose.

Name Tags. The most common form of identification at reunions is name tags. The name-of-the-game with name tags is not just identification, but *easy* identification. Make the letters large and clear enough to be read 6 feet away without squinting. Buy large felt-tip pens for this purpose and find someone who can print well, or have them printed on a computer printer. Letters 1/4" high should be the minimum size, 3/8" to 1/2" is better.

➤ Make name tags in advance for everyone who is registered.

➤ Have all necessary items for making name tags at the reunion. Assign someone to make them on the spot for

last minute drop-ins or re-make any that have errors.
➤ The stick-on type of name tag won't last more than one
day. Use the pin-on or clip-on type for multi-day events.
➤ "Button" name tags look nice, make nice souvenirs, and
can have a family crest on them. But the standard size
(2.25") is too small to be read easily. A more readable
size is 2.75" which can be rather expensive.

Alternatives to Name Tags. As a unique alternative to the
commonplace "peel-and-wear" tag, Virginia Graboyes of Vallejo,
CA, painted a family tree on a big banner (below). The family
has six branches, one for Mr. Graboyes and his 5 siblings. Each
person was listed on the tree with his or her name on a leaf.
Each family branch had leaves of a distinctive color. The beauty

of this family tree is that the leaves were detachable name tags.
For instance, if your grandfather was Stephen, your leaf was red.
If your grandfather was Forrest, your leaf was orange, etc. When
you removed your leaf to wear your name tag, a permanent leaf
below the removable name tag also showed your name. After
everyone had arrived and was sporting name tags, a complete

family tree on a banner was revealed for all to see—and everyone was identified by his or her name tag. The name tags were covered with clear contact paper so they would hold up throughout the several-day reunion.

The organizer of another reunion also created unique name tags—ones that ended up as souvenirs. She cut dry cedar branches into ¼" thick slices, creating circles three inches in diameter. In the top of each circle of wood, she drilled two small holes and inserted yarn long enough to hang the circle around one's neck. The yarn was color coded for different families.

At the reunion, she set up a table with sandpaper, colored pens, and a clear lacquer spray. After families arrived and were settled for the three-day event, people visited the craft table and made their own name tags. On the tag, people wrote their names, hometowns, and year of the reunion. Everyone participated— from the youngest to the oldest—sanding, applying names, and adding other features to individualize their art. As families arrived, children who already had made their name tags took the new families to the craft table and instructed the newcomers on how to make theirs. They loved this duty, feeling an important part of the family and the reunion. Many saved their name tags as a memento of the special time spent together.

Creating name tags can be a rewarding do-it-yourself project. If your reunion is several days long, this is a good first-day "get acquainted" activity.

Decorations (or Don't Get Carried Away)

Decorations are always nice, but aren't absolutely necessary at reunions. You can go without, or you can keep them simple, tasteful, relatively inexpensive, and still maintain the spirit of the reunion. After all, a reunion is not a prom.

Most commonly used decorations are flower arrangements, flags, banners, balloons, and family crests incorporated into place settings and tablecloths. Floral arrangements make nice table centerpieces; however, they are a bit more expensive than balloons. Bud vases with a few bright flowers are attractive and sometimes cheaper.

If you *are* thinking about fancy do-it-yourself decorations, consider whether your group has someone with talent, interest, energy, and the ability to recruit and motivate helpers. Next, consider the cost and budget. Decorations are no longer a nickel-and-dime expense. If the interest and expertise is available in your group, then be sure to draw up a carefully itemized list of materials needed. At a large reunion, an "all-out" decoration job with flowers on each table, banners, crepe paper streamers, imprinted balloons and napkins, etc., can easily run $300–400. If this is the "look" you want, then it may be well worth the time and money spent.

But before launching a full-scale production, find out the facility's rules about decorating. Some indoor places don't allow thumb tacks or tape; others will allow masking tape, but no thumb tacks. Such rules may limit you to table centerpieces and banners. Even if a banquet facility allows you to decorate, the room may be available only an hour or two beforehand. This may severely limit your decorating plans or require a team effort. Consider how much help you will need. No matter how talented, one or two people may only be able to do a limited job in two hours. Also consider who is going to take them down and find out how soon after the event they must be removed.

In some areas, *helium balloon bouquets* can be delivered or you can rent helium tanks and inflate them yourself. Count the number of tables and figure four-to-seven latex balloons with one mylar (foil) balloon in the middle for a nice looking centerpiece. You can write or draw on the foil balloon (easiest when not inflated) in colored ink using marking pens. The super-large markers work best for this. You can use colored gift wrapping ribbon for "string" or the flashy metallic mylar ribbon available in party supply stores. The balloons should be tied to a decorative weighted object that is placed in the center of the table. Make this weighted object (the part that rests on the table) small enough so that during the meal you have room for food and utensils. Some balloon companies use large jingle bells for this purpose. The helium balloons themselves will rise up out of the way and present no problem.

Dessert cakes, just large enough to feed the people at each table, make nice centerpieces. Appropriate words and crests can be used to decorate the cakes. Numbers and letters made of sugar can be purchased at variety stores and drug stores.

Pennants and banners can be made from butcher paper and poster paint. You can embellish them with crepe paper and glue-on stars or glitter which come in many colors. If you are having a group photo taken, a banner can also serve for identification purposes in the picture.

Miniature flags (numbers are from the catalog). See Paradise Products.

There are mail order companies that specialize in *paper products* for parties, for example: theme, ethnic, and holiday table settings, miniature flags of most countries, table fringes, crepe paper, and rolls of table top paper in many colors. Also piñatas. ➠See "Resources."

Imprinted Tableware. Napkins and coasters imprinted with the family name and/or crest can add a classy touch. You can see samples and order these from most stores that sell wedding, graduation, or prom items and supplies. Also try greeting card stores. If you can't find a store near you, call Carlson Craft (507/625-5011) and ask for their customer service department. Carlson is a wholesaler that supplies many small stores around the country, but they don't sell directly to the consumer. Ask for their representative nearest you who has a Graduation Album or an All Occasion Album. These albums have the styles and colors that you are looking for. Some stores have only the Wedding Album which isn't as useful for your purposes.

A visit to a party supply store will give you more ideas. In the Yellow Pages see "Balloons, Novelty and Toy, Retail," "Party Equipment, Renting," and "Party Supplies."

Using Music Effectively

Background music does not normally play an important role in family reunions. However, it can be used effectively. For example, something light, friendly, and "welcoming" during arrival time can set a "fun" mood. It could simply be recorded music, or perhaps a pianist, or a strolling guitarist. Other possibilities: a string quartet; ethnic music such as Irish, reggae, salsa, klezmer, Cajun, mariachi; country or bluegrass.

The menu of musical options is wide since it covers everything from recorded music to a full orchestra, as well as hundreds of types of music. Of course, a lot will be determined by your budget. Can you afford a large band or will you have to settle for a small band, a single musician, a disk jockey, recorded music, or musicians from within your own group?

Before deciding, investigate all options and costs. A reputable talent or music agency can tell you of the local talent available, and can be a lifesaver in case of problems.

Here are some ideas that have worked at family reunions:

> ➤ An ethnic band during arrival time.
> ➤ Special music pertaining to a chosen theme or era.
> ➤ Strolling strings.
> ➤ A rock band for a teen dance.

➤ A DJ and appropriate music for an adult's dance.
➤ An *a capella* singing group.
➤ A barbershop quartet.
➤ A rented jukebox with appropriate music.
➤ Accordion music during registration.

These musicians are performing at their family reunion and included a special song written for the occasion.

➤ A song leader inspiring people to sing well-known favorites.
➤ A family musical group.

If you hire professionals, have a backup plan in case of bad weather, power failures, no-shows, etc. Identify all technical requirements, such as staging, chairs, sound systems, storage and security of instruments, unloading area, changing room, and refreshments in the changing room.

Hardanger fiddler at a Norwegian reunion.

Choosing a Band. If it's a band you want, then there are two key considerations: The kind of music and the amount you want to pay. Most bands require a deposit and a contract. Be sure to reconfirm the engagement a week or two before the reunion. Rates vary widely from $200–300 for an inexperienced three-person group to $1500 or more for a large, established group. The average price is around $300–500.

Vasquez Family Mariachi Band, Williams, AZ.

Check the Yellow Pages under "Entertainers," "Musicians," or "Orchestras and Bands"; in the white pages look up "Musicians' Union." The people who manage bands and DJs are called booking agents, and can be found under "Entertainment Bureaus" or "Professional Talent Management."

Disk Jockeys (DJs) are usually used at dances, though they can also provide background or theme music. A good DJ has a collection of thousands of songs, amazingly sophisticated equipment, and is able to play music from almost any era, as well as take requests. Most of them have lists of the top ten songs for any month and year, and a reference system that allows them to find, cue up, and play any request in a matter of seconds. Remember, it's a lot easier to tell a DJ to keep the volume down than a band. The best thing about having a DJ is that you get to hear the exact rendition of the song you remember, rather than a band's interpretation. For nostalgic purposes, this can be an important consideration.

There are people in almost every community who work as disk jockeys for events such as reunions, dances, and parties. Their rates vary between $300 and $500 per event. Rates below $200 should be viewed with some skepticism; check on what you are actually getting. We strongly urge you to talk to groups that have hired the prospective DJ in the past. Speak with the person who was directly in charge of music for the group. For disk jockeys, look in the Yellow Pages under "Entertainers."

Taped Music. Between events and while people are socializing, taped music can provide a nice background. It could be music that holds special significance for the family, such as ethnic songs or songs that were popular when many of the adults were young. Few commercial records, tapes or CDs can give you the variety you will want, so try to tape individual selections from private collections. Since many people have kept their old records over the years, mention this need in your mailers. Audiotapes are convenient to play, but records and CDs are best because they make it easier to find requests—tapes being more difficult to cue up. If you decide to provide your own music in this way, have one person in charge of music, and acting as DJ.

Cassettes of national anthems of various countries are available from Paradise Products. ➡See "Resources."

Played on a home stereo or boom box, audiotapes and CDs will provide good music in most situations. However, for a dance in a large room, such a system may not have enough wattage (power). The only way to test this is to try it in the room beforehand, but even this is tricky because in a real situation you have "crowd noise" to contend with and bodies absorbing the sound. "Auditorium sized" amplifiers and speakers can be rented, and some DJs offer a "sound system only" for considerably less cost than their usual package.

In Memoriam

A memorial service can be held in remembrance of ancestors, and perhaps as a special farewell to those who have passed away since the last reunion. At a family reunion, there are several appropriate ways of honoring the deceased:

➤ A short prayer during the main program.

➤ A moment of silence before any event.

➤ A memorial breakfast or brunch during which there is a short service.

➤ A wreath-laying ceremony at a nearby chapel, memorial, gravesite, or family cemetery.

➤ A family or local minister, or a family elder could be asked to say a few words.

There are many ways to arrange an altar or memorial display. It's important to keep it tasteful and carefully prepared. When possible, have photographs of the deceased. Give each photo or each name its own "space." Flowers are always appropriate. Votive candle(s) are a nice touch if the local fire codes allow it. If indoors, there could be a soft spotlight setting off the whole display. The important thing is that it should be by itself with no other display or distraction nearby.

The Lowe Family of North Carolina displays this memorial plaque at their family reunions. Names are added as family members pass away. ➠See "Resources."

Planning for Emergencies

It's important to consider possible on-site emergencies, especially for older people. An illness can be brought on or complicated by change in diet, drinking, time-zone changes, fatigue, excitement, weather, and altitude. Be sure to have a plan to cover emergencies, especially for longer reunions.

Become familiar with local medical support systems. For instance, does the area have a 911 number to call? Get the number for the police and nearest hospital. How about a dentist who can be contacted on the weekends or on short notice? Who in your group is CPR trained? Is there a first aid kit handy? Where is it? Where can you rent a wheelchair? Is there a 24-hour drugstore nearby? It is always better to err on the side of caution than to risk inadequate care and treatment. In order for everyone to have access to key emergency numbers, consider publishing them in the program or on a separate flyer.

And be careful of dispensing medicines, even aspirin, to family members (other than your own immediate family, of course). If a child wants an aspirin or other medication, see that the child's parent is the one who does the actual dispensing.

Tipping

Tipping can be an important part of a reunion; professional meeting planners know this, but unfortunately many reunion planners do not. For this reason the quality of service at some reunions can be lacking. If your reunion site is a hotel or resort, these tips on tipping are especially appropriate:

➤ Assume you will tip and budget for it.
➤ Alert your reunion staff to look for (and remember) people who provide exceptional service, then tip accordingly.
➤ Good rule: Expect good service, tip exceptional service. Do not tip in advance. Possible exception: bellmen, front desk personnel.
➤ Tips do not all have to be in cash. A small gift or letter of commendation are both acceptable.
➤ If "automatic gratuities" are written into your contract,

know exactly what they are for and who gets them so that you do not double tip.

➤ Certain positions should not be tipped: general manager, directors of departments, anyone in sales or management.

➤ If, after you get home, you realize you forgot someone, send a tip with a note. It's never too late to recognize good service.

Chapter 8

Activities & Games

Chapter Highlights

▸*Inactive Activities.* ▸*Gathering for a Program.*
▸*Showing the Kids a Good Time.*
▸*Getting Serious About Games.* ▸*Adapting Popular Games.*
▸*Create Your Own Games.*

Inactive Activities

Not all activities at reunions should be "active." This is very important because not all people at reunions *can* be active, especially the elderly. Following are descriptions of various types of "inactive" activity areas. We'll call them "centers." Such centers help people achieve the basic goals of most reunions: catching up with the events in other's lives, doing something enjoyable together, and learning more about the family. These goals, for the most part, don't require a lot of activity.

A visiting area. A quiet place where people can visit and get to know those long-lost cousins is a must. It should be comfortable. Provide chairs, tables, and shade (if it's outdoors). If it's indoors, you might call it the hospitality room.

Family memorabilia adds interest to any reunion.

Memorabilia table. Display old photos, albums, newspaper clippings, a family tree, war medals, genealogies, old letters, etc. Family members can browse through this area at their leisure.

Make sure that items donated for this table are carefully labeled and that one person is responsible for receiving, displaying, and returning them. If you are concerned about documents or old photos being taken, place heavy clear plastic over everything on the table and tape the edges to the underside.

You should also consider keeping a *scrapbook* of each reunion. These will become more and more interesting over the years. For a source of unique, high quality scrapbooks and photo albums, ➠see "Resources."

The BIG scrapbook offered by Scrapbook Partners.

A message center. At a large reunion, it's helpful to have a bulletin board (plus paper, pencils, and thumb tacks) for messages from the reunion committee and for the exchange of personal messages.

Refreshment table. Many people in social situations need something to do with their hands and their mouths (other than talk) in order to feel at ease. Too often, a glass of alcohol or can of beer is the only thing available. Be sure to serve chips and dips, nuts and other "finger food," sodas, fruit juice and coffee to counteract the effects of alcohol, or to offer an alternative to alcohol.

Slides/movies/videos. People enjoy looking at their past. Set up a slide projector and a screen off to the side or in a corner. In your mailers ask people to bring movies and videos to the reunion and assign a volunteer to show them. A projector that automatically cycles slides can be set up for a continuous showing. Don't forget an extra projection bulb and an extension cord. For safety purposes, tape all cords to the floor or carpet with duct tape.

Residence map. A presentation like the one below gives a good overview of the group's geographical mix, and besides it's

fun to see where everybody lives. You will need a map of the United States and (possibly) Canada. Be sure it includes Hawaii and Alaska, if necessary. Use stick-pins (different colors for different families), and a board you can stick the pins into. Tape the map to the board. For large groups, have each family insert a stick pin where they live. With small groups, write or type the family's name on labels, attach each label to a pin, and stick the pin in the appropriate place. Be sure to have a large table to use for this display or hang it on a wall.

A family store. See page 29 for a full explanation of the family store and other fund-raising activities.

Make a quilt together. Families that enjoy quilting can have a quilt frame set up at the reunion so that anyone who wants to participate can add their stitches. Each year a different family can bring their quilt top for the project. Some families ask for quilt blocks to either produce a group quilt to be auctioned or to trade blocks with others.

Opalene Mitchell (l.) showing her quilt, & Dr. Ione Vargus of the Family Reunion Institute.

In the Kenny clan, each family designed a quilt block depicting something about themselves. They made as many copies of their block as there were families in the clan. At the reunion, they traded blocks. Each family then had enough blocks for their own copy of the family quilt. Subsequent reunions were spent putting the quilts together for each family. Men, women, and children all participated and the gab fests around the quilt frame drew the family closer together. Even the letters sent back and forth during the planning stages created new family closeness. See instructions for children creating a paper quilt on page 113. Also there are some photos of quilts in the "Real Reunions" section.

Gathering for a Program

Be sure to have at least a short program where all the clan can get together and share. It's a great way to introduce everyone. It can take place in a formal setting with chairs or informally around a campfire. At large reunions, it can follow the main meal. Often the oldest family member in each branch will introduce his or her family and announce births, engagements, marriages, deaths, special awards, graduations, appointments, etc. All these milestones create a sense of history as well as pride in the accomplishments of the kin. Everyone is included; everyone is important. At the Chamberlin-Shabowski reunion, each person talks about "what I like best about my family." ➠See "Real Reunions."

Here are some possibilities for a reunion program:

Acknowledgements. You may want to thank the organizing committee, and perhaps single out one or two people who worked especially hard. A small gift may or may not be appropriate; use your discretion.

A more formal acknowledgement could be made by presenting an engraved plaque, trophy, or a quality gift. Possible candidates for such an award are the reunion founder, a family elder, someone who has never missed a reunion, your "historian" who finally finished the family history, or anyone who has distinguished himself or herself in some way. ➠See "Resources."

SPECIAL APPRECIATION AWARD

presented to
Mary Ashworth Benson

for serving as our Reunion Chairperson
from 1978 to 1995 and for providing us with
many wonderful family reunions.

from
the ASHWORTH FAMILY ASSN.

Awards. Here are some possibilities:

- ➤ Traveled the farthest.
- ➤ Most children.
- ➤ Youngest grandparent.
- ➤ Most grandchildren.
- ➤ Who has the most descendants present?
- ➤ Who has attended the most reunions?
- ➤ Who arrived first or last?
- ➤ The youngest/oldest present.
- ➤ Longest hair/biggest hair.
- ➤ Least hair.
- ➤ Came in oldest car.
- ➤ Has largest purse.

➤ Longest fingernails.
➤ Tallest.
➤ Biggest feet.
➤ Married longest.
➤ Newest married.
➤ Whitest hair.
➤ Kid with most teeth missing.
  (Thanks to Marianne Muellerleile for many of these categories.)

Prizes awarded for such achievements can be a family memento such as special T-shirts, buttons or caps. Food items and/or recipes are often given as prizes, such as a ham or watermelon, or Aunt Mindy's prize-winning jam. You may have a craftsman in your family who would make a treasured award, as on the next page.

Clever or humorous awards are a tradition for many families. Remember, your goal is not to embarrass anyone, but for the whole group to have a good laugh at itself. One family gave the parents of the most children a shoe with many tiny dolls tied all over it. ➠See "Resources" for a source of joke awards.

If you ask the right questions, much of the information needed to pick the recipients for your awards can come from the surveys sent out in the mailers. However, be prepared to make some last-minute changes based on surveys filled out at the reunion itself. Also, you will discover that some categories will require direct observation ("last to arrive") and perhaps a few discreet questions asked during the reunion. Someone must be assigned to this task. "The Survey" in Chapter 5 gives more information.

Prizes. Door prizes and other special gifts are always fun, but the process of choosing a winner should be quick and easy. The most common way to choose a winner is to place a special sticker on the bottom of a saucer (which is easy to look under, unlike a plate or cup which may contain food or beverage). Plac-

At the Daniel family reunion, a painted saw blade and a framed quilt square were awarded as prizes. The gifts were handmade by family members.

ing it under a chair can cause a tremendous disruption as people get up to turn their chairs over. For multiple prizes, have multiple stickers with different numbers or colors.

Toasts. A toast is never necessary at a reunion, but if done right, can be quite moving and meaningful. The length of a good toast varies anywhere from a few words to a few minutes, though the shorter ones tend to be better. The person giving the toast should be nothing less than "completely willing" to do the job. An appropriate time for a toast would be right after a meal or at the end of the program, just before everyone gets up. Of course, everyone should have a glass with a bit of "spirits" in it—either wine or an after-dinner liqueur. Grape juice, nonalcoholic wine, or sparkling cider would also be appropriate for nondrinkers and for the children. Most facilities will allow you to bring your own wine for "toasting purposes." This will save you money, but check first; and don't forget the corkscrew. ➠See "Resources" and the Internet chapter for books and Web sites on toasts.

Speeches. The rule of thumb is to keep them short or not have them at all. People bore easily, especially the children. An interesting exception is noted in the "Real Reunion" section under the Chamberlin-Shabowski Reunion. Here descendants depicted their ancestors and dressed in costume. Each was given a short speech to read.

Announcements. While you have a captive audience, use your time well. Remind people to buy raffle tickets, visit the family store, donate for the upcoming family history book, participate in planned activities, etc. Let people know who is in charge of the mailing list and remind them to send change-of-addresses to that person.

Showing the Kids a Good Time

The greatest joy of a family reunion is also its greatest challenge: bringing the generations together in such a way that the youngsters are entertained and engaged, and thus will want to continue the tradition as they get older. A family reunion should be so enjoyable that the kids look forward to each gathering as much as the adults, if not more so. For that to happen, it's essential that they be enthusiastically included and involved as much as possible, and not merely babysat or herded off to where they won't bother the grown-ups.

Means of Mixing. Adults bring bountiful memories to share at a reunion. However, children, often from distant corners of the country, need to find their own common ground in order for friendships to blossom. Nearly any topic will work as an icebreaker when you're introducing youngsters to each other: a common interest in video games, in owning pets, in skateboarding, in collecting baseball cards, in popular music and television shows—anything they can talk about comfortably as they get to know each other.

The same is true in getting younger and older family members to know each other. A love of music, sports, nature, or other areas can be used to break the ice between relatives of disparate ages, and may eventually result in multi-generational musical jam sessions, nature hikes, and other spontaneous outgrowths of common interests. Croquet, by the way, is a great game for "mixing the ages."

One of the best and most important parts of a reunion for both youngsters and adults is the building of common memories. This can be done through organized group activities (hay-rides, volleyball games, relay races, family story-telling, a hiking or bicycling trip, a kids-only party with pizza and dancing, a skating party, card games, board games, drawing contests, etc.) and through casual encounters with each other. Ideally, the reunion experience should provide the kids with plenty of stories to tell their friends back home about all the neat things they did and the nifty cousins, aunts, and uncles they met at the reunion.

Adults love to kiss and pinch the children's cheeks, and haggle over who the members of the newest generation most resemble in the family. However, such attention can be overwhelming for youngsters, particularly those who have never been to a reunion. Give kids plenty of space and time to get used to the crowd on their own terms. Don't assume that everyone's going to get along with everyone else at first sight just because they're related. It may take awhile for the kids to warm up to each other, as well as to adult relatives they've never met.

The various needs and interests of different age groups must be taken into consideration in planning a successful family reunion. Activities that delight preschoolers and kindergartners may bore or embarrass teenagers. Your best bet is to consult the experts—the kids themselves. Send a questionnaire to the kids asking them to rate a list of activities they would find most interesting. Or solicit the advice of a few imaginative youngsters (one for each age bracket) about what they think they and their peers would most enjoy doing during the reunion.

Don't over-structure reunion activities, though. Everyone young and old should feel welcome, but not obliged to participate in any of the outings or activities. For some youngsters, unstructured time spent with each other and some favorite elders may yield the best memories. Obviously, multi-day reunions need more planned activities than one-day reunions.

Babysitting. Since many families make a reunion their family vacation for the year, it's important that it be a true vacation for every member of the family. Don't expect teenagers to babysit the younger crowd, except for short stretches of time, and only if they really want to do it (for some teenage girls, this might be their favorite activity). Adolescent resentments can be kept to a minimum by hiring nonfamily babysitters to care for the wee ones who need close supervision, leaving the older kids free to come and go.

Site Selection with Kids in Mind (also see Chapters 1 and 13). For family reunions lasting several days, it's a good idea to choose a location with a lot of recreational options, both at the reunion site and in the general vicinity. When you evaluate possible sites, keep in mind diversions that would have special appeal for young family members, as well as for chaperoning adults. The following list focuses on some considerations:

- Is there a theme park nearby? an amusement park? a zoo? a museum? a playground? a miniature golf course?
- A facility where bicycles, skates, canoes, rowboats, or other recreational equipment can be rented? a hiking trail?
- A public beach or pool with lifeguards? a lake suitable for fishing or waterskiing?
- A bowling alley for a rainy day?
- A shopping mall or interesting downtown area?
- A dairy farm or small factory (a place that makes its own chocolates, for instance) that would make a good field trip?

➤ On the premises of your reunion site, is there a swimming pool? a baseball diamond? a basketball hoop? a volleyball or badminton net, or at least a place to set one up?

➤ A piano? a stage (and maybe even a sound system) that can be used for a talent show or family history skit? a screen for showing family slides and home movies? a large-screen television for showing videos?

You don't need to have all of these options available, of course, but you do want to have enough diversions at hand, so you won't be confronted with that dreaded refrain of youth everywhere: "There's nothing to dooooo!!"

Involving Kids in Family History. Many children's activities can parallel the interests of the adults. If the family is genealogy oriented, the children can also have activities with this focus. To keep their interest, tracking down ancestors should be presented as a game or solving a mystery. Some families create their own versions of Trivial Pursuit or Jeopardy based on family history. Others make a treasure hunt list for the kids in which they have to collect pertinent information about relatives, living and dead.

Materials brought from home can be inserted into family scrapbooks, photographs traded, and stories written. Older children might like to make a video of the reunion. They can also interview older family members, recording the conversation on tape or in a handmade book. Check with your child's teacher to see if extra credit can be obtained for a family history project.

Children of all ages can work together to make a family "quilt" by each decorating a paper square depicting a family memory. Finished squares are taped together or sewn with yarn into a big paper quilt to be displayed throughout the event and at future reunions.

Fun & Games for Family Gatherings, described on page 248, has a chapter devoted to genealogy for beginners. A great booklet for teaching children about genealogy is entitled *Genealogy,* a Merit Badge Series pamphlet of the Boy Scouts of America and available to anyone. Also *Roots for Kids.* ➠See "Resources."

Getting Serious About Games

Games seem to belong at family reunions like cotton candy at a county fair; they are great icebreakers and encourage people to join together. Just don't take them too seriously. The point is to have fun, rather than engage in cutthroat competition. Games and sports can be organized by age or skill level, or you can mix the age groups for a lesson in diversity and tolerance.

Some families organize traditional sports activities, such as softball, volleyball, golf, tennis, or soccer. Others hold team races, track meets, or Family Olympics. Grandparents and rural dwellers may remember such old-time games as sack races, three-legged races, wheelbarrow races, egg or water balloon toss, bobbing for apples, greased pole climbs, tug-of-war, and baby races. Most of these traditional American games are easy to learn and are very physical without being dangerous—a good way to wear out energetic kids!

Fun & Games for Family Gatherings describes over 235 activities and games for family reunions. See p. 248 to order.

Dale Le Fevre is the guru of noncompetitive and cooperative games. He has several books and instructional videos available. ➠See "Resources" for more information.

Some Traditional Games.

The *sack race* is just like a regular foot race, but each contestant has to jump to the finish line in a gunnysack. For the *three-legged race,* put two roughly equal-size participants shoulder to shoulder, and tie their two inner ankles together with a piece of short, soft rope or a cloth belt. The duo must run together to the finish line, which requires cooperation and coordination! In a *wheelbarrow race*, a large child or adult holds the ankles of a smaller person who "runs" forward on his hands.

For the *egg or balloon toss*, each person picks a partner. The partners line up facing each other. This creates two long parallel lines of participants who begin the toss while standing a yard away from each other. Partners throw raw eggs or water balloons to each other with an underhand toss;  everyone tosses at the same time. After each round of tossing, those partners whose egg or balloon survived take a step back and toss again. The others must drop out. The winners are the last two people to keep their egg or balloon from breaking.

All that's needed for a *greased pole climb* is a smooth vertical metal pole, a can of lard, and a piece of bright yarn to tie around the pole. Tie the yarn high on the pole to provide a "goal" for climbers, *then* grease the pole with lard. (Another enticing goal is an envelope with money inside.) Kids take turns shinnying up the pole. There are all kinds of tricks to successful pole climbing. Experienced climbers use dirt, grass, bandannas, socks, and their own shirt sleeves to wipe the pole as they climb. Although the climb seems impossible at first, the smart athletes soon refine their techniques and reach the goal. Obviously, this is not an activity for the faint-hearted or compulsively clean. Old clothes are a must for this game.

Tug-of-war can be played anywhere

Haugen Family tug-of-war, Decorah, Iowa.

with a soft, strong rope. A good summertime variation is to play across a creek or through a stream of water from a hose. The losers get wet and everyone has a laugh. Don't use any type of rope that stretches a lot (like nylon). If such a rope breaks, it can snap like a large rubber band and hurt people.

Baby races are always fun. Put all family crawlers in a row with one parent. Put the other parent at the finish line and see which baby makes it first.

Getting Acquainted Games.

Family Treasure Hunt. Prepare a list of requests or questions to answer. Distribute one copy to each player. For example:

1. Find two people who traveled over 200 miles to the reunion: _____ and _____ .

2. Find the mother with the most children: _____ .

3. Find the oldest and youngest persons: _____ and _____ .

4. How many children did Grandma Bertha have? _____ .

5. Find three people who married into the family: _____, _____, and _____ .

6. Find three children who presently are on a soccer or baseball team: _____, _____, and _____ .

7. What country did great-grandfather Espinoza come from? _____ .

8. Which relative used to work on a fishing boat? _____ .

9. How long has the Nelson Farm been in the family? _____ .

A list of 12 to 15 requests and/or questions is probably enough to keep everyone playing for 30 minutes. The players need a pencil or pen. Each player hunts for the person or persons who meet the requirements of the request or who can answer the question. The first person with all the blanks filled in correctly wins. It's fun to read the answers to the whole group, identifying the persons listed by having them stand up. The whole group learns to identify each other in some special way.

One family that played this game gave the questions to the children while the adults were visiting. This kept the kids busy and the adults didn't mind an interruption from time to time by kids searching for the person who could answer their questions.

A variation of this game is to ask everyone to write down on a small piece of paper a little-known, interesting fact about themselves (like "I climbed the highest mountain in North Dakota," or "I once met President Kennedy"). Make sure they also write their name on the piece of paper. All the pieces of paper are then put into a bag and drawn out, one at a time. The fact is read and everyone tries to guess who it is. The subject of the guessing then draws out the next piece of paper. It's a great way for people to get to know each other and all ages like to play. *(Thanks to Toni Cohig for submitting this example.)*

Family Statistics. This game requires two teams of eight or more players. If all participants are agile, the age span can be 6 to 100. Someone in a wheelchair can participate if the game is played on a flat surface. You can play inside or outside, standing or seated (one chair required for each person). All you need is room for each team to line up.

The point of the game is to get your team lined up according to a single statistic or requirement, such as height, age, birthday order, astrological sign (from Aries to Pisces), distance traveled to the reunion, number of reunions attended, family birth order, alphabetical order by first or last names, city or state of origin, and so on. A leader who is not on either team selects the statistic. Statistics or requirements can be as complicated as the teams can comprehend. The first team to get lined up according to the statistic or requirement is the winner. This game is a good ice breaker to get the family mixing and having fun together. It can also introduce you to facts about family members.

Hula Hoop Race. Teams form straight lines, holding hands, equal number of people per team. The first person in each team is given a hula hoop. At the start signal, the hula hoop must be passed down the line, from person to person with each person passing *through* the hula hoop, without letting go of each other's hands. First team to pass the hula hoop down and back wins.

Napkin Pass. Have two or more teams with an equal number of people on each team, a straw for each person, and a paper napkin for each team. The first person on each team picks up the napkin by sucking in on the straw (no hands) and passes it to the next person. The last person deposits the napkin in a pre-determined spot or location, like in a waste basket. The first team with their napkin in the waste basket wins. If a napkin is dropped, the person who dropped it must get down and suck it up again, and continue to pass it along. *(The above two games were submitted by Opal Frederick of the Crook Family Reunion.)*

Spoon on a String. Divide the group into equal teams; give each team a ball of yarn with a spoon tied to one end of it. The teams line up and at a signal, the spoon is passed down the shirt of the first person of a team, up the shirt of the next person, down the shirt of the next, and so on. The last person (after passing it up or down his shirt) winds up the yarn. The first team to pass the spoon and roll up the yarn wins. Variation: The last person, after rolling up the yarn, starts the spoon back up the line in the same manner. The first team with the spoon back to the front with the yarn rolled up wins. (From *Fun & Games for Family Gatherings*.)

Killer (or Gotcha!). A number of families reported this game as their favorite. Killer can be played inside or outside and needs at least eight participants in order to be fun. Anyone who can wink and keep a secret can play the game. Some prefer to call this game "Gotcha!" to avoid violent connotations and possibly scaring younger children.

First, cut up enough little pieces of paper (1" x 1") for the number of people playing. Put an "X" on one piece and leave the others blank. Fold the papers in half twice and put them in a hat or jar from which they can be drawn. Each person draws a piece of paper. The person who receives the X is the Killer and keeps his or her identity a secret from the other players.

The Killer kills by winking at a person. When a person sees someone wink at them, they must pretend to "die," the more melodramatically the better. The killer takes care to wink so no one but the person he is winking at sees the wink, because everyone else is out to catch the Killer before getting "killed" by a wink. When you think you know the identity of the Killer, you can accuse him or her. If you are right, the game is over and you have won. If you are wrong, you are "dead" and out of the game. The Killer tries to kill all other players with a wink without getting caught.

Adapting Popular Games

A number of families report making their own version of Trivial Pursuit, using family trivia instead of the game's questions. One person makes up the questions ahead of time or has the reunion group submit questions at the reunion. Another variation of a popular game is Family Jeopardy in which information about family members and events must be identified with the correct question. For example, if the answer is "red bow tie," the question may be "What strange thing did Uncle John wear to his wedding?"

Create Your Own Games

As you can see, families can be as adept as game companies in coming up with ideas. The examples we've suggested may inspire new games. Or you can stir up your sense of creativity by adapting popular parlor games to the reunion. For instance, do a version of charades that centers around important family events—births, promotions, important trips, relocations, etc. Write these events on pieces of paper, fold them, have someone draw one, and that becomes the theme to be acted out. Obviously, the family game possibilities you can "dream up" are as limitless as your imagination.

There is a commercial board game, *LifeStories*, that we highly recommend for family reunions. Through cards that are drawn, this game gets the participants talking about past events and experiences. The best part is that everyone wins. See p. 247 for more information.

Watermelon seed spitting contest. Should be self-explanatory.

Chapter 9

Feeding the Family

Chapter Highlights

▸*The Big Question.* ▸*Letting Someone Else Cook.*
▸*Buffets & Sit-Down Meals.* ▸*Bringing Your Own Food.*
▸*Recipes for Large Groups.* ▸*Stretch Your Food Dollars.*
▸*Serving & Cleanup.* ▸*Keep a History.* ▸*A Banquet Checklist.*

The Big Question

Feeding a large reunion group with a minimum of fuss requires careful planning. But first, ask yourself one question: Are you going to provide your own food or hire someone else to do the cooking? Your decision may well be tied to finances, since a caterer or restaurant usually costs much more than preparing your own reunion meal(s). If the gathering is to take place over several days, you may want to have different options for different meals. For example, you could let people find their own breakfasts, get together for a large noon meal, and later split into smaller groups that provide their own dinners.

Letting Someone Else Cook

If you decide to hire someone to do the cooking, survey different caterers and restaurants in the area to get an idea of what they charge. Some church groups, granges and similar organizations also do catering, and very cheaply, too. The local Chamber of Commerce may know of civic groups that will provide meals and facilities.

Create a list of all the information you need to provide to a caterer when asking for an estimate. This list should include the date and time of the event (caterers may be completely booked a year ahead at certain times of year, *e.g.*, for June weddings or Christmas parties), approximately how many adults and children you're expecting, and the type of meal and beverages you would prefer.

When getting estimates or meal prices, be sure to give each caterer or restaurant the same information, reading from your list. This way you're sure to "compare apples with apples." Take extensive notes when talking to different caterers so you don't have to rely on memory when deciding which to hire.

Use a separate page in your notebook for each restaurant or caterer, heading it with the appropriate name, address, and phone number. Follow with the date you phoned and the name and title of the person you spoke to. (Make sure that you speak to the person in charge of group reservations.)

Here are a few important issues to cover with restaurants and caterers (also see Chapter 1):

➤ Ask about their policy on deposits and cancellations.
➤ Request the names of two or three references you can call to make sure everything promised on other occasions was successfully delivered.
➤ If you are planning to serve alcoholic beverages before or with the meal, be sure you know the facility's policy.

Some places forbid alcohol, while others allow you to bring your own—at considerable savings.

➤ Is the restaurant easy to find? This is especially important if you have lots of out-of-towners attempting to locate it, especially if your reunion meal is at night. It may be wise to select a place near your lodging.

➤ Does the restaurant have adequate parking?

➤ Is the restaurant or hall located in a safe neighborhood?

➤ Does the restaurant have easy access and restrooms for persons in wheelchairs (if needed)?

➤ Are highchairs or booster seats available (if needed)?

➤ Can they provide flowers or other decorations? (See the section on decorating, p. 93.)

When you've collected enough information to make a reasonable choice, it's a good idea to visit the restaurant or banquet hall and look at the actual room before making the deposit. If the event is to be in the evening, visit in the evening. Observe the interior and exterior lighting, the distance from the parking lot to the front door, and so on. To check out the ambiance and the friendliness of the personnel, it's best to eat a meal during your visit (without mentioning that you're "scouting").

When you do make a reservation, request a written confirmation letter including all the details you've agreed upon, such as the date and time, menu, number of persons expected, and price per person. Review this letter very carefully and phone your contact person immediately if you find any discrepancies.

Assuming that you're making reservations six months to a year in advance, you should phone the contact person two months before the event, and again one week before, to make sure everything is proceeding smoothly. Make sure you know exactly what is expected of you (if anything) prior to the actual meal.

Buffets and Sit-Down Meals

Generally, a buffet-style meal with several kinds of dishes can offer appetizing choices for everyone, even the vegetarians and dieters. Include salads, hot entrees such as lasagna (some of them meatless, perhaps), meats, rolls, fresh fruit, and desserts. Buffets also reduce the need for servers; however, you may want some servers replenishing the serving dishes, removing empty dishes, circulating among tables, providing and replenishing beverages, and generally tidying up.

When it comes to organizing, a "sit-down" meal involves more work than a buffet. If you opt for a "sit-down" meal, offer several choices (*e.g.*, entrees featuring meat, chicken, fish, or vegetarian), and you must tell the restaurant how many diners have chosen each entree. Guests select their entrees when they make reservations for the reunion, marking choices on a card they return with their checks. This way, the restaurant is given an exact meal count well before the event. Keep duplicate records and take them to the reunion, in case people forget what they ordered.

Or you can offer only one menu for the sit-down meal. This is easier on the organizers although less accommodating to guests. The restaurant you choose may have a particular specialty (such as prime rib) which becomes the reunion dinner entree. This option can work well if the restaurant has a substantial salad bar, so that vegetarians, small children, and dieters can find plenty to eat while skipping the entree. If such selective dining is acceptable to the restaurant, ask if they offer a two-tiered pricing system, dividing those who choose the entree from those who eat only the salad, bread, and dessert.

When talking to caterers and restaurant staff, be sure to tell them about any special dietary and/or religious restrictions which could present problems. For example, if many reunion members are elderly, you can anticipate that they'd prefer a low-salt, low-fat, low-sugar meal. If you expect a lot of young children, you need to consider their tastes. (Along that line, providing a loaf of sliced bread and the ubiquitous peanut butter and jelly may head off a tantrum or two.)

Bringing Your Own Food

Cooking your own reunion feast is certainly more work, but home cooking provides a personal touch that few restaurants can match. The key here—to avoid complaints like "I did all the work…"—is to make sure the jobs and expenses are equitably distributed.

The easiest (and, therefore, the most popular) approach is to have a potluck, where everyone contributes food to share. You could encourage people to bring special family dishes—such as Uncle Harry's barbecued ribs or Grandma Parker's strawberry/rhubarb pie—along with written recipes for each dish. These recipes can be incorporated into a special keepsake cookbook (see p. 33). To add interest, label each dish at the potluck (*e.g.*, "Aunt Liza's Pickled Beets").

However, to make sure a potluck doesn't end up consisting of 26 salads, you need to organize who brings which items. The best way to cover all the bases is to make a master list of everything essential to the meal. To avoid forgetting something major, it helps to run this list by at least three friends—or get them to help you prepare it in the first place.

The system of using last names "beginning with A–F bring salads" won't work for a family reunion since many people will have the same last name. Using first names can also create confusion—whose first names do you use (mom's, dad's, kid's)? Instead, *assign* salads, main dishes, desserts, beverages, breads, fruits, etc. Be sure to keep track of what everyone is bringing.

Remember, people traveling long distances will find it easier to bring something from a nearby supermarket instead of dragging a casserole across the country. These out-of-towners can be assigned items such as ice, paper plates, cups and napkins, plastic utensils, charcoal and lighter fluid if you're barbecuing, beverages, fresh fruit, meats, hamburger and hotdog rolls, mustard, ketchup, and other condiments.

Some important items you may want to put on your potluck list include:

➤ Decorations—either for the serving tables or the tables where people are eating. Is someone in the family eager to show off her roses? Family gardeners near the reunion site may be a good source for flowers. How about something big and striking—like a flag representing the family's ethnic origin or a welcoming banner—hanging above your serving table? Children are a good resource for imaginative drawings—and may pass rainy afternoons for months before the reunion drawing pictures on paper tablecloths or creating suitable centerpieces. Also see the section on decorating, p. 93.

➤ Condiments—list all that are needed for the items you are serving, starting with easily-forgotten salt and pepper.

➤ Equipment for your cooking area (if there is to be one) and for last-minute preparations. A couple of cutting boards and some sharp knives are essential. And how about barbecue gear such as tongs, potholders, and aprons? Don't forget the matches. Paper towels and trash cans are handy.

➤ Extra seating—it can be anything from comfortable folding lawn chairs to rented chairs to bales of hay. Don't forget highchairs or booster seats.

➤ Miscellaneous equipment—such as items needed to keep food and drink cold or hot. You may need to rent or borrow a coffee urn or a big punch bowl. Ice-filled washbuckets and ice chests are useful to keep beverages cold and prevent perishables from spoiling.

➤ Shelter—if it's an outdoor event, you may need to rent some sort of tent or pavilion in case of rain or for shade.
➤ Cleanup gear—such as detergent, scouring pads, sponges, paper towels, dish drainers, and large washtubs. Don't forget brooms, dustpans and trash cans with liners.

There are several variations on the "potluck" approach. One is to have people bring their own meat to barbecue, while the salads, desserts, rolls, and other side dishes are assigned in potluck fashion or are provided by the committee. Another approach is to have guests contribute money (the amount based on the number of adults and children attending) to a general fund from which the committee buys meat to barbecue, charcoal, ice, beverages, utensils and paper plates, etc. The salads and desserts are contributed via potluck. If you choose this option make sure to collect everyone's money before the reunion.

Even if most of the food is purchased by the committee, you can still ask guests to bring one special dish to be judged in a contest. It's fun to ask the family to vote for their favorite, awarding an appropriate gift (an apron, chef's hat, potholders, etc.) to the elected Champion Cook(s). Provide a ballot box, small paper ballots, and a couple of pencils tied to the box with strings. Ask people to vote after they've finished eating (including desserts) and appoint a committee of older children to run the election, tally the votes, and hand out the prize(s).

Other types of potlucks are limited only by your imagination and the location of the reunion. You can have a "chili cookoff," where many variations of that specialty simmer all day, with the committee providing cold drinks, corn bread, and ice cream or watermelon for dessert. Or tie your meal to an event such as a clam dig. The clams go into huge pots of chowder with different family members providing the remaining ingredients (bacon, onions, celery, milk, bottled clam juice, parsley, sherry, etc.). Don't forget the garlic bread, drinks and desserts.

Depending on where you hold your reunion, there may be other regional favorites that influence your menu. Let's say one family lives on a ranch and offers to roast a whole pig. This porker becomes the focal point for a theme meal—whether it's an Hawaiian Luau or a Cowboy Cookout.

Little details can also shape your meal into something more fun and more memorable than the usual potluck. For example, a luau theme will be a lot more convincing if you hire a ukulele player (or play taped Polynesian music), ask people to wear Hawaiian-style flowered shirts, buy paper leis and have them handed out by a child dressed in a grass skirt, serve drinks with little paper parasols in them, make some fake palm trees from painted cardboard, and haul in some sand for a photo backdrop.

Recipes for Large Groups

Recipes for large groups are a bit beyond the scope of this book, but we can certainly point you in the right direction. "Resources" in the back lists some books you may want to purchase or check out from the library. The Web is also a great source of such recipes. See the Internet chapter on how to search for subjects. If you don't have a computer with Internet connection, try your local library.

Stretch Your Food Dollars

➤ If you are having your reunion at a hotel, don't ask what they charge for the meal. Tell them how much you wish to spend per meal and have them prepare a meal accordingly. If necessary, eliminate desserts and extra vegetables. Ask the chef about special food buys, food on hand, and concurrent meals with other groups.

➤ If unsure of attendance, select "stretchables" such as pastas and stews.

➤ Avoid delicacies such as shrimp, lobster, crab, and caviar unless you are in an area where the prices are reasonable.

Same reunion, different meals.

Serving and Clean Up

Whatever kind of meal you're creating, don't forget to give some thought to serving and cleaning up. Buffet style is certainly the easiest way to serve a crowd. Set up your buffet tables so that people can access the food from both sides at once, serving themselves faster. Some older children really enjoy helping and can be mobilized for serving beverages or desserts.

When laying out your serving area, be sure to include several beverage stations for easy access. Cold sodas, mineral waters, juices, and nonalcoholic drinks should be separated from the beer and alcoholic drinks. Provide recycling boxes for aluminum and glass containers.

It's easier to serve and clean up a buffet if it's in a slightly different location than the pre-meal snacks and the desserts.

Separate them so they don't create traffic jams if groups are serving themselves from different tables at the same time.

Be sure to appoint a cleanup committee which oversees the details of trash pick up and disposal, making sure all fires are out, utensils washed, and so on. If you're using a rented facility, such as a campground or hall for your meal, the return of the security deposit is often dependent upon a good cleanup job. One person (Chairman of Cleanup) should be assigned to do a final site inspection and collect the deposit, turning it over to the Reunion Committee's Treasurer.

Keep a History

Soon after the reunion is over, whether you used a caterer, restaurant, or the wits and generosity of your own family for the group meal(s), it's a good idea to haul out that dog-eared notebook again and write down what worked and what didn't. This is the best time to record your thoughts about how you would do it differently next time. You may want to solicit opinions of several others for this analysis. Your notes, however brief, will be of tremendous help to the next person (even if it's you) who feeds the group.

A Banquet Checklist

Here's a check list for a large banquet (also see p. 12):

- ➤ When, during the reunion, will the banquet be held?
- ➤ Size of the room: seating capacity, dance floor space, etc.
- ➤ How will you be charged by the facility: signed guarantee, collected tickets, or by quantities? Remember, it's your job to know the number of people that will attend, and you should assume the burden of incorrect projections.
- ➤ Taxes and gratuities.
- ➤ Decorations. Ask if the site has table decorations in stock.
- ➤ Flowers: what type, size and how many?

➤ Entertainment: band, DJ, taped music, space to perform, staging, dressing room.
➤ Rental equipment, costs.
➤ Check on local liquor laws. Some regulations may affect you. Some counties are dry, or are dry on certain days.
➤ Alcohol controls. Types of bars: host, cash, your own. Will you sell tickets? Bartender to guest ratio: 1 to 75 is average.
➤ Time span of the event. When is dinner to be served? When will the meal end?
➤ Will there be a reception? Will you need a separate room?
➤ Give the facility manager a diagram of what the room should look like when set up.
➤ Type and color of linen you will use.
➤ Audio-visual equipment.
➤ Will there be a head table? Who will sit there?
➤ Type of dress.
➤ Smoking, no smoking?
➤ Who will collect tickets?
➤ Signs for event.
➤ Type of service: buffet, individual plates.
➤ Menu: variety, creativity, cost?
➤ Are vegetables canned, frozen, or fresh? Accept only fresh, maybe frozen.
➤ Special dietary requirements? Vegetarian, low sodium, low fat, no sugar, no wheat, religious.
➤ Waiter-to-guest ratio? This can mean fast or slow service. (No greater than 1 to 20 for plated meals.
➤ Distribution of materials: menu cards, programs, favors.
➤ Will you need security?
➤ Room lighting, electricity, spotlights, public address system?
➤ Parking.
➤ Checkroom for coats?

➤ Location of rest rooms. Signs, if necessary.
➤ Photography/video coverage. Costs? Instructions for how to obtain photos or tapes.
➤ What other events will be going on at the facility simultaneous to your event?

Useful Books

The Black Family Reunion Cookbook has great recipes but serves best by showing how a cookbook can be layed out in a clear and organized manner—useful information if you intend to create your own family cookbook. ➠See "Resources" for more information.

Family Reunion Potluck has 100 potluck recipes from a professional home economist. Categories include beverages, appetizers, salads, vegetables, entrees, breads and desserts. ➠See "Resources" for how to obtain.

Chapter 10

Making History
Documenting Family Memories

Chapter Highlights
▶ *Photography.* ▶ *Videos.* ▶ *The Art of Interviewing.*
▶ *Approaches to Interviewing.* ▶ *Reunions for Genealogical Research.*
▶ *Family Histories.* ▶ *Family Directories.* ▶ *Coats of Arms.*
▶ *Time Capsules.* ▶ *Using Photocopy Shops.*

Reunions are perfect occasions to gather family history; after all, a family reunion itself is part of your family's history. Common methods of gathering and preserving family history are presented in this chapter.

Photography
Be sure that some type of photographic or videographic documentation takes place at your reunion. At the very least, maintain a reunion scrapbook of candid photos. If necessary, hire a professional photographer. An "on-going" scrapbook will become valuable and add interest to future reunions. ➠See sources of scrapbooks in "Resources" and page 104.

Group photos are the most common photos taken at family reunions. If indoors, they should be taken by a professional because indoor settings present lighting problems few amateurs can overcome. Most pros don't like to take group photos of more than about 80 people. More than that and the faces in the photo become indistinct. A larger photo format, say 11" x 18", can be a solution to this problem. Of course, it will cost more.

One difficulty in setting up a group photo is to keep faces from being hidden behind other faces. People think if they can see the camera, then their entire face will appear in the photo; this isn't necessarily the case. It takes a lot of time and an experienced photographer to arrange everyone properly so all faces show. For large groups, figure at least 30–40 minutes for setup, and warn the group ahead of time so they don't get disgruntled during the wait.

An 8 x 10 color print should cost between $9 and $15 each, depending on quantity. It's best to include the cost of the photo in the registration fee, rather than charge separately for it. Be sure to offer the photo to those who can't attend. Have a special place on the registration form for this, and don't forget to add the mailing cost to the price.

An experienced amateur photographer with good equipment can usually take a decent outdoor group photo. With a tripod and camera with a timer, the photographer can also get in the picture. Be sure to schedule the photo session well before anyone has departed for home. Many groups miss the opportunity to get everyone in the picture by not scheduling it early enough.

A big problem at family reunions is disorganization at photography sessions. It's helpful to plan ahead. Find a site that will hold everyone, and where the lighting is proper at the time of day when the photo session is scheduled. Set up the camera on a tripod beforehand to see how wide a group can be photographed. If it's helpful, set out side markers to indicate the maximum width. If your group requires three rows of people, it's also helpful to have a row of chairs so that the middle row is sitting.

The Graham Family are champions.

A new form of photography called *event photography* is gaining popularity these days. Watch for it. The photographer uses a digital camera hooked up to a color printer. The photo comes out of the printer a few seconds after the picture is taken. Kind of like Polaroids, only much higher quality. A good photographer will also bring various props and backgrounds to use. Some may have these mock Wheaties boxes that you can attach a group photo to.

If you meet at a site that has particular meaning to your family, you may want to photograph the location. Homes built by ancestors, tombstones in a family cemetery, the church that your family helped build, the college your mom attended, the old family busines, an uncle's collection of antique cars, are all important. Include an interview of a person who remembers the most about each special place.

Nancy Dahl took this photo in Durand, WI, of the building that was her grandfather's shoe shop from 1892–1924.

The Fun of Videos

Videotapes of reunions are becoming increasingly popular as video recording and playback equipment become cheaper and of higher quality. Nearly 80% of American households own VCRs, and that percentage will only increase over the next few years. Of course, you don't need to own a VCR to enjoy a reunion video. The machines are inexpensive to rent for one evening; all you need is a TV.

Video cameras are getting easier to use and amateur videography is getting better. However, if you intend to sell or distribute videos of your reunion, don't even *consider* amateur videography unless the tape will be edited. "Editing," at the very least, means cutting out portions of the tape that are of poor quality or redundant. It's better if the editing process also adds narration, titles or captions, music, still "shots" of memorabilia, old photos, etc. It can even include a "The End" sign. This type of editing can sometimes be done through a video camera to a VCR—it depends on the camera. Otherwise it's done "VCR-to-VCR," and if you want to get fancy, it can be done on a desktop computer that's properly equiped. VCRs can be rented along with "titling boxes" and special effects generators.

If you elect the amateur route, the first thing to do is get Mary Lou Peterson's video, *Gift of Heritage*, on how to do family videos. This award-winning tape explains exactly how to make use of video to record and document your family's history. ➠See "Resources" for information. Also, *Fun & Games for Family Gatherings* has five pages of information on how to do amateur videos. See page 248 for more information on this book.

There is a wide variety of services available from video professionals. They, of course, can do the whole process from beginning to end. But they can also do part of it, such as tape duplication, editing, photo montages (like a slide show of your old photos), and film-to-tape (putting your old movies on video).

Please remember: professional videographers will *always* do a better job than amateurs. Their equipment is of better quality, they know how to minimize "camera shake," they can edit, add captions and background music, etc. Video footage of old photos and memorabilia, even old movies, can be added. The difference, of course, is cost.

Some professionals charge a base fee plus so much per copy sold; others do not charge a base fee, but must be guaranteed a minimum purchase. In the latter case, the committee or the company advertises the tape through the mail beforehand. If not enough videos are pre-sold, then the service is cancelled or a higher price is negotiated.

Reunion videos usually contain two types of live footage. One is the "interview" where each person is asked questions to which he or she replies on camera. The other concentrates on "candid shots": the camera operator wanders through the reunion taking footage of people talking, playing, eating, etc.

Whatever you do, make sure that everyone present—from the youngest to the oldest—is on the tape somewhere. About the only disadvantage of using a professional is their lack of familiarity with the family. Assign a "helper" from the family to assist the camera person. This assistant should have a list of all attendees and check off people as they are videotaped. Be sure to include special performances and set up interviews with key people.

If you hire a professional and your reunion is two or three days long, you can save money by videotaping during one day only. Schedule important events for this day.

A large reunion group may be able to find a professional willing to videotape on a completely freelance basis. There is no charge to the reunion committee, and the sale of the product is done through the mail by the video company several weeks after the reunion. However, an arrangement of this kind often involves beginners who are trying to break into the field. This doesn't necessarily mean that quality will be compromised, but it does mean that you should be careful. Even though the video service is not costing you anything, your group will expect a high quality product, and you are the one in charge of selecting the videographer. The quality of a videotape depends on the skill of the person operating the camera, the skill of the editor, and the skill of the interviewer. For low-budget assignments, this may be the same person. It's very important to preview a reunion video that the company has already produced. Then call someone in that reunion group to find out how they liked their video and the video company.

The Art of Interviewing

Much of a family's history exists only in the memories of the family members. If these memories are not "drawn out" and preserved in some way, they are lost forever as people pass away. To prevent this loss, plan some interviewing and recording sessions to preserve the oral history of your family. Interviewing is the means by which these memories are coaxed from people's minds and onto paper or audio/video tape.

However, an interview is only as good as the interviewer. We encourage you to become familiar with this art form and its techniques. We recommend reading *Instant Oral Biographies*, *Keeping Family Stories Alive*, or some of the other books mentioned in "Resources."

To make the most of your interviewing time at the reunion, be well-organized. If the reunion is only one day long, you need to know exactly who to talk to and what to ask them. If the reunion lasts several days, create a schedule for each day. To be sure of including certain people, you might make appointments by mail or phone ahead of time. Also, send your potential interviewees a list of questions you intend to ask and facts that you are looking for. Prior knowledge of the questions can help tremendously by giving people a chance to remember or gather the facts and chronology.

Interviews can go off on tangents that might be interesting, but never gather the information you want. On the other hand, tangents can sometimes get you information you never expected. Overall, you should strive for a balance between the scripted and the spontaneous.

The traditional method of taking notes is with pencil and paper. However, using tape recorders and video cameras can be most helpful during interviews. Because you can review the answers later, they allow you to concentrate on the interview instead of on note-taking.

The tapes can be important additions to a family's archives or they might be used to create a composite tape to share with other members of the family. And videos not only add to the family "scrapbook," they provide a "feature film" to show at the next reunion.

Two Approaches to Interviewing

There are two basic approaches to interviews. One collects oral history; this requires talking directly, one-on-one, with a person—often for hours at a time. A family reunion is not the best place to do this type of interviewing because of various distractions. For example, an audience may gather, causing self-consciousness. Scheduling "private sessions" a day or two before or after the reunion can help.

The other approach concentrates on collecting facts and figures for charts and family trees. Because "in-depth" interviewing is not required, this way is custom-made for family reunions.

Collecting oral history. If oral history is your goal, here is a list of questions you can ask during an interview:

1. When and where a person was born; incidents they have been told about their birth.

2. Information about the person's parents: birthplace, where they grew up, schools they attended, professions, physical characteristics, medical history, circumstances of death, where they were buried.

3. Preschool times: memories of siblings, where they lived, life events, medical problems.

4. Childhood memories: where they went to school, their friends, family events, teachers, pets, adventures, vacations, dreams of the future, what life was like, what things had or had not been invented, transportation they used, how far they had to walk to school, cost of common items such as milk, bread, gas, postage stamps, etc.

5. Teenage years: how they felt about growing up, what high school was like, what they did in the summers, how or why they made choices after high school (to work, go to college, get married, or join the military), how they spent their leisure time.

6. Dating and marriage: customs surrounding these events, special friends they didn't marry, how they met their spouse, how they proposed, the wedding, the honeymoon, early marriage, divorce, remarriage, etc.

7. Having children: pregnancy events, where they gave birth, birth circumstances, how children's names were chosen, baptism and blessings, children's personalities, memorable childhood events.

8. Career: jobs they held (what, where and when), salaries, their attitudes about work, what they did, their successes and failures, reasons for occupational changes, how the times affected what they did.

9. Hobbies: how and where they pursued their hobbies, changes in hobbies, any collections and where they are now.

10. Spiritual development: their philosophy of life, beliefs, commitments to ideals, spiritual experiences, psychic events and premonitions, callings they followed, ordinations, promises they made, near death experiences, attitudes and stories about adversity and recovery, attitudes about death and dying, immortality, the meaning of life.

11. Civic activities: involvement in organizations or politics, churches attended, offices held, service to the community, awards won.

12. World view: hopes for future generations, what they still want to accomplish in their lives, attitudes about prosperity and how one gets what they want out of life, their attitudes and feelings during major world events.

13. Medical information: illnesses, diseases, allergies, addictions, causes of death, genetic weaknesses, overcoming terminal illnesses, epidemics, causes for hearing loss or blindness, paralysis, etc.

14. Outstanding people they knew and how their lives were affected: mentors, memories of well-known people, favorite teachers, best friends.

15. How their way of life changed over the years: inventions in their lifetimes, how they traveled and communicated, attitude changes of the young and old, how leisure time was spent, responsibilities of men, women, parents and children, world problems that affected lives, results of world events, times of prosperity, hard times, etc.

16. Family ceremonies and traditions for holidays, religious events, pilgrimages, births and birthdays, marriages, deaths, funerals.

17. Where family items are located: old family homes, graves, diaries, wills, journals, scrapbooks, school annuals, Bibles, homesteads, churches, old family businesses.

18. Family pets, work animals, incidents with animals.

19. Adoptions, second marriages, step- or half-siblings or children, stillborns, childhood deaths.

20. Family recipes and cooking secrets.

After an interview, transcribe it to paper verbatim, even if the grammar is not proper. It can be valuable to other researchers in the "raw" form. Remember that every writer will take a different slant. One writer may like facts; another may try to convey personal philosophy. If you know beforehand what slant you intend to take, develop questions that will elicit the information you need.

Collecting facts. If you want to collect facts—names, dates, places—at the reunion, announce in one of the mailers what you are looking for and what kinds of things people can bring to help you. Ask for old Bibles, journals, wills, letters, birth and death certificates, newspaper clippings, old genealogies, church records, old photos, military records, naturalization papers, marriage certificates. At the reunion, collect these items in a central location where researchers can view them. Perhaps someone in the family can bring a portable photocopier or computer with scanner.

If you must rely on the memory of those present for facts, create lists of what you need, question those who might know, record what you find out and, most important, *document your sources*. If the reunion is so large that you cannot personally interview everyone who has information you want, make a fact-gathering chart that people can fill in at their leisure.

Medical history. The Crom family had a medical chart available at their reunion. They were interested in certain types of medical problems that seemed to be cropping up in the younger generation. They listed these medical problems down the side of the chart and asked people to fill in the names, dates, and

Checking over the medical history charts.

addresses of others in the family who suffered from these ailments. Helpful pamphlets are available from the March of Dimes to aid you in collecting medical information from your family. ▸See "Resources."

Reunions for Genealogical Research

Some reunions are held specifically to do genealogical research. The family of Helen Hardin Hoots has such reunions. She reports that the "most memorable part [of the reunion] was meeting correspondents...and learning of their work and ancestral research." If your reunion is for this purpose, careful planning will help researchers achieve their goals. Query the researchers ahead of time to determine what they would like to accomplish at the reunion; set up a schedule based on these needs. This may mean scheduling library time, interviewing time, touring time, etc. However, your plans should be flexible; for instance, if people doing research in the library don't want to quit, they should be able to continue there as long as they want. But constant study and research can be tiring, too. Plan some rest and recreation to give people a break.

Producing a Family History

A family history is the story of your ancestors, but can also

include living relatives. What better way to present special family qualities and philosophies than by preparing the story of the past in an easy-to-read form. A well-written, well-researched family history can be as exciting to read as a good biography. It's a fact, however, that most family histories are rather boring, factual accounts of family chronology. But this is okay! If you aren't a great writer, get the facts down anyway. A great writer may come

Specialized companies can produce your family history. Photo courtesy Family History Publishers. See address in "Resources."

along later, maybe generations later. Or funds may someday be available for professional assistance.

If writing from memory, be careful of errors. Often family histories have little genealogical value due to an abundance of erroneous facts, such as dates, places, names, and relationships. Use the best documented sources you can find to back up your memory; however, check these sources against others, and have a person familiar with the family proofread to look for factual errors. The proofreader may remember dates and events differently. Rather than having such discrepancies lead to disagreements, use this information to research more extensively.

Then have someone unfamiliar with your history read over the preliminary drafts and make suggestions. Often events you portray are so familiar to you that you are unaware of the lack of clarity.

No "fact" is assumed correct in genealogical research until it is verified a number of different ways. There is much room for error, especially if you are relying on people's memories. Even printed materials such as newspaper articles can be erroneous. One woman reported finding nine errors in her mother's obituary! If you feel that facts in your sources, or in your history, may not be totally correct, communicate this to the reader. Qualify this information. Document your sources in a bibliography; future generations will be grateful and you won't be adding to the world of misinformation.

Problems with grammar, punctuation, syntax, and spelling may also be encountered. If you are using a computer, get a spelling checker. Have a proofreader who is a good speller and grammarian help polish your final draft. There are a number of good style manuals which clarify grammar, punctuation, and word usage. *The Chicago Manual of Style* and *The Gregg Reference Manual* are the most used.

A desktop publishing system can be used for creating family histories. All aspects of book design can be handled by the software including line spacing, type styles, headings, page numbering, etc. (This book is a good example.) The cost depends on how much work you do yourself. Compiling, writing, and editing are the most expensive elements. If your family can do these things, a 300-page hard cover book can be produced for around $15–50 per book, depending on the quantity printed.

There are many books available on the subjects of self-publishing, printing, book design, writing and editing, how to copyright your work, and anything else you need to know to produce a high quality family history. For more information, read some of the books mentioned in "Resources."

A tip: Printing color photos in a book is very expensive, especially for a small number of books. A cheaper alternative is to paste a few color photographs or high quality color photocopies into your book by hand.

To keep histories up to date, print them in numbered volumes. This method can also allow you to concentrate on one period of time, rather than facing the overwhelming task of covering three or four centuries in one work. Any time period can be chosen; volumes can cover one or two generations, one century, or just fifty years. Another advantage of producing one volume at a time is that the work and costs are spread over a longer time period. Also, smaller volumes at a lower price will be easier to sell (if that's how you finance the project) than one huge volume.

If your family history is carefully researched and of high quality, you may be able to sell it commercially. Genealogy libraries, specialized book dealers, and genealogy societies are the usual buyers. ➤See "Resources" for more information.

Family Directories

A family directory is a directory or reference booklet of family-related information, usually published annually. Family directories differ from newsletters in that they contain addresses, facts, dates, lists, and not much news. For example they might list births, deaths, marriages, graduations, anniversaries, people serving in the military, family association officers and committees, as well as the current mailing list. The size is usually 5.5" x 8.5". Directory costs can be covered by membership dues, or they can be sold, either as a fundraiser or just to break even.

Family associations can use the directory as their annual report including, beside the items above, the year-end financial statement, and the minutes of the board meeting(s). The directory is usually mailed at the end of the association's fiscal year; however, a November mailing brings the most recent mailing list to the members before holiday cards are addressed. The association's constitution and bylaws can also be printed, along with its goals and purposes.

Most directories can be produced following the steps used to create newsletters (see Chapter 5). However, you will want a more durable cover on a directory; it may be referred to many times during the year. Most printers and copy shops carry card stock that makes a substantial cover, and comes in a range of colors and textures. It's helpful to print a different color cover each year to avoid confusing one issue with another.

It's critical that a directory be proofread at least twice before printing. With so many details—addresses, phone numbers, names, and zip codes—it's easy to transpose numbers, forget a middle initial, or leave out a "Jr." in a name. Carefully proofread anything produced by a typesetter as well. Typesetting looks more official, but there still may be errors.

Coats of Arms

Originally worn into battle, coats of arms were used to tell friend from foe. Colors and designs were chosen to show status, allegiance, personality, and profession and to reflect the traits and traditions of the original bearer. They were as distinctive as fingerprints and can tell an interesting tale.

The examples to the right were created by Marcia Rainaud of The Ship's Chandler in Wilmington, Vermont. Left is a wall shield and right is a hand-painted rendering.

Also available are embroidered blazer patches, framed needle-work renderings, rubber stamps, signet rings, etc. ➠See "Resources" for more information.

Time Capsules

A time capsule is an interesting way of preserving family history and traditions. And it creates a very exciting event when being opened, especially for children. It can be buried if you are reasonably sure the burial spot will be accessible to the family when the time comes to open it. Otherwise, it can be placed on a mantle or simply stored in an attic or garage. The interval between sealing and opening can be anywhere from a few years to a century or more. It depends on who you wish the audience to be. If it's today's children, then try 5 or 10 years—this may seem a short time to older folks but is forever to a child. If your audience is future generations, then a century or more would be appropriate. ➠See "Resources" for more information.

Using Photocopy Shops

Many of the larger photocopy stores like Kinko's and Sir Speedy have services and products that are useful to reunion planners. For example:

- ➤ Blank, pre-printed forms for announcements, postcards, and newsletters (with matching envelopes). These forms have colorful designs and a blank area for your message. You can use your own printer at home or the photocopy machines at the store.
- ➤ T-shirt transfers. Your design or photo is color copied onto a heat transfer sheet which is then ironed onto the shirt.
- ➤ Personalized calendars. Your color photos can be added. Birthdays and anniversaries also appear.

It's possible to take a photo at your reunion in the morning and get back postcards, calendars, or t-shirt transfers by afternoon, or at least the next day. Call ahead to smooth this all out with the manager.

Chapter 11

Family Associations
& Surname Associations

▶*Why a Family Association?* ▶*Purposes of a Family Association.*
▶*Surname Associations.*

Why a Family Association?

Once you have organized a couple of successful reunions, and have discovered both interest and leadership ability in your group, you might consider forming a family association. To do so legally, requires that you draw up by-laws, file articles of incorporation with your state government, file for tax-exempt status with the IRS, and elect a board of directors.

In a family association, the leadership for your family projects—including reunions—shifts from an individual or small group to an elected board with appointed committees. This is similar to a small business expanding into a corporation. There are some advantages to making this move, other than legal. First, it's easier for a family association to continue with its projects if a leader dies or loses interest. Another is that in the long run, more people will volunteer both time and money to help a legal organization than a one-person show. This is especially true of newcomers joining an organization that's already in existence.

Purposes of a Family Association

The LDS church, which encourages its members to form family associations, publishes the following list of reasons to create an association. It could very well speak to all families.

> ➤ To foster love and understanding among family members.
> ➤ To produce something to leave future generations.
> ➤ To do family research, compile records, avoid duplication of research, and provide copies to family members.
> ➤ To share finances for genealogical research, thereby improving the quality of research.
> ➤ To preserve family records and memorabilia, store keepsakes, photographs, valuable papers, and documents.
> ➤ To hold annual meetings or reunions where all can meet and share their common bond.

Other, more specific, reasons might be:
> ➤ To preserve a family homestead, house or farm.
> ➤ To create a museum housing family keepsakes and genealogical research.
> ➤ To create a scholarship fund for needy or deserving students.
> ➤ To create an endowment fund to provide donations to churches, schools, the arts, science—whatever is dear to the hearts of the family.
> ➤ To preserve a family cemetery.
> ➤ To publish a family history book.

Families of any size can form an association. You should first decide whether you have the need, interest, finances, and resources to run one. Some serious discussion and commitments must be made before tackling such a project.

After determining that there is reason to create an association, and that it can be administrated and financed, then decide what families will initially be included. Usually the descendants of a common ancestor or married couple are chosen. For example, it may be the descendants of the first person or couple who immigrated to this country. If such a choice makes the group too large to administrate, perhaps a more recent ancestor can be selected. This ancestor may be a grandparent or a great-grandparent. If in doubt, start with a smaller group and expand.

Often the first plans for a family association start at a family reunion. If attendance represents most of the family branches, a decision to start an association can be brought to a vote.

For early input, send a mailer before the reunion describing your intentions. Include a survey form for each family to write comments and mail back. From this data, you can determine if voting on an association at the reunion is appropriate.

Surname Associations

Surname associations are family associations that are open to anyone with a common last name. Some of these groups have hundreds of officers and thousands of members. Christine

The Rose Family Association meets every three years near a national repository.

Rose of the Rose Family Association explains:

"A family does not have to be related to have a successful reunion. Surname organizations, for instance, have many members who are not related. It's important that people feel welcome; that those coming alone have a place to meet others. If meeting at a hotel or motel, a hospitality suite is a must, and should be open at least two days before the start of the event. For those who are not related, there must be something that will bring them together. Our association makes available 8–10 huge scrapbooks of newspa-

A display at the Rose Surname Reunion.

per items on Roses collected over the years."

It should be noted that related families can also have their family reunions at these surname gatherings.

Sources for More Information

We have chosen to go no further into the subject of family associations in this book because a very fine book on the subject already exists:

If you are serious about starting a family association, get *Family Associations: Organization and Management* by Christine Rose. Mrs. Rose has "been there," tells you everything you need to know, and includes sample by-laws. See p. 248 for ordering information.

Chapter 12

Finding People

Chapter Highlights

▸*Find a "Sherlock."* ▸*Covering Costs.* ▸*Grapevine Leads.*
▸*Using the Media.* ▸*Historic Sources.* ▸*Database Searches/the
Forwarded Letter.* ▸*Public Records.* ▸*Using Computers*
▸*Using the Telephone.* ▸*Phone Books/City Directories.*
▸*Using Mailers & Newsletters.*

*   *   *   *

This chapter is limited to the basics of finding people and does not pretend to get beyond the beginner stage. For books on the subject, ⇒see "Resources." One of the best books, *Find Anyone Fast*, is described on p. 248. Also see Chapter 14 (Using the Internet).

*   *   *   *

Depending on the family, "finding people" can be easy, hard, or seemingly take forever. Some families are so small or so tight-knit that locating people is not a problem; everybody knows where everybody is. Other families may be looking only for a few cousins who "disappeared years ago." Still others may conduct an on-going, world-wide search for anyone with a particular last name.

The truth is, it takes a lot of hard work and persistence to find "missing" people. More than 99% of the information you are looking for is in someone's memory or in some file or computer somewhere in the country. It's just a question of how to get to it. Diligence and persistence are the name of this game.

Find a "Sherlock"

To really dig for those "hard-to-finds," it takes someone with curiosity, a knack for detective work, and persistence in following leads. Some people hate to do this and others love it. Find someone who loves it and give them the authority and resources they need. You may find that some of these "Sherlocks" are not interested in helping with the reunion in any other way. This should be fine with you as long as they get results. You might offer a "Sherlock Holmes" award during your reunion program to the person who finds the most people. This could be a joke prize such as a toy detective kit or a more serious award, such as a plaque or trophy.

One person should be in charge of finding people (of course, this person can have many helpers). Her name, address, and phone number should be in all your mailings and correspondence. If possible, give this person year-round authority and funding to do research by mail and telephone. And, of course, she should be willing and able to do such research. Such a person (or persons, if you are lucky enough to have more than one in your family) is one of your greatest assets.

Professional genealogists are located throughout the U.S. and many of them will search their local public records and libraries for you at an hourly rate. For information on finding professional genealogists, ➡see "Resources"

Covering Costs

The money budgeted for finding people usually pays for actual expenses such as telephone calls, mail costs, and search fees. You might pay for some gas and travel expenses, depending on the particular situation. Since the job is voluntary, labor costs (hourly wages) are almost never covered.

However, you should understand that it *does* take money to find people; and the harder and longer you look, the more it will cost per "found" person. When your group is small, every "find" is a minor celebration and the money is considered well-spent. But later on, as leads and interest wear thin, the cost per "found" person may become too high. Every year, your family should re-evaluate its policy, funding, and techniques for finding people. By taking this periodic "long, hard look," your family can optimize the interest and resources it has, and change accordingly.

Since most people must use their own phones, they may shy away from a volunteer job that costs them money. These days even dialing Directory Assistance costs money. It's necessary to budget for telephone calls as part of the reunion expense, and to let volunteers know they can be reimbursed. It's also a good idea to put a limit on the cost (or time) of each long distance call since some people may find it awkward to cut short a conversation with a long-lost relative. A set limit will give them an excuse to keep the conversation brief. You might also have a policy that if they exceed the time limit, they pay for the additional charges. Of course, such a policy would require them to keep a list of the phone calls they make. If anyone in your group has access to an outgoing WATS line, you might see if it can be used in the evenings or on weekends.

"Grapevine" Leads

The "grapevine" can lead to 80–90% of the people you are trying to find *if* you learn to ask the right questions. The most important point to remember, and get across to others, is that *any small clue can help.*

In many instances, a relative or former friend may have the information necessary to find a person—they just don't realize that their knowledge is useful. In some cases, the combined information from two or three people may eventually lead to a "find." It's the searcher's job to orchestrate this process and coax people to give the right information. The searcher must be willing to constantly ply people with questions that will lead to useable answers: "Do you remember what school she went to?" "Do you recall his middle name?" "What was his father's occupation?" "Did she marry someone from her hometown?" The usefulness of extracting this type of information cannot be overemphasized.

A LIST OF INFORMATION TO ASK FOR:

1. Hometown or hometown area.
2. Schools attended, years graduated.
3. Special interests or training.
4. Approximate age, if not exact birthdate.
5. Parent's occupations.
6. Nickname and middle name.
7. Religious affiliation.
8. Married name, approximate date and place of marriage.
9. Community affiliation and service clubs (Elk's, 4-H, Lion's, PTA, etc.)

ALSO, ASK THE PERSON YOU ARE TALKING TO:

1. Do you have any old photos? (Look for names, dates and other information written on the back.)

2. Do you have any old letters or diaries that might mention names or help you remember?

When talking to someone about a particular "missing" family member, ask for information on the topics in the preceding list. Give copies of this list to all the people helping you search and ask them to keep it by the phone.

Note: When talking with a stranger, *always* mention that your purpose for finding the person is to notify them about a family reunion. And remember the first rule of finding someone: If you can't find the person directly, find someone who *can* find them.

The "hometown" lead. If you know a person's hometown, and if that community is relatively small, you have a big advantage. A letter or phone call to the mayor's office or library will secure the names of the local high schools. Get the names of the newspapers while you are at it. Write or call the school secretaries requesting a check of school records (of course, it helps to know the approximate year of graduation or age if the person didn't graduate). Any address you receive from a school will be the parents' or guardians' address at the time the person was in school, which could be very old and useless. However, the school record can also yield some very useful information, such as full name, birthdate, full names of parents, and their occupations.

Be sure to ask the school secretary for addresses and phone numbers of reunion organizers for class reunions plus-or-minus 8–10 years from the year your relative graduated. Class reunions are great sources of information and the organizers have done the work for you. The "plus-or-minus 8–10 years" allows you to find siblings or cousins with the same last name. Of course, this works best with unusual or uncommon last names.

Let's say you find the parents' first names and the father's occupation. You could place an ad in the local paper that reads like this: "Looking for James Q. Doe and family, age 56, graduate of Hometown High School, class of '61, son of John and Mary Doe, father employed as carpenter. Please write: (give address) or call collect (give phone number)." The father's occupation helps in this case because all the retired carpenters and the retired carpenters' wives are going to be racking their brains trying to remember John Doe who had a son named James. In this instance, another source worth tracking down is the local carpenters' union.

You can find the name and address of any newspaper or magazine in the U.S. through *Gale's Directory of Publications* in your local library. These directories are indexed by location (as well as other ways), so you don't need to know the name of the newspaper in order to find the address.

Members of ethnic or close-knit religious groups within a community are very likely to be in touch with each other, at least through the "grapevine." You might want to check with a church, temple, or synagogue which the family may belong to, or contact ethnic or community organizations, especially those offering memberships and newsletters.

If someone in your family lives in the area, and has the time and inclination, she could go to an old address to ask the neighbors for information on the person being sought. Just the name of the town the person moved to could be of help. (See list of topics to cover, p. 156). Speaking with neighbors usually works if the family lived in the neighborhood for a long time. See how to do such a search using city directories on p. 166.

Using the Media

Putting a reunion announcement in the newspaper is another way to contact missing family members. However, getting an announcement printed free of charge is not likely and not easy. Most large daily newspapers will not print them, though there are exceptions to this rule. In some papers they are gathered together and printed all at once. Smaller newspapers, especially the local weeklies, are more obliging. A few regional magazines will use reunion announcements as "fillers." Most notable among these is *Yankee Magazine* which covers the New England area.

You should send a reunion announcement to a newspaper in the form of a press release as shown below. Notice that the press release contains only the pertinent facts. Editors appreciate succinct, complete information. If, for some reason, you think a particular publication may be interested in more information for an article, either inquire first or send the information separately from your short press release.

If your press release is cut to a bare-bones minimum (as below), it can also be used as a public service announcement (PSA) for radio stations. (It's even acceptable to keep the title of "press release.") However, keep in mind that most radio stations are not interested in airing family reunion announcements. If they have any interest in reunions at all, it's usually in school reunions, though there may be exceptions to this rule. The best way to get the phone numbers and addresses of radio stations is in the Yellow Pages under "Radio Stations." Otherwise look under sta-

```
PRESS  RELEASE
For release:  Immediately
Contact: John Jones (717) 555-3333


Johnson Family Reunion
Descendants of Jonah and Anne Johnson
of Albany. To be held August 21-22,
2001 at Sander's Park, Yourtown, NY.
Contact: John Jones, 333 Oak St.,
Pineville, PA 19123.
(717) 555-3333.
```

All press releases should be typed and double-line spaced.

tion call letters in the very front of the K's or W's in the white pages (C's in Canada). The only TV stations that will carry reunion announcements are the small local cable stations. Look under "Television Stations" in the Yellow Pages.

Historic Sources Provide Clues

Diaries, old letters, old photos, scrapbooks, and old newspaper clippings can contain useful information about missing people. Always solicit these through your newsletters and mailers, and when talking with members of your family. Be persistent! These items are often lying in the bottom of a trunk somewhere, completely forgotten. The owner doesn't even know they are there. However, when "bothered" enough times, they may actually look for them.

Database Searches/The Forwarded Letter

All colleges, trade schools, large corporations, unions, fraternal organizations, military publications, the Department of Veterans Affairs, military associations, etc., have databases (files) containing addresses of members, former members, alumni, employees, etc. Often these files will be searched if you provide a stamped envelope to be forwarded to the person you seek.

The procedure is to write a letter to the person you seek and place the letter in a stamped envelope with the missing person's name on the outside of the envelope. Also write on the envelope your return address and the words, "Return Service Requested" (explained on p. 83) under the return address. Send this envelope to the person or department in charge of the database, along with a note giving all identifying information about the person in question. If applicable, include the search fee. If the search is successful, the person's last known address is written on your envelope, and the envelope is mailed. (Note: Some organizations prefer the envelope to be sealed. Others want the envelope to be unsealed, so they can see the contents. If in doubt, leave it unsealed, or ask for their procedures first.) Furnish as much identifying information as possible.

This "forwarded letter" approach is one of the best investments available. The cost is two stamps, two envelopes, and some paper. Be sure to include all pertinent information in a cover letter to the organization that owns the database. It really helps to throw in some phrases like: "last resort," "I've been looking for this person for 10 years," "you're my only hope," "I know you are extremely busy, but…," etc.

The "forwarded letter" procedure protects the privacy of the individual. You cannot learn her address unless she decides to respond to your letter. A word to the wise: Don't be discouraged when a letter is not answered. Some people just aren't enthusiastic about reunions or may have reasons not to respond.

Public Records

Public records are available at the registrar of voters, the Department of Motor Vehicles (each state has its own name for this department, and some states don't allow access), the county tax office or assessor's office, the county recorder's office, and the county or state hall of records (vital statistics).

Searching these records can be rewarding in many different ways. But it's beyond the scope of this book to go into detail on what you can find in these records and how to go about doing so. There are many good books on the subject. Two of the best are *Find Anyone Fast* and *Checking Out Lawyers*. ➟See "Resources" for more information.

Using Computers

The great news concerning computers and tele-communications these days is that many libraries are now on-line with the Internet. In the next few years, most libraries will be on-line. That means you can do a lot of searching for free. See Chapter 14 (Using the Internet) for more information.

Using CD-ROMs. Digital technology has finally developed to the point of allowing a lot of information to be put into a very small package. This means that the names, addresses, and phone numbers of over 100 million people can be crammed onto a few CD-ROM discs, each under 5" in diameter. Of course, to read the discs you must have a computer with a CD-ROM reader. Or use the one at your library.

The latest reviews of such products list only two that are worth using: PhoneDisc and Select Phone. However, these two products are now owned by the same company which means they may soon be merged into one product. Another, Phone Search USA, is a distant third. Prices range from around $20 for a "home" version to $250 for a full-blown professional version. The pro versions are often worth the price because the data are more current and there are more ways to find the information. Still, expect only 45–50% accurate "hits." Remember, these are directories of *listed* phone numbers. ⇒See "Resources" for more information.

Using the Telephone

Let's say you find a name you are looking for in a phone book. Even the middle name or initial is the same, and you are reasonably sure the person is (or was) somewhere in the area. You phone the number and are informed the number is disconnected or no longer in service. Don't give up! Call Directory Assistance to see if another number is listed. The number published may not be right. The person may have recently moved and the phone company erred in referring the number. If that doesn't work, send a postcard to the address in the phone book (if one is listed). Remember, if the person moved, the Post Office is likely to forward mail longer than the phone company is likely to refer the phone number. Next, follow the instructions on p. 167 for sending a letter to the current resident asking her help. Persistence is the name of this game.

The cheapest times to call long distance are usually from 11 p.m. to 8 a.m., all day Saturday, and Sunday until 5 p.m. (local time). But it depends on the rules of your long distance carrier.

All long distance carriers have money-saving plans you can sign up for. Call to find out what's currently available.

Some interesting facts about unlisted phone numbers:

> Over 40% of all residential phone numbers are unlisted, and the more affluent a person, the more likely the number is unlisted.
> Sometimes an unlisted number will appear in a city directory (see page 166).
> Directory Assistance in some areas will tell you if the name you are looking for has an unpublished (unlisted) number. You won't get the number, but at least you know that the person (or a person with that name) is in the area. Unfortunately this convenience is slowly being phased out all over the country.

Dealing with Directory Assistance. Some information operators are not very personable, and many of them are talking to each other between calls (and, therefore, not giving you their full attention). Some are actually prison inmates. And since they must average a certain number of calls per hour, they are not too anxious to "linger" while you collect your thoughts when the name you ask for doesn't immediately turn up.

Our experience since 1982 has been that Directory Assistance is wrong or misleading about 15% of the time. Sometimes operators give you the wrong number (if you report this back to an operator, you will get credit for the call). Other times the name is there; they just can't find it. Or more precisely, they don't check various spellings or initials; they look only under the exact name and spelling you ask for and if it's not there, you lose. There is no way for you to know if they are checking other options or not. So you have to be explicit. If you ask, for example, for the number of a David Charles MacKenzie, and are informed that it's not there, then ask for "initials D.C.," "initial D.," "D. Charles," and MacKenzie spelled with "Mc" instead of "Mac." If you are very interested in finding a person, you should try Directory Assistance more than once. You are likely to get another operator next time you call.

You are usually allowed three directory checks (sometimes two, depending on the area) per phone call to Directory Assistance, but you must tell the operator first that you are looking for more than one number. Then you will get the first number(s) by live human voice and the last by an electronic voice called an audio response unit.

Many people don't realize that in most areas it is possible (and legitimate) to get an *address* from the Directory Assistance operator. Obviously, this could ultimately save you a phone call. You must ask for the address right from the start. You will get the address (or be informed that there is no address listed) from a live operator before being turned over to the electronic voice for the phone number.

Using the telephone for contacting family members is a personal approach. This can be a great advantage. A real live voice on the other end of the line is a lot different from a notice in the mail, and can easily elicit the "nostalgic interest" necessary for the person to say "Yes, I want to be there!" We suggest phoning all the "nonresponses" 6 to 8 weeks before the reunion. A good time is right after the last mailer is sent. If possible, have someone call who "best knows" the family or person being called.

Using the phone in this way can definitely be cost-effective. If you convince only five extra people to attend, at (say) $20 each, that's $100. And at the very least, you get to verify some addresses in your "unverified" address file.

Phone Books & City Directories

When looking through phone books, and when calling Directory Assistance, remember that the main objective is to get the address. The phone number is important, too, but your first attempt at contact should be through the mail. It will be cheaper to mail the information, and besides, you have to send the reunion mailers anyway. Use the telephone if the person doesn't respond to the mailing (it may be that the address is incorrect and the envelope was not returned), or if the person is "found" just before the reunion and has no time to receive your notice.

When using phone books, of course you should check under the full name of the person. But also check for possible relatives, especially if it's an unusual or uncommon name. This may be hopeless for a Smith or a Johnson, but let's say you are looking for a Kradowsky. You notice a Kradowsky in the phone book, but the first name is wrong. You phone that particular Kradowsky and find that the person you are looking for is his first cousin who moved to Pittsburgh, PA, ten years ago and they have been out of touch. Next, dial "0" and ask the operator for the area code for Pittsburgh, PA. Then dial the area code plus 555-1212 for information in Pittsburgh. (Remember, you will be charged a small fee for Directory Assistance calls.)

All public and college libraries have a large assortment of current phone books from the major metropolitan areas around the country. To save yourself a lot of time, phone first to find out if they have the ones you need. Libraries, or sections within libraries that are specifically designed for genealogical research, have truly amazing collections of both out-of-date and current phone books and city directories. For example, the Sutro Library in San Francisco, which is by no means the largest, has on hand 15,000 city directories and 10,000 telephone books. For genealogy libraries in your area, look under "Libraries" in the Yellow Pages. Your state library system, LDS Family History

Centers, and the National Archives System should be the best sources. ➡See "Resources" for more information.

City directories (sometimes called criss-cross directories) are published by private companies and contain two separate listings: alphabetical by name and numerical by street address. The alphabetical listing often includes the person's occupation, but you will have to turn to the address listing to find the phone number. Occasionally, unlisted phone numbers are found here.

With the help of a street map that shows the city block numbers, you can find the phone numbers of neighbors. Then by comparing the old city directories with the new, you can figure out who is still living in the neighborhood. When you call, remember to mention that it is for a family reunion. Also, leave your name and phone number with them in case they remember something later. If you are really persistent, call back in a week or two to see if they have remembered something after having had a chance to think about it.

Using Your Mailers & Newsletters

Be sure to include a list of missing persons in *every* mailer and newsletter you send out. In addition, make a plea for help in locating people. It's easy for people to forget about notifying you or put it off until later, assuming that someone else will do it. Mention in the mailer that the reader may very well be the only one with information on a particular individual, and not to assume someone else will send in the information.

Make it easy for people to contact you. Include a phone number (two, if possible) in all your mailers. Some people are very impulsive and "phone oriented." They will make a call, but won't take the time to write. Give the phone numbers of people who 1.) are willing and able to field phone calls, 2.) are reasonably gregarious and enthusiastic, 3.) are near the phone much of the time, especially in the evening, and 4.) have a phone answering machine.

Old addresses are often wrong. But if you can't get an address any other way, send an announcement to an old address. Remember, if it's not sent back by return mail, you can't assume the addressee received it. The person now living at that address (if it slipped past the Post Office's mail forwarding system—which is quite possible) may have thrown it away. Also, "mail forwarding" is good for only one year at the most, and in metropolitan areas, 6 months. You might consider writing a letter to the "occupant" or "resident" of the address to see if they know the whereabouts of the person you are looking for. The exact address may not be known, but they may know the city to which your relatives moved. Ask for clues (give a list), hand-address the envelope and write "Important!!" and "Personal" on the outside (since many people throw away letters addressed to "occupant"), and include a self-addressed, stamped postcard or ask them to call you collect. And *always* mention that it's for a reunion.

➠More information on mailing and postage is available in Chapter 6.

Chapter   13

Special Places for Reunions

This chapter is entirely noncommercial. None of the places listed in this chapter have paid to be here. For commercial listings, see our annual Directory of Reunion Sites *described on p. 247 and sometimes bound into the back of this book.*

*   *   *   *   *

Most family reunions are held in backyards, neighborhood parks, state parks, or local community centers. And well they should be. After all, these are the cheapest places, and inexpensive reunions better serve the family because more people are able to attend.

But there are a couple of very good reasons to eventually try a reunion in a more "interesting" place. One is just because it's fun. The other is because there's no better way to spice up reunions that are getting a bit boring.

These "special" reunions can celebrate a special event, investigate a special interest, answer a special concern, or fulfill a special wish. For instance, a reunion might honor the day that

Grandma Sophia immigrated to this country from Naples. Or a reunion might explore a family's interest in Native Americans and how they live. Another reunion might address environmental concerns and involve tidying up a forest preserve. Yet another reunion might find family members fulfilling a long-held dream of vacationing at a luxurious resort or going on a cruise together. Such reunions deserve (sometimes require) special surroundings—distinctive, off-the-beaten-path sites and activities.

To stir up your imagination and get the creative juices flowing, this chapter suggests a variety of places to go and things to do. However, most of these suggestions will be more expensive than a reunion in Grandma's backyard. Please bear in mind that these are not necessarily suggested as candidates for yearly reunions—rather for very special, once-in-a-decade or lifetime events. Fund-raising efforts of several "regular" reunions might be directed towards financing a special reunion the family will never forget. Announce this type of reunion several years in advance so that people have time to plan and to save money, and you should have very little trouble.

➡️See "Resources" for recommended books, and the Internet chapter (14) on how to find more information.

Special Tips

Some of the categories in this chapter are listed below, along with tips and suggestions.

Cruises

When shopping for a cruise via a travel agency or a cruise company, remember that the prices cited in the brochures aren't cast in stone. In most instances, they represent "high hopes" on the part of the cruise lines. Price cutting is pretty much the norm. While cruise companies cut their rates like the airlines, unlike the airlines, they often don't advertise the reductions. And they don't offer the same rates to every travel agency. So the name of the game is shop around! And don't hesitate to deal directly with the cruise company, especially if you have a large group. For a list of travel agents in your area who specialize in cruises, contact The National Association of Cruise Oriented Agencies, 7600 Red Rd. #128, South Miami, FL 33143, 305/663-5626. (*www.nacoa.com*)

Condominiums

Condos are a better deal for family reunions than most people realize. Here's why:

1. Most condos have 2 or 3 bedrooms, sometimes 4. Throw a few sleeping bags on the floor for the kids and it adds up to a low cost per person per night.

2. Most condos are someone's second home. Some even have a guest register to sign and family photos on the wall. They are a *lot* homier than hotels.

3. All have full sized kitchens.

4. Most are located near scenic or recreational attractions.

5. If you choose an area's "off" season, you can enjoy some great discounts. For example: a ski area in the summer.

To find a condo in your chosen area, contact the Chamber of Commerce and ask for condominium management companies. For recommendations on a nationwide basis (plus Mexico and the Caribbean) contact: Condominium Travel Associates, 2001 W. Main St. #140, Stamford, CT 06902, 203/975-7714.

Houseboats

Houseboats are great fun for the whole family, and can be rented throughout much of the U.S. and Canada. Piloting a houseboat is easier than driving a car and you don't need a special license. For a list of houseboat rental agencies, see Houseboat Association of America in "Resources."

Cowboy Adventures

Dude ranches and guest ranches are wonderful places for family reunions; however, many of these places require a one-week minimum stay.

A great resource for "scouting" a cowboy-style family reunion is Eugene Kilgore's *Ranch Vacations*. Eugene also has a great Web page. ➠See "Resources" for lots more information.

Luxury Resorts

During their busy season, luxury resorts can be quite pricey. However, it's an entirely different story during their respective off-seasons. For instance, as Arizona's temperatures soar from Memorial Day through Labor Day, rates at its resorts can drop by as much as 70–75 percent.

YMCAs and Church Camps

Some YMCAs and church camps are among the best places in the world for family reunions. That's because you can get reasonably comfortable accommodations, reasonably good food, and great recreational facilities for a rock-bottom price (in most cases; there are exceptions). The Ys listed in this chapter are the ones that actively seek family reunions. Many other Ys and church camps have family camps that small reunions can join.

Campuses

Many colleges rent out student's rooms very inexpensively during the summer. The advantage of campuses is that they are clean, cheap, safe, and many have cafeterias or restaurants and sports facilities. Most do not allow alcohol. See *Campus Lodging Guide* in "Resources."

*   *   *   *   *

The following facilities are (more or less) in geographical order from East to West.

Maine Windjammers

Accommodating up to 40 passengers, a seagoing windjammer is a great way for family members to get to know one an-other without outside attractions and distractions. The season is Memorial Day to Labor Day, with the peak season in July and August. Rates are lower in June and September. For more information, call the Maine Windjammer Association at 800/807-WIND, or write: PO Box 1144P, Blue Hill, ME 04614. *www.midcoast.com/~sailmwa*

The age limit for "general" cruises is usually 15 and up. However, if you rent the entire boat (capacities vary between 20 and 44, minimum of 3 days), then the boat is "yours," and any age is permissible. One company with such an arrangement is Maine Windjammer Cruises (capacity of their boat is 29). For more information, call them at 207/236-2938, or write: PO Box 617, Camden, ME 04843.

Hofstra University

For an affordable family reunion within sight of a large city, try Hofstra University, located 23 miles east of New York City on 240 beautiful acres. There are 1681 air-conditioned rooms available during the summer months. Save money on cafeteria-style food service, or try their catering service for anything from a

specially prepared meal in a private dining room to an outdoor barbecue under a pavilion. Meeting rooms can accommodate up to 1000. Tennis courts and play fields are available.

Hofstra University, Conference Services, 111 Student Center, Hempstead, NY 11550, 516/463-5067.

Holiday Hills Conference Center (YMCA)

This year-round conference center is located in historic Pawling, New York, in the foothills of the Berkshire Mountains,

70 miles north of Manhattan. It has accommodations for 20–175 people in comfortable air-conditioned rooms with private baths, excellent facilities, and scenic lakeside dining—the perfect natural setting for a family reunion.

There are endless opportunities to relax, refresh and invigorate your mind and body and breathe in fresh country air. The 500-acre property has a lake for water sports, or play tennis, basketball, softball, volleyball, or hike on the many trails. In the winter months you'll find a toboggan run, ice skating, ice fishing, sledding and miles of cross country ski trails.

Call 914/855-1550 or write to Holiday Hills Conference Center, 2 Lakeside Drive, Pawling, New York 12564.

Frost Valley YMCA

Frost Valley YMCA is located on 6000 acres, 2 hours northwest of New York City. Forests, meadows, ponds, a lake, waterfalls, and mountain streams make up the scenery. Activities include hiking,

climbing, boating, fly-fishing, archery, challenge courses, games, sports, crafts, campfires and more. A variety of lodging options include family-style and hotel-style lodges, rustic cabins, the historic Forstmann Castle, and the country inn atmosphere of the Straus Center. Many styles and sizes of meeting rooms are available, some with fireplaces. Contact: Frost Valley YMCA, 2000 Frost Valley Rd, Claryville, NY 12725, 914/985-2291. *www.frostvalley.org*

Silver Bay Association (YMCA).

Founded in 1902, Silver Bay has been serving family reunions for nearly 100 years. Its location on Lake George, "Queen of American Lakes" in upstate New York, is ideal for fun and festivities. Enjoy two beaches, sailing, hiking, tennis, crafts, music, arts, a state-of-the-art workout gym, rock climbing on a 40 x 40 foot climbing wall, or just relaxing. There's something for all ages.

Some families have come to Silver Bay through four generations. It's on the National Register of Historic Places, and more than half its 70 buildings are nearing or passing the century mark.

Silver Bay Association, 87 Silver Bay Rd, Silver Bay, NY 12874, 518/543-8833. E-mail: SBAMCJ@aol.com. Web site: *www.silverbay.org*

Watson Homestead Conference and Retreat Center

This is a year-round conference and retreat center affiliated with the United Methodist Church and serving all religious, educational, social service and charitable organizations. Located in the heart of the beautiful central southern tier of New York State,

Watson Homestead is situated on 600 acres of scenic valleys and hills, formerly the home of Tom Watson, founder of IBM.

This perfect reunion site offers space for large or small groups. Accommodations include hotel-style air-conditioned rooms with private baths, or bunk beds with shared baths. Recreational opportunities include a heated indoor pool, volleyball, basketball, softball, minia-  ture golf, hayrides, hiking trails and more. Watson Homestead is located only a few miles from the Corning Museum of Glass, Rockwell Museum of Western Art, the National Soaring Museum, Watkins Glen State Park, the Finger Lakes vineyards, and more. The airport is 20 miles away. Call 607/962-0541 or write Watson Homestead, 9620 Dry Run Road, Painted Post, NY 14870.

Smithsonian, Washington DC

Why not consider a family reunion with an educational twist? During the summer, the Smithsonian Institution in Washington DC offers their "Campus on the Mall." Among one-weekend classes offered are subjects that might appeal to some ethnic groups, such as "A Pilgrimage to China" and "Classic Arab Folk Tales." Since Washington DC is very much geared to touring families, your group could stay at a nearby hotel (enjoying group rates) and conduct group meetings in a conference room. For more information on classes, call the Smithsonian at 202/357-3030, or write: 1100 Jefferson Dr. #3077, Washington, DC 20560. For accommodations, call the District of Columbia Visitor's Bureau at 202/789-7000, or write: 1212 New York Ave. NW #600, Washington, DC 20005. *www.washington.org*

Colonial Williamsburg

Located midway between Norfolk and Richmond, Williamsburg is the re-creation of an 18th century Virginia community and is one of America's premier historical resorts. Brought to life with busy shops, horse-drawn carriages, and costumed characters, Williamsburg consists of 88 original structures—homes, businesses, public buildings—that have been restored and preserved.

Experience Williamsburgs' past by visiting museums, shops, mansions, and slave quarters to see how men, women, and children of that time lived, worked and played. The site can be enjoyed as "history brought to life" by taking part in various activities. Discover how people traveled two centuries ago with the Stage Wagon Tour. Explore the life-styles of African-Americans with the Other Half Tour. Join 18th century dancing and lawn games; learn how to make ornaments from that time period.

Special children's activities are offered throughout the year at various times. These include ox cart rides, fife and drum presentations, tours, and magic shows. Special programs are available for children 4–12 at a nominal cost.

Lodging options can be contemporary or colonial. Ideally located between the Historic Area and Visitor's Center, the Governor's Inn is recommended for families. Reduced packages are available during the off-season. Groups of more than 15 receive discounts. For more information, call 800-HISTORY, or write: PO Box C, Williamsburg, VA 23187. *www.history.org*

YMCA Blue Ridge Assembly

This is a full-service conference center situated near Asheville, North Carolina, on 1200 acres of woodland with mountain streams, wildflowers, and spectacular views. It was founded in 1906 and serves 20,000 guests annually.

Sleeping arrangements range from modern rooms with private baths to dormitory-style residences. Individual cottages are available, too. Buffet-style dining and meeting rooms (large auditoriums and small break-out rooms) are available to accommodate any size group.

Activities include swimming, hiking, tennis, volleyball, basketball, orienteering, environmental studies, biking, square dancing, archery, crafts, and campfires.

YMCA, 84 Blue Ridge Assembly, Black Mountain, NC 28711, 828/669-8422. *www.blueridgeassembly.org*

African-American Roots

With the publication of Alex Haley's *Roots* in 1976, both African-American and families of other origins developed a greater interest in their respective histories. As a result, Mr. Haley was a driving force behind the continued growing popularity of organized family reunions (this book is dedicated to him).

With the current emphasis on ethnic origins and pride, this interest is destined to become even more intense. In ethnic family reunions, the trend is dramatized by the record numbers of African-Americans seeking their past in the South. Among the most popular destinations visited by both individual families and groups are The Black Heritage Tour (800/647-6724, PO Box 1485, Natchez, MS 39121-1485), and the birth home of Dr. Martin Luther King Jr. (522 Auburn Ave., Atlanta, GA 30312). *www.natchez.ms.us* or *www.natchez.com*

Ridgecrest Conference Center in NC (see Glorieta in NM)

Cedar Hill Resort

Located on beautiful Dale Hollow Lake with 620 miles of shoreline to explore, this complete resort in the Cumberland Mountains offers 31 cottages, 6 motel rooms, 20 houseboats, a swimming pool, a restaurant, and a marina. Houseboats hold a maximum of 12 people. Excellent fishing, scuba diving, and water skiing. Calm waters, no mosquitos, average summer water temperature of 82°. Send for 4-color brochure.

Cedar Hill Resort, 2371 Cedar Hill Rd, Celina, TN 38551. 800/872-8393, 931/243-3201.

Living History Farms

Located in Urbandale, Iowa (10 miles from downtown Des Moines), Living History Farms is a 600-acre, open-air museum that re-creates the history of agriculture in the Midwest. The buildings, planting methods, and livestock are authentic from the time periods represented. Interpreters dressed in historic

clothing re-enact the daily routines of early Iowans and help visitors appreciate the artistry of the craftsmen who founded the state's first town. By joining the numerous activities scheduled through the summer, reunion members can experience the "living history" of the farm on another level. For instance, during the summer, games include leap frog, greased pole climbing, sack races, pig calling, and foot races. (If this is a little "too active" for older members, they might try square dancing.)

Summer day-camp sessions are available on a weekly basis for children entering grades 3–6 in the fall. Group accommodations and discounts for 20 or more are available. For more information, call 515/278-5286, or write: Living History Farms, 2600 NW 111 St., Urbandale, IA 50322. *www.lhf.org*

YMCA of the Ozarks

This Y is located 90 miles south of St. Louis in the Ozark Mountains on 5000 acres, which includes a 360-acre lake and 3 trout ponds.

They have year-round accommodations for 2 to 200, and offer customized family reunion programs that include everything from group photos to t-shirts, a private chuck wagon dinner, or a private party on a deck overlooking the lake. Free activities include tennis, boating, fishing, swimming, campfires, and hiking. Commercial activities include horseback riding, hayrides, crafts, climbing towers, zip lines, miniature golf or a full round of golf at Forche Valley Golf Club next door.

YMCA of the Ozarks, Rt. 2, Box 240, Potosi, MO 63664, 888/FUN-YMCA.

Overland Wagon Train Trips

For more than a decade, a Kansas company has offered "weekend pioneers" the opportunity to relive the adventures of their forefathers, enjoy the scenic beauty of the famous Flint  Hills area, partake of chuckwagon meals over an open fire, and sleep out under the stars. Wagon train trips are overnight, returning to the point of embarkation the next day. Excursions are scheduled from the middle of June to the middle of September. Group rates are available.

For more information, call 316/321-6300, or write: Overland Wagon Train Trips, Box 1076, El Dorado, KS 67042. Space is limited. Reserve early.

Delta Queen Steamboat Co.

For adults and children alike, there's nothing like the excitement of a steamboat coming into view, calliope playing, paddle wheel churning. Representing an important part of the Ameri-

can Heritage, a steamboat provides a marvelous setting for a family reunion.

The steamboatin' lines' famous *Delta Queen, American Queen,* and *Mississippi Queen* embark from a number of cities: Minneapolis/St. Paul, Pittsburgh, Cincinnati, Louisville, St. Louis, Nashville, Chattanooga, Memphis, and New Orleans.

While a dizzying number of themes and options are available, the "Celebration of Heartland America" vacations are described as the perfect setting for a family reunion. Staged in different areas of the country, this steamboat theme trip can range from 3–11 days. Minimum group size is 10 full-fare passengers and discounts can add up to 40%. If you want to discuss group discount fares with the company, call 800/458-6789, or write: Delta Queen Steamboat Co., 1380 Port of New Orleans Place, New Orleans, LA 70130-1890. *www.deltaqueen.com*

Dixie Dude Ranch

Don't go callin' this a resort ranch. The Dixie Dude is a 725-acre old-time working stock ranch founded in 1901. But of course, you don't have to

do any work at all. Just take it easy and have a good time with your family. Activities include horseback riding, hayrides, campfire sing-alongs, dancing, hiking, arrowhead hunting, and barbecues. Located in the Texas Hill Country, 55 miles northwest of San Antonio. Airport pickup is available with prior arrangement. Dixie Dude Ranch, PO Box 548, Bandera, TX 78003, 800/375-Y'ALL. *www.tourtexas.com/dixiedudranch/*

Prude Ranch

Established as a cattle ranch in the late 1800s, the Prude spread has been welcoming guests since the 1920s. Located in west Texas, six miles west of Fort Davis, the ranch is recognized as a fun place for the entire family. Guests can enjoy open-range riding, hayrides, country-and-western dancing, etc. Accommodations (for up to 250) include ranch style cottages and bunkhouses. Open around the year, the Prudes accept weekend as well as weeklong reservations. A summer camp program for kids is offered mid-June to early August. Baby-sitting services are available. For more information, call 800/458-6232, or write: PO Box 1431, Fort Davis, TX 79734. *www.tourtexas.com/pruderanch/*

YMCA of the Rockies

In operation since 1907, the YMCA of the Rockies (to the best of our knowledge) hosts more family reunions than any other organization in the world—over 650 per year. There are actually two separate facilities, Estes Park Center and Snow Mountain Ranch.

Located 65 miles northwest of Denver, Estes Park Center offers affordable accommodations of all kinds, and provides nearly 40

Pattie Hyde Barclay Reunion Lodge.

meeting rooms on the 860-acre property. Extremely popular with family reunions is the Pattie Hyde Barclay Reunion Lodge (capacity 72), designed from the ground up with family reunions in mind. This lodge is booked several years in advance.

Located 80 miles west of Denver, 5000-acre Snow Moun-

tain Ranch enfolds forests of pine and fir as well as cozy cabins, spacious lodges, and numerous meeting facilities. Accommodating meetings from 20 to 1300, the ranch has 5 family reunion cabins (capacity: 25 each) with sweeping views of the surrounding

Snowberry Cabin, Snow Mountain Ranch.

wilderness. Recently added is the Heritage Reunion Cabin with a capacity of 32.

Both the Center and the Ranch offer numerous recreational activities, from swimming to hayrides, nature hikes to crafts. Call 800/777-YMCA, or write: YMCA of the Rockies, Estes Park, CO 80511-2800. *www.ymcarockies.org/*

Winter Park, Colorado

One of my favorite areas for family reunions happens to also have great condo rates in the summer—that's Winter Park, Colorado. This part of Colorado probably hosts more family reunions than any other area in the country—over 600 per year. Snow Mountain Ranch (see above) hosts over 250 alone. Another great reunion site in this area is The Inn at Silver Creek (800/926-4386).

What I like best about the Winter Park area is that there are so many great things for families to do without experiencing the super-distraction of a Disney World. The main attraction is Winter Park Resort which is a 7-acre playland with an alpine slide, a maze, volleyball courts, miniature golf and a lot more. In and around Winter Park, you can go on hayrides and sing around a campfire; there's a small rodeo once or twice a week; a ski lift to Sunspot Lodge where you can dine with an unsurpassed view; white water rafting; horseback riding; biking; hiking. And there's even an Amtrak station nearby.

Here are some Winter Park condo management companies: Beaver Village Condos (800/824-8438); Iron Horse Resort (800/621-8190); Winter Park Adventures (800/832-7830). The latter can also arrange all kinds of recreation for you.

The Nature Place

Located 35 miles west of Colorado Springs, Colorado, The Nature Place welcomes family reunions to a quiet, relaxed year-round mountain retreat. Designated by the National Park Service as a "National Environmental Study Area," the 6000-acre center offers numerous programs, including astronomy, botany, geology, ornithology, and wildlife observation. Lodge and studio apartments constructed of natural wood, native rock, and large expanses of grass can accommodate up to 100. Conference facilities are available. A deluxe sports complex contains a pool, Jacuzzi, sauna, and exercise room; tennis and volleyball courts are outside. For more information, call 719/748-3475, or write: Colorado Outdoor Education Center, Florissant, CO 80816. *www.iex.net/ sanborn/tnp.htm*

Glorieta Conference Center/Ridgecrest Conference Center

Glorieta Conference Center in New Mexico, and its sister property, Ridgecrest in North Carolina are two of the best facili-

ties in the U.S. for family reunions. Owned and operated by the Sunday School Board of the Southern Baptist Convention, both sites rival the YMCA of the Rockies in activities,

Activities at Glorieta.

prices, scenery and safe, Christian environment. Glorieta is situated 18 miles east of Santa Fe right on I-25; Ridgecrest is 17

miles east of Asheville. Activities at both facilities include volleyball, basketball, softball, tennis, ping pong, badminton, frisbee, horseshoes, billiards, miniature golf, and white water rafting nearby. Accommodations are available with or

Parachute games at Ridgecrest.

without kitchen facilities. Glorieta Conference Center, PO Box 8, Glorieta, NM 87535, 800/797-4222. Ridgecrest Conference Center, PO Box 128, Ridgecrest, NC 28770, 800/588-7222.

Lake Powell Resorts and Marinas

Lake Powell, the dramatic centerpiece of the Utah/Arizona area which includes Monument Valley, the Grand Canyon, and Zion National Park, is one of the centers of houseboat activity in the U.S. With 2000 miles of shoreline, 2 lodges, 4 full-time marinas, an 18-hole golf course, plus tennis, hiking, bicycling, dam and museum tours, Lake Powell is truly a reunion planner's paradise. Their houseboats come in three sizes, each with creature

comforts that include a bathroom
with hot shower, refrigerator/
freezer, fully-equipped kitchen
with stove, etc. Seasonal pricing
and packages can offer substantial
savings on both lodging and boat
rentals. For more information, call
800/528-6154 or 602/484-9090,
or write: Lake Powell Resorts and
Marinas, 2233 W. Dunlap #400,
Phoenix, AZ 85079. Minimum
rental for houseboats during the

summer season (mid-May through mid-October) is three days.

Grand Canyon Railway

Located in Williams, Arizona, less than 3 hours from Phoenix, the Grand Canyon Railway Depot offers a preview of the

exciting trip to and
from the Grand Can-
yon. As the 1910
steam locomotive
pulls up and passen-
gers get ready to
board, a mock shoot-
out between the mar-
shal and some "var-
mints" takes place.
Despite all the hullabaloo, the train pulls out at precisely 9:30
a.m. and everyone is on their way in the comfort of authenti-
cally restored 1920s Harriman coach cars.

During the leisurely 2 hour 15 minute trip, passengers are
entertained by beautiful vistas, wildlife sightings, and live music
provided by banjo and guitar players. Stepping off the train at
the Grand Canyon Depot—the only operational log depot in
the United States—everyone has plenty of time to take a bus

tour, go sightseeing, visit the museums and stores, or hike around the majestic South Rim. On the return trip, there's great excitement again when the train is "held up" by some bad hombres who come riding in on horseback. However, the marshal comes to the rescue, peace is restored, and the passengers arrive back in Williams safely.

While everyone enjoys the Grand Canyon Railway, railroad buffs think they've died and gone to heaven. As a family reunion site, it uniquely combines an historical trip with a visit to one of the world's greatest sights. (It should be noted that parking has become difficult at the Grand Canyon, especially during the summer.) Large reunions (80 or multiples of 80) can have their own railroad cars, thus ensuring greater privacy and enjoyment. Groups of 10 or more receive a discount. For more information, call 800/843-8723, or write: Grand Canyon Railway, 1201 W. Route 66 #200, Flagstaff, AZ 86001. *www.thetrain.com*

Edgewater Resort

Located 100 miles north of San Francisco, the Edgewater Resort is an ideal choice for family reunions. With over 150 shade

trees, plenty of sunshine and fresh air, you'll enjoy the peaceful serenity of this natural park-like setting. It's located in Soda Bay, on the shores of Clear Lake, the largest natural lake in California, known as "The Bass Capital of the West Coast."

There are a variety of accommodations to suit everyone, including RV sites, tent sites and cozy cabins with lakefront views. Activities include swimming in the pool or lake, sunbathing on the 300' beach, lawn or pool volleyball, horseshoes, ping-pong, video games or billiards, fishing off the 230' pier, or any kind of water sports including water skiing, parasailing, kayaks, and paddle boats.

The lakefront clubhouse is a great place for families to relax, visit and enjoy meals together. An indoor commercial kitchen facility and an outdoor group barbecue area are available to pre-pare your own group meals together. For those special memo-ries, meals can be catered so that you can do what you came for......cook? No! To visit and relax.

Only minutes away you can enjoy golf, hiking, tennis, fine dining, casinos, wine tasting, cycling, live concerts, or a cruise aboard the *Clear Lake Queen*, a 150-passenger paddle wheel cruiser. Contact the Edgewater Resort at 800/396-6224 or write: 6420 Soda Bay Rd., Kelseyville, CA 95451.

Alisal Guest Ranch

Located 35 miles northwest of Santa Barbara on a 10,000-acre working cattle ranch secluded in the Santa Ynez Valley, The Alisal is Calif-ornia's only full-ser-vice guest ranch. For half a century, the same families have returned year after year, and The Alisal is now hosting the 4th generation. The ranch features 73 cottage studios and suites, all with wood-burning fireplaces and refrigerators, two championship golf courses, 7 tennis courts, many kinds of horseback activities, a swimming pool, a 90-acre lake for fishing and water sports, and a year-round children's program. The Alisal Guest Ranch, 1054 Alisal Rd, Solvang, CA 93463, 800/425-4725. *www.alisal.com*

Rafter Six Ranch Resort

Forty-five miles west of Calgary, Alberta, at the threshold to the Canadian Rockies, you'll find the Rafter Six Ranch. Offering endless activities—trail rides, hayrides, carriage rides, western entertainment, numerous nearby sightseeing attractions—the ranch accommodates up to 60. Children's facilities include a play area and petting zoo. Whether your group stays for a day or a weekend, they'll enjoy downhome hospitality here. For more information, call 403/673-3622, or write: Rafter Six Ranch Resort, Seebe, Alberta, Canada T0L 1X0.

Chapter 14

Using the Internet

Chapter Highlights
▸*Where to Search.* ▸*How to Search.*
▸*More Tips on Searching.* ▸*How to Find Books.*
▸*Searching for People.* ▸*Subject Trees & Search Engines.*
▸*Family Web Pages.*

Don't skip this chapter just because you don't have a computer or don't have an Internet connection. In most parts of the country you can get on-line for *free* down at your local library—if not right now, then soon. It won't be long before all libraries are on-line.

Searching the Internet for information is *not* rocket science. The librarians can help you get started. Then buy a book that explains the browser your library uses (probably Netscape or Explorer). The basic techniques of searching for information on the Internet can be learned in just an hour or two.

What's available for reunion planners on the Internet? Here are just a few catagories of information:

➤ Finding people
➤ Newsletter production and design
➤ Suppliers: t-shirts, photography, videography, catering, imprinted gifts, scrapbooks, personalized calendars, plaques, awards, etc.
➤ Recipes for large groups or potlucks
➤ Books on any subject
➤ Games and activities
➤ Reunion sites and accommodations
➤ Transportation schedules and fares (airlines, buses, trains)
➤ Family Web sites
➤ Much, much more

The Internet (and the World Wide Web which is part of the Internet) is evolving so quickly right now that listing URLs (Web addresses) in this book is probably a lesson in futility. That's because at least some of these Web addresses will be changing, if not in the next few months, then certainly in the next few years. So, in order to best serve the reader, we will list a few current Web addresses at the end of this chapter, but mostly we will explain *how* to search for the information you are looking for. That way you can find what you need, including what has come into existance since this book was printed.

A URL (or Web address) is like a phone number. It's the unique information you must type into the browser (the software that accesses the Internet) to display a particular Web site on your computer screen. Useful URLs can be found throughout the "Resources" section.

Where to Search

There are *subject trees, search engines,* and *metasearch engines.* They all help you find what you're looking for on the Internet. We'll call them all search engines here.

Might as well start with one of the best: *www.yahoo.com.* (By the way, *http://* always comes before the *www* part. Most browsers nowadays are smart enough to know this. If not, put it in.) The figure below shows what the home page of *www.yahoo.com* looks like (a home page is the first page of a Web site). Forget about all those categories you see, like "Arts and Humanities,"

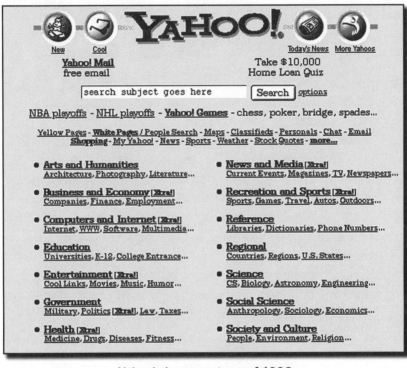

Yahoo's home page as of 1998.

etc. If you start clicking there it will take forever to find what you're looking for. Instead, fill in the search box with a few well-thought-out words pertaining to your subject. Let's say you're looking for a company that will print t-shirts for your reunion. In the subject box, type in "family reunion shirts" (without the quotes). Click on the Search button, wait awhile, then start sifting through all the information that comes your way. You might just try "shirts" but by adding "family reunion" you are likely to find companies that cater specifically to family reunions and have ready-made designs. (The reason for not putting "t-shirts" is because it can be spelled "tshirts," "T-shirts," "tee shirts," "teeshirts," "Tee shirts," etc.).

Notice the underlined word, <u>options</u>, to the right of the search box in the figure on the previous page. Click there for a list of the search parameters. Or go directly to the first help page: *http://search.yahoo.com/search/help?* Or the advanced search page: *http://search.yahoo.com/search/syntax?* Briefly, the parameters are:

➤ Anything within quotes will be found exactly as is. If you type *"family reunion"* you will get anything with that exact phrase (the word "family" immediately before the word "reunion"). If the quotes are excluded, you will get anything containing either the word "family" or the word "reunion" or both words. There's a big difference.

➤ A + sign before the word means that the word *must* be found. For example, *+family +reunion* will return anything containing both words. The words don't have to be together.

➤ A – sign (hyphen) before the word means that the word must *not* be found. For example, *+reunion –school* will return anything with the word "reunion" in it and not the word "school" in it.

➤ Each Web page has a title (though some are blank). Putting *"t:"* (without the quotes) before your request searches the titles for the words that follow.

➤ *"u:"* (without the quotes) before a request searches the URLs (Web addresses). For example, *u:reuni* will find all URLs with the string "reuni" in them. This will catch such URLs as *www.reunited.com* which, by the way, is a great site for school reunion planners.

There are other parameters, too, such as *wildcards*. Each search engine has an explanation of its parameters. Luckily, most of them are the same or close to the same. In the future, they will converge even more. Some search engines now have a box with clickable choices, such as: "exact phrase," "contains all of these words," "contains any of these words," etc. This is a quick way to the same parameters as described above.

By the way, you may be wondering just exactly what gets searched. When you send out a search request, the search engine is *not* looking though every Web site in the universe. Instead it is looking though its own index of information collected ahead of time from various Web sites. That's why it's important to search every few weeks or so. Things change rapidly on the Internet. Information is constantly being added, updated, and deleted. It takes time for the various search engines to update their indexes of information. And some Web sites get missed altogether.

Each search engine collects information it deems important from each Web site. Some index every word; others index certain key words that it thinks appropriate; others index the first hundred words or so; others index just the page titles and what's known as the meta header (a place for the Web site creator to put key words to be found by the search engines).

So that's why you should use several search engines. We sent you to Yahoo first because it's what's known as a *subject tree.* It searches through many search engines at once and compiles the information for you.

Now here's a trick for finding other search engines and Web references: From *www.yahoo.com* do a search (any search; we just want to get the the next page). After the search is complete, go down to the bottom of that page where there is a section called "Other Search Engines." You will see a few individual search engines listed, such as Alta Vista, WebCrawler, HotBot, Lycos, etc. At the end of that list you will see the word <u>more</u> underlined. Click on that word and something like the figure on the next page will appear. As you can see, there are more search engines and references listed than you know what to do with. But that's the nature of the Internet. It can overwhealm you if you let it.

URLs for other subject trees and search engines can be found at the end of this chapter.

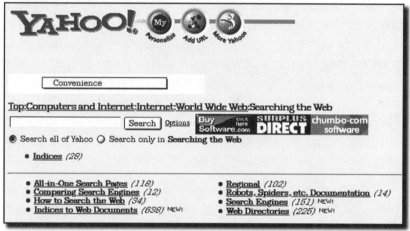

Yahoo's index of search-related Web sites, indices, and directories. The number to the right of each category is the quantity. For example, if you click on *Search Engines*, you will be presented with a list of 151 search engines to choose from.

How to Search

Here are some suggested ways of searching for certain topics related to family reunions:

Looking for companies that print family reunion t-shirts:
    +reunion +shirts

Looking for imprinted giftware:
    +gift +imprint or *+reunion +gift +imprint*

Looking for decorations:
    +decoration +party

Looking for recipes for potlucks:
    +recipe +potluck

Looking for recipes for large groups:
+reunion +recipes or *+recipes +group* or *+recipes +crowd*
or *+recipes +quantity*

Looking for information on how to produce newsletters:
+newsletter +design

Looking for ways of finding people:
+find +people or *+search +people*

Looking for games and activities:
+reunion +games

Looking for family Web sites:
+family +web or *+family +site*

Looking for sites and accommodations:
+reunion +hotel or *+reunion +resort*

Or you can be a lot more specific with some searches. For example, if you are looking for pinatas, try: *+pinata*. If you are looking for personalized pencils, try: *"imprinted pencils"*.

A Few More Tips on Searching

> ➤ Take a few minutes to learn the search parameters of a particular search engine, especially if there are indications of not returning the right information. These parameters are usually under "help" or "options."
> ➤ Don't use plurals. Use "reunion" instead of "reunions."
> ➤ Be careful with capital letters. "Rose" will most likely find Rose Kennedy and nothing about flowers (except perhaps the Rose Society).
> ➤ Use different spellings, even misspellings. Try "recipies" instead of "recipes."
> ➤ Try again a week or two later. The Internet changes constantly.

How to Find Books on Your Subject

Check into *www.amazon.com* and, in the title search box, en-ter the word or words that you would most expect to be in the title of a book. For example, enter the word "reunion" (without the quotes) for a list of books with the word "reunion" in the title. The list will include books that are out of print. If you don't want to purchase right away over the Internet, take the list to a library or book store.

Possible search parameters for reunion-related books:

For books on t-shirt design try:
   shirt, design

For books of recipes for large groups try:
   recipes, group or *recipe, crowd* or *recipe, quantity*

For books of recipes for potlucks try:
   recipe, potluck or *family, potluck* or just *potluck*

For books on games for reunions try:
   reunion, game or *family, game*

For books on newsletters try:
   newsletter, family or *newsletter, design*

For books on clip-art try:
   clipart or *clip art* or *clip-art*

For books on how to find people try:
   find, people or *search, people*

For books on video instruction try:
   videography or *video, beginner* or *video, how* or *video, family*

For books on storytelling try:
   storytelling or *family, story*

For books on scrapbooks try:
   scrapbook

For books on family reunion sites and accommodations try:
> *family, vacation* or *family, resort* or *ranch, vacation*
> or *kids, vacation* or *family, lodging* or *family, accommodation*

For books on how to collect family history try:
> *family, collect* or *oral, history* or *family, history*

You get the idea. You just have to start thinking like the computer programs that index this information in the first place.

Searching for People?

We could give you a long list of phone and address directories, but there's no need. Just go to *www.CyndisList.com/finding.htm*. This page has lists of phone directories, e-mail directories, and address directories. It's a long list; scroll down. It's updated every month or so and will probably be there 10 years from now. Thank God for lists like this.

A List of Subject Trees & Search Engines

> *http://www.yahoo.com/*

My favorite is SavvySearch at:
> *http://guaraldi.cs.colostate.edu:2000/form*
> *http://www.cyber411.com/main.htm*
> *http://www.mckinley.com/*
> *http://www.metacrawler.com/index.html*
> *http://www.dogpile.com/*
> *http://www.altavista.com/*
> *http://www.excite.com/*
> *http://www.hotbot.com/*
> *http://www.infoseek.com/*
> *http://www.lycos.com/*
> *http://www.WebCrawler.com/*

Family Web Pages

Family Web pages will become more and more popular over the next several years. That's because the software for creating

these pages is becoming a lot easier to use, and home computers are becoming more common. The Web "space" itself is already very cheap or free.

Items that can be posted on a Web page are about the same as
those printed in newsletters: photos, puzzles, artwork, stories,
etc. Web pages have it over newsletters because they can contain video and sound clips, and of course they are in color.

Check out a few family Web pages to get some ideas. From a
search engine, search for family, sites or family, web. Or check
www.CyndisList.com for its list of family Web sites.

A great book on designing family Web pages is *Home Sweet
Home Page* by R. Williams. ➡See "Resources."

Other Tips

➤ To verify an address or a zip code, try the Postal Service's
  Web page at *www.usps.gov/*
➤ To see a map of telephone area codes:
  www.555-1212.com/aclookup.html
➤ Please understand that all the Web addresses in this book
  will someday be out of date; it's just a question of when.
  Please check our Web site at *www.reuniontips.com* for the
  latest tips and updates.

➡Also see "Resources."

Real Reunions
A Gathering of Ideas

Nothing beats real examples for getting the point across. The following pages are straight from the horses mouth.

Future editions of this book will have even more examples like these. We would love to add your input to these pages. Please document part of your next reunion for us. Take photos. Write a few words of explanation. You will earn a free book, meager compensation, and something very interesting for your great-great-grandchildren to look at while they are trying to figure out what to do at their next reunion. Send information to the address on the back cover.

The BECK
Family Reunion

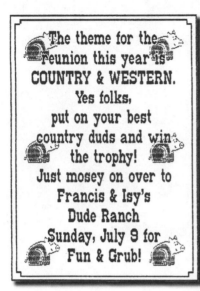

The theme for the reunion this year is COUNTRY & WESTERN. Yes folks, put on your best country duds and win the trophy! Just mosey on over to Francis & Isy's Dude Ranch Sunday, July 9 for Fun & Grub!

As our family comes from all over the U.S., we asked everyone to bring "scratch-off" lottery tickets, which became the most coveted prizes for contests. We have scavenger hunts; trivia games; win, lose or draw with a large easel; softball; balloon tosses (always popular on hot sunny days). The kids love to guess how many pennies or M&Ms are in a jar.

We ask people to bring baby pictures and graduation photos. We then make a photo display and have people guess who is who. This year's hit was story-telling in front of a video camera — stories of growing up.

Site: Family farms are where we first had our reunions — fresh, home-grown vegetables, and the kids loved the new farm animals.

Every reunion is followed with a newsletter. We even have friends who want to become honorary family members so they can come to our reunions.

Each year our expert kite designers bring us new high-flyers.

Lisa dressed as a '60s hippy. Other themes: Polynesian, Monte Carlo/Las Vegas, wild & crazy, country & western, etc.

The Briss Family Reunion

The First International Briss Family Reunion was held in Bridgewater, Massachusetts, in 1996. Cousins came from Canada, Israel, South Africa, and all parts of the U.S. The Briss family originated in Lithuania and there are now over 300 living descendants.

We posted a long printout of all seven generations of the family tree and supplied pencils for each person in attendance to mark their initials. Some cousins brought photographs of children or siblings who could not attend.

A world map was mounted on a foamcore board with pins marking the states, provinces and countries inhabited by family members. This display really interested the kids.

Most people like old photos but children are usually bored with pictures of people they don't know. So we displayed a few generations of wedding portraits. <u>Everybody</u> likes to look at wedding pictures.

A commemorative cross-stitch, designed and executed by Joyce Rowland, presented here to Philip Briss, the patriarch of the American branches of the family. It shows the original Hebrew spelling of the family name.

Always get a good photo of the oldest and youngest together. Here is Jack Miller (l.) who came from South Africa for the reunion and Jen Alexander Rowland.

The BULLOCK Family Reunion

The Bullock Family of Parmele, North Carolina, are descendants of George Bullock Sr., who was one of seven offspring of Caesar Bullock Sr., born into slavery in 1819.

Now our family meets each year with around 200 of our 600 members getting together from New York to North Carolina. The site and hosting of our reunion rotates among five regional committees.

The family crest was designed by 16-year-old Renee Brown in 1985 and is now on T-shirts, hats, plaques, etc.

We begin with an invocation and the singing of the Negro hymn "Lift Every Voice and Sing." We also have a family song. We incorporate surprises into the reunion with a "Family Member of the Year Award" and birthday parties. An essay contest about the family, with prizes for the children has worked well.

We ask "What does our family need?" Out of this has grown the Bullock Family Scholarship Fund to assist academics. Also individual medical histories can help us trace any predisposition to illnesses.

One family member donated a 3-foot-wide candelabra that is now used during our memorial service and then passed on to the group hosting next year's reunion.

And no reunion would be complete without the recitation of a special family poem.

Plan a fashion show.

SOME POINTERS:

➤ Form committees to look for a site, food, entertainment, accommodations, special events, and youth activities.

➤ Keep searching for your family — do genealogical work.

➤ Document the reunion well. Videotape stories and recollections to share with those who could not attend and to show future generations.

Sharing long-lost photos at the banquet.

Have a talent show, an art show, or a concert.

Family Weekend

The Chamberlin-Shabowski Family Association was formed in 1995 to promote family togetherness, to honor those who came before us, and to preserve our family history.

Our reunion took place in Park City, Kentucky, in 1996. When participants registered, they all received tote bags containing a schedule of events, tickets for the Mammoth Cave Tour, name tags, a family cookbook, contests to enter, and family genealogies.

After registration was a barbecue in a picnic area. While the cooks grilled burgers and hot dogs, the children participated in an autograph hunt and the adults got acquainted. After the meal we introduced ourselves, telling how we were related to the Chamberlin or Shabowski families, and what we liked best about our families.

The next day the Chamberlin-Shabowski Family Olympics

The One-Minute Timed Walk

began. Teams had been previously assigned so that each team had an equal representation of all ages. We had Team Ireland, Team England, and Team Poland, representing the ethnic backgrounds of most of us. Contests were the back-

Back-to-Back Race

to-back race, the three-legged race, "what age are they" (guessing the ages of celebrities), "guess the product by the slogan," the one-minute race (object: cross the finish line as close to one minute as possible. No wearing watches!), egg toss, etc. Team Poland won our first Olympics.

Our reunion theme was "In the service of Their Country." After the banquet meal, the Chamberlin-Shabowski

Players presented a wonderful program based on this theme. The narrator introduced to the audience various ancestors who told about their lives and their service to our country. The Chamberlin-Shabowski Singers sang songs which represented the times these people lived in. We met a colonial ancestor who outlived 3 husbands and yet died at the age of 40 in 1673, a Revolutionary War ancestor and his wife, a Civil War ancestor and his wife, and not a dry eye was in the house as we heard from our WWII relative who was missing in action. The program ended with a moment of silence. The audience then joined the choir in singing "This Land Is Your Land" and "God Bless America."

The Chamberlin-Shabowski Singers.

John Chamberlin and Jamie Schabowski as ancestors John Chamberlin, Civil war veteran, and wife Hannah Stevens Chamberlin.

Robert Shabowski as relative Ted Schabowski, WWII pilot missing in action in 1944.

Picture contest. All these people are attending the reunion. Guess their names. Warning! In some photos, the people appear much younger than they presently are.

The Coberly Tradition

Our family reunion was held in Amana, Iowa. Approximately 190 people came — mostly from the Midwest, but some from Washington and California. Any Coberly clan member was invited — no matter how they spelled the name, from Cubberly to Koberleigh. The Name came from the Cotswolds in England with a village there still called Coberly.

As people arrived we had them sign their names in a numbered guest book. This made it easy to give door prizes by just putting numbered pieces of paper into a fish bowl. Very simple. Many prizes were donated (like the family cross-stitch pictured above), so lots of folks went home with a "freebie."

Of special interest to newer clan members were the several family trees, each representing a different branch. They're drawn on boards and are over 5 feet tall.

We publish "The Coberly Tradition" twice yearly to keep our folks connected with family and reunion information. We plan reunions every two years with locations often chosen for their special outside interests: museum exhibits, galleries, etc. And do remember to prepare entertainment for the children.

The CONNOLLY Family Reunion
of Nova Scotia and Ontario, Canada

The Connolly Family Mini-Olympics pits Ontario vs. Nova Scotia. Some officially approved events are:
1. egg toss
2. ski race (photo)
3. limbo stick stretch
4. basketball race
5. 3-legged race
6. obstacle course, etc.

Spot drug checking is permitted, so no steroids; no name calling; no punching; no pinching; no telling jokes to distract the other team; having fun is permitted; do laugh; yelling & screaming is encouraged; no stealing or kidnapping members of the opposite team. Points will be awarded according to the fancy of the official.

The Nova Scotia branch of the Connolly Family Ski Team.

Our family has nicknames for each other and a "family dialect." Here is part of our glossary:

glasses = giglamps	carrots = rots
radio = rond-a-rurd	awful = ickbait, etc.

In the evening we have a bonfire with story-telling and "famous moments" in Connolly music. We employed a local mentally handicapped workshop to make buttons and key chains for all the family. Good prices and a good cause.

CONNOLLY
19   91
FAMILY REUNION

PREMIUM WINE
12.08% alc./vol. 750 ml
PRODUCED AND BOTTLED BY
SAINTE FAMILLY WINES LTD.
FALMOUTH, NOVA SCOTIA

We specially ordered wine from a nearby vineyard with our own label showing a map of Nova Scotia superimposed over one of Ontario with the home towns circled.

The Graham Reunion

Each family branch takes turns planning our reunions. The location is their choice. Our last reunion was held at Butman Methodist Camp and Retreat, Merkel, Texas. Our theme was Western. The family in charge wore sheriff's badges.

Signs were posted, pointing the way.

We had western-type place cards at the meals. The cards were switched after each meal allowing folks to mix and mingle.

G R A H A M O

COWS	DEVINE	PRAIRIE LEE	DEACON	COUSINS	NERD	AIR FORCE
TENNESSEE	ROY	TERRELL	BILLY	CLAYTE	GRAHAM	FIREMAN
SUDAN	BETTY	GRAHAM	COTTON FLAT	FARMER	KNAPP	COAHOMA
RICHMOND	WESTFALL	WTBU	FREE	MERKEL	RONALD	DIGHTON
GREENWOOD	CANYON	TEACHER	TERRELL	ARMY	LITTLEFIELD	RONALD
NAVY	BULA	ANNABETH	CISCO	JOYCE	RUSHING	THOMAS
LUMS CHAPEL	DAVIS	BILLY	DIGHTON	COTTON	PASTOR	COWBOY

We played "Grahamo," like Bingo but we used names, places, occupations, etc, of family members.

We put together a 45-minute homemade video of old photos and old 8mm movies and had a "movie night" to show this video. A little family history was included in the narration of the video. We all laughed and cried.

Each person was asked to bring one can of food which was donated to a children's home in Abilene.

We always take a group picture. One family member does a scrapbook of all the reunions.

The children participated in bashing a pinata which was in the shape of a cowboy boot. They all had fun dashing for the prizes that fell out.

We also played "We I.D." where old pictures of family members are posted and numbered. Then everyone tries to identify each photo (no talking allowed during this time, but laughing is okay). Each person is given a sheet of paper with numbered blanks to fill out with the names of the people in the photos. Prizes were awarded to the person with the most correct guesses.

Owns an Elvis album	Last Name Zachry	Owns a vehicle that doesn't run	Has seen 101 Dalmations
Has a tan.	Less than 4 foot tall.	Lived out of state	Chicago Bulls Fan

Here's part of our game called "Match-A-Relative." The idea is to write a relative's name in the box who fits the description. First one to find a name for all boxes wins. The complete game has 25 squares. It gets people talking to each other.

HASEGAWA-KAZATO-TAJIRI-YAGYU
FAMILY REUNION

Our group of 70 people stayed in condos on the beach near Monterey, California. Condos may seem expensive but are actually quite affordable. We rented eight units (3-4 bedrooms per unit) and the total cost for three nights was #110 per person which also included two group dinners. Condos are great for reunions because they have living rooms and other areas where families can get together and visit and share meals. Our reunion was held mid-week to save money on condo rates.

It's best to get announcements out early to allow people to make vacation plans. We started 18 months beforehand. We sent out 5 newsletters over a period of 18 months to stimulate enthusiasm. The newsletters featured computerized clip-art such as this take-off on a traditional Japanese print. Also included were lists of things to do and places to go in the area.

The welcoming banquet was a traditional meal at a Japanese restaurant. Our BBQ at a state beach featured teriyaki chicken and fresh salmon (in foil in photo) caught during an ocean fishing expedition by some of our group. A huge platter of sushi was part of the feast, purchased from a local restaurant.

A special early morning hot air balloon ride was arranged.

- 212 -

The HENSON
Family Round-Up

Held at the Llano, Texas, Community Center and Rodeo Barn

At each reunion we have a calendar of all birth-days and anniversaries; genealogy books; lots of photo albums; videos & cassettes from past re-unions; a "growing" cookbook; and an heirloom quilt as wall decoration.

Some Favorite Activities: Story-telling from past reunions and family experiences; gathering native wildflowers to decorate tables; playing music and singing; lots of games and sports; field trips; birthday parties for the kids.

Each year we have an auction with the help of a local cattle auctioneer. The families find things in attics & garages and make hand-crafted items to be auctioned off.

Another favorite is the "country store" where we sell lots of fun items. The kids love it and get to ring up prices on an old-fashioned cash register.

Remember: Pick a site that's good for children's play. And to quote grandfather Welborn Lee Henson, "Ask ques-tions if you don't know the answers. No question is dumb if you don't know the answer."

The stories of 4 generations of Hensons were hand embroidered by Fern Bland into this "4-generation quilt."

The HERNANDEZ Family Reunion

Titino, a Spanish clown

Many years ago my father, Antonio Hernandez, migrated to Southern California from Guadalajara in his native Mexico. Today he and his siblings' descendants meet yearly in a park near San Fernando for a day-long picnic.

Well over 100 family members come from all over (Tijuana in the South to San Jose in the North).

When my cousin Letitia, and I (Gabriel Hernandez) got together a few years ago, we found we really did not know our family. But the idea of a family reunion was a hard sell because people said we already get together a lot. But not the whole family. So we created a family support system to start the reunion.

A committee agreed that the food would be potluck and that individual families would share the other costs — soft drinks, T-shirts, children's entertainment, and so on. Some ideas were ruled out, like hiring a mariachi band, because we decided we wanted to be our own entertainment.

What matters to us is that the reunion helps reinforce our commitment to family in an American culture of increasingly broken homes and fragmentation.

We had a pie-eating contest, volleyball, soccer, sack race, pass-the-hat contest, water balloon toss, and a lot more games.

- 214 -

JUNKINS FAMILY ASSOCIATION
of Aston, Pennsylvania

We held our reunion in NW Ohio in a public county park surrounded by cornfields. Lapel name tags were given to everyone. Two self-styled gene-alogists had family-tree printouts to inspect and add to.

A county historical museum was located next to the park and proved very interesting to all. We also toured local family farms and a cemetery with many grave markers of revered ancestors.

We came across this road sign (left) on one of our trips. "Roots" activities provided a common bond for folks — some strangers to each other.

Family archaeological digs are being worked on around New England. With the help of professionals, these projects bring family members in contact with their roots, and give people great projects to work on season after season. Gravestones in old family plots have been found, unearthed, and reset.

Our meals were prepared by the ladies of a local church. Such groups are especially great for this sort of thing. They are inexpensive, sincere, and completely reliable.

The Kennelly '99

I organize 2 reunions. One is a small reunion of first cousins and their families every year. The other is a larger group on my mother's side every 5 years. We want our children to experience the joy and comfort which comes from strong family ties.

We have rented luxury condos, rented lakeside houses in upstate New York, rented a run-down kid's summer camp, and for the last 2 years have been renting a mansion in Rhode Island for a week.

We plan activities where all family members partici- pate. This helps avoid the cliques that can form with the younger children.

On one night we have an elaborate meal, but the other nights we use the low maintenance meal plan: pizza, subs, spaghetti. The spaghetti is a lot of fun. Each family brings a jar of store-bought sauce that goes into a big pot.

We sometimes rent the Walsh Mansion in Newport, Rhode Island.

One night is devoted to tie-dying t-shirts.

Tie-dyed t-shirts.

Postcards. I make postcards for the kids to mail to their friends back home. I also use the postcard to clean my mailing list and to motivate people to attend next year. Postcards can be done in a few hours by running down to Kinko's or Sir Speedy.

Name Tags. We use different color paper to color code the name tags. I prefer the clip-on tags because pins make me nervous with the kids running around.

- 216 -

Record Keeping. I use File Maker Pro and build my own tracking method, but the software includes some basic templates for family records.

Talent Show. We do a talent show every year and video tape it. We now have about six years on tape. The year at the summer camp, we actually had a Little Rascals-type auditorium with a stage. We roast an adult at each show.

Event Photography. This is the new procedure using a digital camera. The photos are printed on-location using a very high quality printer. Make sure the photographer has a good selection of borders and backdrops for the photo shoot.

Newsletters. I write several newsletters the months before the reunion to help build excitement and grow anticipation for the reunion. I include funny stories of the older generation. It helps to keep it humorous.

E-mail. Our family is approaching 20% with e-mail. But that 20% keeps tabs on almost 80% of the families. It saves on postage.

Logos. We design our own. See top of previous page and postcard below.

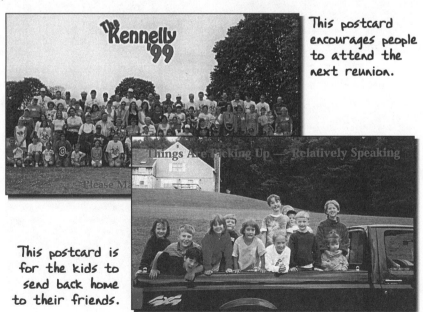

This postcard encourages people to attend the next reunion.

This postcard is for the kids to send back home to their friends.

Reunion Roundup, Paris, Texas

We have a six-trunk family tree consisting of the Goodman, McFatridge, Keener, Priddy, Rook and Stockton families. Our reunion is the last weekend of June each year. Last year 165 attended. We meet at the Main Exhibition Hall of the Red River Valley Fair Grounds in Paris, Texas. You might look into renting fair ground facilities. We find them fairly inexpensive.

We begin each reunion with our "Circle of Prayer."

A rented piano adds a special touch for Saturday evening's Family Night and Sunday's morning services. After the banquet we start Family Night with a "leaf hanging" ceremony. Everyone, young and old, individually places their leaf upon a felt tree, then introduces themselves to the gathering. We then have a talent show with singing, skits and poetry readings.

On Sunday we have a cemetery tour by convoy. Beforehand, cleanup crews tidy up the gravesites. Some of us go on a genealogy library trip to a nearby town.

One of our members has quilted over 100 coverlets for her relatives. Some of these are used as hangings and wall coverings at the reunion and make a perfect photo backdrop.

LEMASTER-PATTERSON
Family Reunions of Snyder, Oklahoma

We all enjoy going "back home" — a place which is associated with childhood memories, where our forebears trod and were laid to rest, where our bonds with loved ones are strengthened and renewed.

Here are some ideas and things we do at our reunions:

The **Reunion Tablecloth** (pictured above) — the family tree is embroidered in the center — individuals coming for the first time sign-in on the tablecloth — after the reunion, their names are permanently embroidered onto the tree.

The **White Elephant Auction** — we have an auctioneer in the family and every reunion we raise over #200 on our "elephants."

The **Family Cookbook** has become a treasure. We chose a cookbook publishing company in Kansas to print it. They added scads of free pages and a beautiful color cover. We included pictures of our grandparents, plus some of their old recipes.

Surprise birthday parties are fun. We also have a skit prepared by a "ham" in the group.

A bulletin board is useful. Full of information, photos, cartoons, etc.

Our reunion is covered by the local newspaper and a copy of that article is reprinted in the next family newsletter.

Mylius Family Reunion

In Minnesota in 1994 our family celebrated the first U.S. reunion of the Norwegian Mylius family. Over 200 people attended. Most had never met before, and most knew very little about Norwegian life and customs. We were honored that 12 cousins came all the way from Norway to introduce themselves and to teach us about our history. They presented everyone with a lapel pin (pictured above) featuring the family crest and the Norwegian and American flags.

The reunion was held in a local park where we rented a building with kitchen facilities and a pavilion, in case of rain. We hired a local woman to inexpensively cater the

Centerpiece.

luncheon. The hall was simply but brightly decorated in red, white, and blue streamers, Norwegian and American flags, white tablecloths and red geraniums (later given away as doorprizes).

Many people participated in country western line dancing lessons and listened to traditional Norwegian folk music on the hardanger fiddle. A time was set aside so that family members could take the microphone to tell stories about the histories and emigration routes of each branch of the family.

These young Norwegian cousins are wearing traditional costumes called "bunads," worn only to important events.

Before lunch we had country line dancing lessons which all ages enjoyed. Meanwhile, the food was being set up inside the building which had kitchen facilities and provided protection in case of rain.

After lunch we listened to Norwegian folk music played on the hardanger fiddle. The musician is wearing a bunad from the Hardanger area of Norway.

Prints of an ink drawing of the Mylius family homestead (ca. 1825) were brought from Norway and were available for purchase.

Nash Reunions of Salem, Missouri

We celebrated our 50th reunion on June 1, 1997. It was started in 1947 by my grandparents. At this reunion, my grandfather got drunk on his own home brew, climbed on a table, and announced to all, "This is great! Let's do it every year!" He passed away the next year and never got to attend another one.

For the 50th, we made a family tree quilt, and a family cookbook with our grandparent's picture on the front and some of grandmother's recipes in her own handwriting. I (Joanne Beers Helton) also wrote a family book titled "Patchwork of Memories — the Nash Family Story."

It took us a little over 2 years to complete our family tree quilt. The center square has 3 sets of our ancestors, their names, marriages, and photos. The rest of the quilt consists of 120 quilt blocks. 116 of them were handed out

to married couples to record their family history on. Eventually we will donate the quilt to the historical society in my grandparents hometown of Salem, Missouri.

Our display of old photos, done so artfully by a cousin and his wife.

Mummy Wrap Race using toilet paper.

Toothpick Lifesaver Pass Race.

- 223 -

The Olson Family Reunions

We've had 2 reunions with 5 years between them and attended by about 125 people. The setting was a family member's home about 25 miles from Boston — a large property which included a barn with kitchen facilities.

We asked everyone to dress "Farm Casual" or to choose an ancestor to dress like. Those who complied with the second request put on a fashion show. Here are two sisters modeling old-time swim suits, much like their mother and aunt in the right-hand photo.

Many Swedish touches were included: a Swedish flag, a stand-up cutout (Sven and Olga) provided a photo opportunity along with a tomten (Swedish elf) for the smaller folks, plenty of Swedish coffee bread, two relatives dressed in native costume, and a Swedish blessing was sung by several before the noon cook-out.

Our first-ever family auction resulted in proceeds that would off-set the cost of publishing a book of family memories. Family members were strongly urged to search their attics for instant heirlooms or to create some handmade treasures to donate to the auction. The highest priced item was a quilt which several family members worked on throughout the year. One very popular item was a barrel stave, painted with the likeness of the Olson homestead and a Swedish welcome.

Sven + Olga cut-out.

Swedish elf cut-out.

A word of caution, however: no matter how wonderful the activity, limit the amount of time devoted to it. Even though it was fun for most, the auction lasted

The auction in action.

a long time and many wished some of that time could have been spent interacting with long-lost relatives.

Experience has taught us that many folks are willing to help out with most anything when asked specifically, whereas calls for volunteers often go unheeded. No matter how many newsletters, chock full of information, are sent out, endless phone calls must still be made.

A few months after the reunion, a follow-up newsletter was sent out to remind everyone of the wonderful event, thank the many helping hands, and hopefully to interest more to attend next time.

A painted barrel stave and a hand-made quilt brought high prices at the auction.

An impromptu fingernail painting clinic resulted in a wide array of designs in Swedish blue and yellow.

Smucker
Schmucker Smoker

The first North American reunion of the Schmucker-Smoker-Smucker Family (run by the SSS Family Association) was held in 1976 in Smoketown, Pennsylvania. So far we have had 5 reunions at 5 year intervals with attendance from 300 to 800.

We have sponsored two European Swiss heritage tours (our progenitor, Christian Schmucker, came from Switzerland in 1752), and printed a cookbook that sold out. We publish a newsletter 3-5 times between the 5 year reunions. Our reunions have included keynote speakers, hymn singing, craft shows, games for the children, photography sessions, tours of the nearby countryside, and seminars on such diverse topics as genealogy, religious history, and fraktur design. The J.M. Smucker Company or Orrville, Ohio, often sends a truckload of their jams and jellies to the reunion site, donating much of the sales profits to the reunion fund.

Special mementos of the events have been a fraktur design by Emily Smucker-Beidler (elements of which appear on this page) depicting some of our family's history, and a custom-made redware plate.

from Switzerland to America
1752

from Pennsylvania to Ohio
1828

If it's a Smucker's reunion, it has to be good!

These are all John Schmuckers, Smokers or Smuckers.

At our last reunion, a special program was organized for children K-5. The activities were based on what our ancestors experienced when they arrived: how they lived, worked, played and worshipped together. Craftsmen from Lancaster County, Pennsylvania, (the reunion location) gave demonstrations and the children made functional items that Schmucker children would have helped their parents make in the 1700s.

A copy of Christian Schmucker's 1782 will and a copy of the September 1752 Pennsylvania Gazette (the week Christian arrived in Philadelphia) were displayed.

Our next reunion will be at College Mennonite Church on the campus of Goshen College, Goshen, Indiana.

One of our family trees.

The STREBE Family Reunion

Our family had little information concerning our German roots. Strebe was an uncommon name. With the opening of the East and West German border our curiosity intensified. In 1990 a family member traveling in Europe made contact with an individual sharing our ancestor's name — Edward Strebe. He also had a great interest in Strebe genealogy. Much correspondence led him and his wife to be invited to our Strebe Family Reunion. It would be their first trip to the United States. This news was quickly circulated and helped make this reunion something special indeed.

Activities and Displays: Our first 3 reunions were kept simple, due to inexperience and cost. We sat in a large

outdoor circle, shared information and played music. Some problems: rainy weather, hearing each other, and disorganized children's activities.

We rented indoor space with video equipment, display tables and chairs, a podium with audio equipment, easels with paper tablets. We displayed genealogical information, photo albums of past reunions, a U.S. map with home location, quilts, photos of our ancestor, and a hand-painted family tree.

We also had information on the pitifully neglected East German church where our ancestor had been confirmed. To raise money to help restore the church, we held an auction and a raffle at the reunion. Our European guests agreed to get the funds to the church. This project gave us all a sense of pride and history.

Sites: State parks with full accommodations and outdoor activities have been chosen for all our reunions. The children loved the organized games, swims, frisbee throws, horse-back riding, hiking, boating — the list goes on.

Group picture of WHAT NOT TO DO. A professional photographer would be a wise investment. Set a definite time for group pictures. We have not done this and consequently our pictures have been very poor. They even looked chaotic with quilts hanging about in disarray and chairs scattered around in front.

Urness Family Gathering

We restarted the Urness reunions in 1981 after not having any since the 1950s. We meet in a small air-conditioned hall with kitchen facilities in Browntown, Wis. Here (right) we are listening to the only surviving grandchild (born in 1902) of our Norwegian immigrant couple. She's at the headstone of her grandparents talking to us about the importance of religion to our ancestors.

Occasionally we meet at Wrigley Field to see our cousin, Robby Thompson, play professional baseball.

- 229 -

The Stevens Family Centennial Reunion
1891-1990

In 1891, five brothers & sisters — the children of Hanson and Lavina Stevens, pioneers who came to Oregon by covered wagon 40 years earlier — met with their families at the home of the eldest brother for a family reunion. They enjoyed themselves so much that it was agreed to meet annually. A tradition was begun that has faithfully endured for over 100 years.

The Centennial Reunion Committee first met in 1987 (four years early). Decisions were made regarding the reunion: its site, publicity, announcements, activities, etc.

Other meetings were held — perhaps one or two a year. The reunion was to take place over four days in the latter part of July (traditionally, the reunion occurred only on the third Sunday of July). The last surviving farm in the family, over 125 years old, was chosen as the venue; a family "logo" (above) was designed for t-shirts and coffee mugs; "upscale" announcements were printed; a Saturday barbecue followed by a lawn dance with a live band was organized.

There was a host of things to consider: toilet facilities for an expected 200-300 people, night lighting, electrical and water hookups for RVs. The list was endless, and there was continuous brainstorming.

The reunion went splendidly. The weather cooperated. Family members came from across the country: some stayed in motels, others camped in RVs, tents and under the stars. Every night we had a campfire. On Saturday a hog was barbecued underground. We danced later, with a family member as band-leader. The traditional meeting on Sunday was attended by 350 people, 10 times the number of the first reunion 100 years ago.

Perhaps most important, we truly did give a great deal of thought to every feature of the reunion. The goal was to anticipate <u>everything</u>. We did not hope for the best: we <u>planned</u> for the best, but had contingency plans for the worst. Again, this was possible because we began early.

Wofford, Lottie, Brinker
Family Reunions

When 5 generations of Woffords, Lotties, and Brinkers come together for a reunion, it's more like a mini-convention. Our reunions have been held in various places since the mid-1980s, including Arkansas, Missouri, Tennessee, South Carolina, and Indiana.

One of the most memorable was at Wofford College, Spartanburg, South Carolina, where the family traces its

origins back to the early 1800s. Our reunion and a white Wofford family reunion were combined.

Reunion activities include a family picnic with games and prizes for the children, a family scholarship banquet with door prizes, and a memorial worship service. Family members come from all over and are encouraged to bring items which represent something about their city or state; for example, Gates BBQ sauce from Kansas City or a Chicago Bulls cap. These items are used as door prizes or raffled away to generate money for the family scholarship fund which was established to help graduating seniors attend college.

We have pooled our resources to publish a hard-cover book of the family's history called "The Homecoming."

Black and white Woffords meet for the first time.

Norman Family

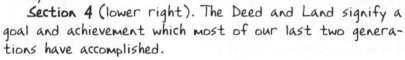

We created our own family crest. Each element has some significance to the family, past or present.

Section 1 (upper left). These elements indicate various Norman family interests, past and present.

Section 2 (upper right). Bible and Cross signify our spiritual belief and faith in the Christian Church.

Section 3 (lower left). Our family motto.

Section 4 (lower right). The Deed and Land signify a goal and achievement which most of our last two generations have accomplished.

Acknowledgements

Thanks to these individuals for their contributions to this section:

Jill Keener & Peggy Ann Beck of the Beck Family; Joyce Rowland of the Briss Family; Sheila Linton of the Bullock Family; Carol Sheedy of the Chamberlin-Shabowski Family; Mary Burkholder of the Coberly Family; Christine Connolly & Thelma Bliss of the Connolly Family; Sharon Graham of the Graham Family; Bruce Hasegawa; Fern Bland & Marjorie Sayles of the Henson Family; Gabriel Hernandez of the Hernandez Family; Alan Junkin & Richard Pugh of the Junkins Family; William Griffin of the Kennelly Family; Hester Stockton; Vicki Albu of the Mylius Family; Joann Helton of the Nash Family; Janet McCabe of the Olson Family; John R. Smucker of the Smucker Family; June Van Dusen Smith of the Stebe Family; Matt Figi of the Urness family; Phyllis Rhodes of the Lemaster-Patterson Family; Tom & Virginia Ewing of the Stevens Family; Dorothy Wofford Witherspoon of the Wofford Family; Curtis Brasfield of the Norman Family.

Resources

A Listing of References & Resources by Chapter

(Books, videos and Websites are in *italics*.)

◆ **CHAPTER 1 — Early Decisions**

Phone Books—

To purchase any current phone book in the U.S., call 800/848-8000, 8 a.m. to 5 p.m. (PST). Visa or Mastercharge can be used, or if your local phone company is Pacific Bell or Nevada Bell, the charges can be added to your phone bill. The prices vary per size of phone book. The following phone books can also be purchased through this source:

• *The Directory of 800 Numbers*, Consumer Edition or Business Edition.

• *The National Directory of Addresses and Telephone Numbers*. Over 200,000 listings, published and updated annually. This book may be available at your local library in the Reference Section. Among its many listings are the addresses and phone numbers of: Chambers of Commerce and convention bureaus of all major cities; Conference centers and major hotels of all major cities; Important state offices including Information Offices; County seats of every county in the U.S.

Reunion Sites—

• See resources for Chapter 13 in this section.

◆ **CHAPTER 3 — Money & Finances**

Roll Tickets—

• Paradise Products, PO Box 568, El Cerrito, CA 94530, 510/524-8300.

Fund-raising Items—

Personalized calendars—

• Daily Memories, RD #1, Box 69R, Bear Lake, PA 16412, 814/489-3123. This company creates a personalized calendar with up to 4 special events per day (birthdays, anniversaries, etc) and a new photo for each month.

Cookbooks—

The following printing companies specialize in creating cookbooks for fund-raisers and have how-to instructions available:

• Walter's Publishing, 215 5th Ave SE, Waseca, MN 56093, 800/447-3274, 507/835-3691. Send for free fund-raising kit. *www.custom-cookbooks.com*

• Cookbook Publishers, PO Box 15920, Lenexa, KS 66285, 800/227-7282. Send for their free cookbook kit and price list. *www.cookbookpublishers.com*

• Brennan Printing, 100 Main St, Deep River, IA 52222, 800/448-3740, 515/595-2000. Send for free sample and kit.

Lottery tickets—

• Scratch-It Promotions, 1763 Barnum Ave, Bridgeport, CT 06610, 800/966-9467, 203/367-5377. This company has scratcher tickets (generic or custom-made) and scratcher disks that you can apply to your own tickets. Invent your own scratcher fund-raiser or ask for ideas. Rush service is available.

Merchandise—

• Quality marble paperweights make great take-home gifts. You can incorporate your family crest into the design. Order from Paperweights, Ltd, 3661 Horseblock Rd, Unit O, Medford, NY 11763, 516/345-0752.

• Preserve a precious photo in needlepoint or cross-stitch. Custom chart made from original photo. Designs by Karen, PO Box 65490, Vancouver, WA 98665-0017, 360/694-6881.

• Button making machines: Badge-A-Minit, PO Box 800, LaSalle, IL 61301, 800/223-4103. *www.badgeaminit.com/*

• Reunion t-shirts using photos: 800/347-4482. *www.bowplus.com/t-shirts/*

◆ **CHAPTER 4 — Keeping Records**

• Quill Corp, 100 S. Schelter Rd, Lincolnshire, IL 60197-4700. Imprinted and plain envelopes; file card trays, metal or plastic, 3 sizes; file cards, 3 sizes, lined or plain and in 6 colors plus white; address labels.

• Walter Drake and Sons, Colorado Springs, CO 80940 (that's all the address you need). Return address labels, and imprinted envelopes in quantities of 100.

◆ **CHAPTER 5 — Family Communications: Newsletters, Flyers, Surveys**

Sources of example newsletters—

• *Genealogical Helper Magazine*, Everton Publishers, PO Box 368, Logan, UT 84323, 800/443-6325. Six issues per year for $24, over 285 pages per issue—a real bargain. It will put you in direct contact with things genealogical. Many ads on helpful books, videos, T-shirt companies, family history printers, etc. *www.everton.com*

• *The Directory of Family Associations*. Genealogical Publishing, 1001 N. Calvert St, Baltimore, MD 21202. 800/296-6687.

Facts, Figures and Trivia—

Chronologies, yearly histories, old newspapers, and encyclopedia yearbooks (annual volumes) are good for finding interesting facts and figures for mailers, newsletters, and reunion programs. Your local library reference section is the place to start looking. Some good sources are:

• *Chase's Calendar of Annual Events* by W. and H. Chase, Contemporary Books, Chicago. Source of ideas, facts, and sayings. Expensive, found in most libraries.

• *The Almanac of Dates*, Linda Millgate. Pub. by Harcourt, Brace, and Javanovich.

• *2500 Anecdotes for All Occasions*, Edmund Fuller, Dolphin Books.

• *The People's Chronology*, edited by James Trager. Holt, Rinehart and Winston, arranged by years, 30,000 entries, 1200+ pages. Especially good.

• *The Timetables of History*, Bernard Grun, published by Simon and Schuster, 700 page paperback. Especially good.

Graphics Supplies and Books—

• *Creating Family Newsletters* by Elaine Floyd. A unique book by the foremost authority on creating newsletters; covers the whole gamut from hand-crafted to computer-generated newsletters. Highly recommended. Order from 800/289-0963. Also check Elaine's Website at *www.newsletterinfo.com*.

• *Editing Your Newsletter* by M. Beach. Newsletters and mailers are often what sells a reunion. This is one of the best books on the subject. Order from 800/289-0963.

• The Printers Shopper, PO Box 1056, Chula Vista, CA 91912, 800/854-2911. Free catalog. Clip art, rub-on type, borders, graphics books, clip art book of humorous certificates, art and graphics supplies, mechanical and electric paper folders, saddle stitch staplers, hand waxers.

• Dover Publications, 31 East 2nd St, Mineola, NY 11501, 516/294-7000. Clip art books. Ask for a catalog of their Clip Art Series.

• Graphic Products Corp, 1480 S. Wolf Rd, Wheeling, IL 60090. 847/537-9300. This company makes Formatt, one of the largest lines of cut-out graphic art aids. The product is available only from graphic art stores. However, the catalog, which costs at least $3 in the stores, is available free from them just for asking.

• Personalized crossword puzzles to dress up your next newsletter or flyer. $20 each. See page 250. Reunion Research, 3145 Geary Blvd #14, San Francisco, CA 94118.

Stationery Supplies—

• Quill Corp, 100 S. Schelter Rd, Lincolnshire, IL 60197-4700. Imprinted and plain envelopes; file card trays, metal or plastic, 3 sizes; file cards, 3 sizes, lined or plain and in 6 colors plus white; address labels.

• Walter Drake and Sons, Colorado Springs, CO 80940 (that's all the address you need). Return address labels, and imprinted envelopes in quantities of 100.

• The U.S. Postal Service can provide you with personalized stamped envelopes in quantities as few as 50, and in either regular or business size. Ask your local Post Office to send you a Personalized Envelope Order Form which explains the options and prices.

• Rootstamps, 6479 White Pine Dr, Lakeside, AZ 85929. Special rubber stamps for genealogists and family reunions. These will really dress up your next mailers. $2 for catalog, refunded with first order. *www.whitemtns.com/~roots/*

• Special reunion stickers for envelopes and mailers. These are designed to get more people to attend your next reunion. See page 248 for details.

Historical printouts—

• Window In Time, 4321 Laurelwood Way, Sacramento, CA 95864. Send a date and get a computer printout of the history and other trivia of that time; a real value at $8 per printout (1998). However, prices may change. For the current price, send a stamped self-addressed envelope to the above address. See page 74.

◆ **CHAPTER 6 — Mailers/Postage** (see Stationery Supplies, above)

◆ **CHAPTER 7 — Getting Ready: Services, Supplies & Special Touches**

T-shirts—
• See under "Games and Activities" in next Chapter.

Button Name Tags—
• Button making machines: Badge-A-Minit, PO Box 800, LaSalle, IL 61301, 800/223-4103. *www.badgeaminit.com/*

Decorations and Table Settings—
• Paradise Products, PO Box 568, El Cerrito, CA 94530, 510/524-8300. Theme, ethnic and holiday table settings and party supplies. Miniature flags of many countries, table fringes, crepe paper decorations, paper tabletop rolls in many colors. National anthems of many countries on cassette tape. Roll-type numbered tickets. Also spell out your own family name with Make-A-Banner. Lots more. Free catalog.

• B. Palmer Sales Co, PO Box 850247, Mesquite, TX 75185, 800/888-3087, 214/288-1026. Good prices on piñatas, piñata goodies, and crepe streamers.

• Party goods and decorations: *www.beistle.com/*

• Custom piñatas: *www.pinatadesign.com/*

• Inexpensive piñatas: 800/228-2269. *www.oriental.com*

Plaques and Awards—
• See "Recognition Awards," below.

◆ **CHAPTER 8 — Games & Activities**

Photo Albums and Scrapbooks—
• All reunion groups should keep photo albums and scrapbooks. For a truly BIG scrapbook (25" x 20") of archival quality (that means it will still be around in 200 years), contact Scrapbook Partners, 419 N. Larchmont Blvd. #21, Los Angeles, CA 90004. 888/904-1016. This company also has hard-to-find scrapbook desks. *http://mall.scrapbooking.com/*

• Exposures, PO Box 3615, Oshkosh, WI 54903, 800/222-4947. This company has a good selection, including an Oversize Scrapbook. Free catalog.

• Enduring Memories, 7 Dogwood Ln, Willow Street, PA 17584, 717/464-0963. Albums, scrapbooks and supplies. Acid-free, archival quality. Photo labeling pencils. Free catalog.

Recognition Awards—
• Emblem and Badge Co, Providence, Rhode Island, 401/331-5444. Inexpensive recognition awards and plaques. *www.recognition.com*

Humorous Awards—
• Funny Side Up, PO Box 2800, North Wales, PA 19454, 215/361-5142. A good source of inexpensive joke awards. However, in recent years their catalog has had some items of poor taste. Be forewarned. Free catalog.

Toasts—
• *Toasts: Over 1500 of the best toasts, sentiments, blessings and graces* by P. Dickson. Crown Publishers.

• Virtual toasts: *www.thevirtualbar.com/~willie/Toasts/*

Genealogy for Kids—

• *Genealogy*, a Merit Badge Series pamphlet from the Boy Scouts. A good resource that anyone can order. 800/323-0732.

• *Roots for Kids* by Susan Beller, Genealogical Publishing Co, 800/296-6687.

Games and Activities—

• Animal Town, PO Box 485, Healdsburg, CA 95448, 800/445-8642, ask for their free catalog. Lots of great board games for kids and families, face painting kit, tapes, puzzles, many great books including: *Co-operative Sports & Games Book* (Vols. 1 & 2), *Festivals, Family and Food*, and much more.

• Chinaberry Book Service, 2780 via Orange Way #B, Spring Valley, CA 91978, 800/776-2242. Books and music for children and families. Free catalog.

• *Questions and Ancestors*. A game to celebrate your family and to share discoveries with each other. Order from Conestoga Book Service, Box 7, West Willow, PA, 17583, 717/464-0963.

• *Lifestories*. A fun board game that gets participants talking about their past. Both young and old have such experiences which makes this a great game for mixing the ages. See page 247 for a description and page 249 to order.

• Dale Le Fevre, PO Box 1641, Mendocino, CA 95460, 707/937-3337. Dale is the guru of noncompetitive and co-operative games. His books are *New Games for the Whole Family* and *Parachute Games*. His videos are *The New Games Video*, *New Games from Around the World*, *Sunny Day Games*, *Rainy Day Games*, *New Soccer*, and *Cooperative Group Games*. He's on the Web at *www.mcn.org/a/newgames/*

• National Association for the Preservation and Perpetuation of Storytelling (NAPPS), 116 W. Main St, Jonesborough, TN 37659, 800/525-4514. This association can put you in touch with a professional storyteller near you. *www.storeynet.org*

• Youth Specialties, PO Box 668, Holmes, PA 19043, 800/776-8008. This company has truly great books on games, skits and entertainment ideas for kids of all ages. Their *Ideas Combo* series runs from #1–53 with over 3500 ideas listed, but get the *Ideas Combo Index* first to determine which Combo you want. Also check out *The Greatest Skits on Earth*, Volumes 1 and 2. Free catalog has lots more.

• *Decorative T-Shirts & Sweats Made Easy* by Susan Figliulo. Signet.

• *The Ultimate T-Shirt Book: Creating Your Own Unique Designs* by Deborah Morgenthal. Lark Books.

• EDC Publications, 10302 E. 55th Place, Tulsa, OK 74146, 800/475-4522. This company has *Decorating T-Shirts* (comes with paints). Highly recommended. Catalog is $2, refunded with first purchase.

• *Painting Faces* by S. Haldine. Penguin USA, 800/526-0275.

• *Balloon Hats and Accessories* by A. Hsu-Flanders. NTC/Contemporary Publishing, 4255 W. Touhy Ave, Lincolnwood, IL 60646, 800/323-4900. How to make hats and other items from pencil balloons. Comes with balloons and small pump.

• Klutz Press, 455 Portage Ave, Palo Alto, CA 94306, 800/558-8944. This company has lots of great books that explain how to do fun things and the necessary equipment or props comes with the book. Here are two good ones: *The Unbelievable Bubble Book* by J. Cassidy shows how to make huge bubbles (necessary equipment included); *Face Painting* comes with paints. Free catalog.

• Personalized crossword puzzles to dress up your next newsletter or flyer. $20 each. See page 250. Reunion Research, 3145 Geary Blvd #14, San Francisco, CA 94118.

◆ CHAPTER 9 — Feeding the Family

• *Cooking for a Big Family & Large Groups* by M. Meredith. Countrywoman's Press.

• *The Black Family Reunion Cookbook*. Published by Wimmer Companies, 800/727-1034. Has a great design that can be an example for other cookbooks. See p. 132.

• *Family Reunion Potluck* by Carol McGarvey. Sta-Kris, PO Box 1131, Marshalltown, IA 50158. 515/753-4139. Has many good potluck recipes. See p. 132.

• BBQ information: *www.cyber-kitchen.com/pgbbq.htm*

• More BBQ information: *www.ces.uga.edu/pubcd/b1039-w.html*

◆ CHAPTER 10 — Making History: Documenting Family Memories

Photo Albums and Scrapbooks—
• See resources for Chapter 8 in this section.

Photography—
• Seattle FilmWorks, 1260 16th Ave. W, Seattle, WA 98119, 800/345-6967. Quality film processing. Receive slides, prints, or photos on disk (or any combination) or download your photos from the Internet. *www.filmworks.com*

Videography—
• *Gift of Heritage*. An award-winning instructional video from Mary Lou Productions, PO Box 17233, Minneapolis, MN 55417, 800/224-8511. *www.giftofheritage.com* Explains simple video techniques that will allow you to effectively tell your family story on video.

• *Basic Camcorder Guide* by S. Bryant. Everything you need to know to get started and have fun. Amhurst Media, 155 Rano St #300, Buffalo, NY 14207, 800/622-3278.

• *Video Family History* by D. and P. Sturm. Published by Ancestry, PO Box 476, Salt Lake City, Utah, 84110, 800/531-1790.

• *Family Treasures: Videotaping Your Family History* by S. Bannister. Explains about equipment, technique and interviewing. Genealogical Publishing, 800/296-6687.

Interviewing/Oral History—
• *Oral History for the Local Historical Society*, and *Transcribing and Editing Oral History*, both by W. Baum. These books explain how to interview and how to transcribe, index, store, and present oral history tapes. Sage Publications, 2455 Teller Rd, Thousand Oaks, CA 91320, 805/499-9774.

• *Instant Oral Biographies: How to tape record, video or film your life stories* by W. Zimmerman. Guarionex Press, 201 W. 77th St, New York, NY 10024, 212/724-5259.

• *Keeping Family Stories Alive* by Vera Rosenbluth. An excellent book on how to interview family members on audio tape or video tape. Order from Hartley and Marks Publishing, PO Box 147, Point Roberts, WA 98281, 604/739-1771.

Medical History—

• March of Dimes, National Office, 1275 Mamaroneck Ave, White Plains, NY 10605, 914/428-7100, or contact your local chapter, listed in the white pages of your phone book. Ask for their free pamphlet, *Genetic Counseling.*

• *Family Medical Census Kit* by A. Anderson. This kit gives you all the information and forms necessary to conduct a survey of genetic diseases and medical problems within your family. Genealogy Plus, PO Box 69, Langdon, Alberta, T0J 1X0, Canada.

Family History—

• Family History Publishers, 845 S. Main St, Bountiful, UT 84010, 801/295-7490. This company specializes in processing family histories into any desired form and then publishing them into the desired size, cover, and quantity. Send for their free brochure, *How to Prepare Your Family History and How to Get It Published.*

• *The Complete Guide to Self-Publishing* by Tom & Marilyn Ross. Writers Digest Books. 800/289-0963.

Genealogy—

• *The Complete Idiot's Guide to Genealogy* by C. Rose and K. Ingalls. Alpha Books.

• *Roots for Kids* by Susan Beller, Genealogical Publishing Co, 800/296-6687.

• *Family Memories* by S. McNeill and L. Stiles, Betterway Books. Inspires readers to create family albums. Hundreds of ideas on how to organize and decorate scrapbook pages. Full-color. Order from 800/289-0963.

• *Writing Family Histories and Memoirs* by K. Polking. Betterway Books. 800/289-0963.

• *Unpuzzling Your Past: A basic guide to genealogy* by A. Croom. Betterway Books. 800/289-0963.

• Genealogy forms such as Family Group Sheets and Ancestor Charts can be purchased from Ancestry (800/531-1790) or Everton Publishers (800/443-6325).

• *Genealogical Helper Magazine*, Everton Publishers, PO Box 368, Logan, UT 84323, 800/443-6325. Six issues per year for $24, over 285 pages per issue—a real bargain. It will put you in direct contact with things genealogical. Many ads on helpful books, videos, T-shirt companies, family history printers, etc.

• *The Family Tree.* A newspaper focusing on genealogy of the British Isles but includes other countries, too. *The Family Tree*, Odom Library, Moultrie Public Library, PO Box 2828, Moultrie, GA 31776-2828. Has an annual newsletter contest. Published bi-monthly for postage contributions.

• *Heritage Quest Magazine*, PO Box 329, Bountiful, UT 84011, 801/298-5446. A genealogy magazine & mail-order bookstore and lending library.

• *The Researcher's Guide to American Genealogy* by V. Greenwood. Genealogical Publishing Co, 1001 Calvert St, Baltimore, MD 21202, 800/296-6687.

• *Kinship: It's All Relative* by J. Arnold. Explains everything there is to know about kinship. From Genealogical Publishing, see above.

• Board for Certification of Genealogists, PO Box 5816, Falmouth, VA 22403. To locate a professional genealogist near you, write for their Roster of Certified Persons. There is a small charge.

• National Genealogical Society, 4527 17th St. N, Arlington, VA 22207-2399, 703/ 525-0050. This is a membership society that offers annual conventions, a mail-order lending library, a home-study course, and many books, forms and resources. To find someone near you who can speak to your group on the subject of genealogy or local history, get their *Speaker's Directory*.

• The National Archives. This federal agency has available regionally-created federal records located in regional archives in or near Boston (Waltham, MA), New York, Philadelphia, Atlanta (East Point, GA), Chicago, Kansas City, Fort Worth, Denver, Los Angeles (Laguna Niguel, CA), San Francisco (San Bruno, CA), Seattle and Anchorage. For phone numbers, ask directory assistance for The National Archives in the cities mentioned above, or write to: The National Archives, Washington, DC 20408.

• The Family History Library of the LDS Church, 35 N. West Temple St, Salt Lake City, UT 84150, houses the most extensive collection of genealogical information in the world. Documents from around the world have been microfilmed and are available for inspection. The library is open every day except Sunday and holidays. The library information number is 801/240-2331.

The LDS Church also has over 2000 Family History Centers located throughout the world. These Centers are small repositories that are linked to the main library in Salt Lake City, and are good places for beginners to learn about genealogy. Look in the white pages of your phone book under Church of Jesus Christ of Latter Day Saints, then under that title look for genealogy library or Family History Center. Or write to the main library in Salt Lake City (address above).

Coats of Arms—
• Originally worn into battle to distinguish friend from foe, coats of arms can add much to the pride and lore of any family. To research a crest or to have a new one created, contact: The Ship's Chandler, Wilmington, VT 05363, 800/375-9469. Lots of options from a simple hand-painted crest to a 3-dimensional wall shield to a blazer patch, rubber stamps or signet ring. Free catalog. See p. 147. *www.coatsofarms.com*

• *Design Your Own Coat of Arms* by Rosemary Chorzempa. Dover.

Time Capsules—
• Time capsules are a great way to introduce yourself (and this generation) to future generations. They can be buried or placed on a mantle. Items to include are stamps, coins, paper money, a letter to great-great-grandchildren, photos, etc. Order from Erie Landmark Co, 14110 Sullyfield Circle, Chantilly, VA 20151-1615, 800/874-7848.

• Jack Mallory serves as a consultant and source of time capsules—any use and any price. Contact him at 12258 Kirkdale Dr, Saratoga, CA 95070, 408/252-7447.

• *Make Your Own Time Capsule* by Steven Caney. Workman Publications.

Tombstone Rubbings—
• How to do tombstone rubbings: *www.firstct.com/fv/t_stn1.html*

◆ **CHAPTER 11 — Family Associations/Surname Associations**
• *Family Associations: Organization and Management*. This book tells you exactly why and how to go about forming a family association. See page 248 to order.

◆ **CHAPTER 12 — Finding People**

• *Find Anyone Fast* by R. Johnson and Debra Johnson Knox; *How to Locate Anyone Who Is or Has Been in the Military* by R. Johnson; *Checking Out Lawyers* by Don Ray. Great books by the leading authorities on finding people. Order from 800/937-2133.

• *Get the Facts on Anyone* by Dennis King. Prentice Hall/Macmillan, NY. One of the best books available on how to do background checking. 800/428-5331.

• Board for Certification of Genealogists, PO Box 5816, Falmouth, VA 22403. To locate a professional genealogist near you, write for their Roster of Certified Persons. There is a small charge.

• CD-ROMs: *PhoneDisc* and *Select Phone*, both from American Business Information, 5711 S. 86 Circle, Omaha, NE 68127. 800/284-8353 or 800/992-3766. Windows or Mac. These CDs are available in most libraries. As of 1998, the information on these two CD sets is identical but the software interface is different. In the future, they will probably be combined into one product.

• Cyberdix Investigative Services, 419 Oak St, Roseville, CA 95678, 800/788-4895. This company will check a name or a roster of names against its many databases very cheaply. *www.cyberdix.com*

• For National Archives information, see under Chapter 10 in this section.

◆ **CHAPTER 13 — Special Places for Family Reunions**

Reunion Sites—

• *Campus Lodging Guide*. Updated yearly. Listing of inexpensive lodging, campus accommodations, YMCA centers, home exchanges, much more. B&J Publications, PO Box 5486, Fullerton, CA 92838, 800/525-6633. *www.campus-lodging.com*

• *The Best Bargain Family Vacations in the U.S.* by L. Sutherland. St. Martins Press. 200+ destinations: state parks, resorts, beaches, historical and cultural sites, learning vacations. All kid-friendly.

• *Super Family Vacations: Resort and Adventure Guide* by M. Shirk and N. Klepper, HarperCollins, New York. Excellent, highly recommended.

• *Ranch Vacations* by Eugene Kilgore. Lists over 200 guest ranches in the U.S. and Canada, and includes information on children's programs, rates, and nearby attractions. John Muir Publications, PO Box 613, Santa Fe, NM 87504, 800/888-7504.

• Gene Kilgore's dude ranch Web site: *www.ranchweb.com*

• Dude Rancher's Association, PO Box 471, LaPorte, CO 80535, 970/223-8440. *www.duderanch.org*

• *Dude Ranches of the West* by J. Franklin. Homestead Publishing.

• *Floating Vacations* by M. White. A great book but out of print. Try your library.

• Travel books and maps: *www.randmcnallystore.com*

• Houseboat Association of America, 4940 N. Rhett Ave, Charleston, SC 29405, 803/744-6581. Send $3 for a listing of houseboat rental companies in North America.

Phone Books—

• See resources for Chapter 1 in this section.

◆ **CHAPTER 14 — Using the Internet** (also see other Web sites listed throughout this section)

Web addresses go out of date faster than phone numbers. It's best to learn to search for what you want. See Chapter 14 for how to search for a particular subject.

Family Web Pages—

• *Home Sweet Home Page* by R. Williams. Peachpit Press. A great book on how and why to create family Web pages. 800/283-9444.

• A beautiful family web page: *www.surnames.com/organizations/peacock/*

◆ **MISCELLANEOUS**

Reunion Conferences and Classes—

• Family Reunion Institute, School of Social Administration, Ritter Hall Annex, Temple University, Philadelphia, PA 19122, 215/204-6244. Sponsors an African-American Family Reunion Conference. This is by far the most serious family reunion conference in the U.S. to date. Everyone welcome. Founded by Dr. Ione Vargus, Professor Emeritus, Temple University (see photo page 106).

• Myra Quick has taught a family reunion planning class since 1990 through the Continuing Education Department of the University of Memphis. She can be reached at her office at the University of Memphis, 901/678-4030.

• Matt Figi is an experienced genealogist and teaches classes in northwest Indiana on the subjects of beginning genealogy, writing a family history, and reunion planning. He can be reached at 219/924-0947.

• Reunion planning consultant. William Griffin, PO Box 521, Marlboro, MA 01752, 508/485-0424. *bgriffin@ultranet.com* Bill has lots of experience with family and school reunions.

Genealogy Software—

• *Reunion* from Leister Productions, PO Box 289, Mechanicsburg, PA 17055, 717/697-1378. *www.LeisterPro.com*

• *Family Tree Maker* by Broderbund Software, PO Box 6125, Novato, CA 94948, 415/382-4770. *www.familytreemaker.com*

Positive Family Traits

Some families seem to be particularly strong, emotionally healthy, and enduring, with a minimum of internal bickering and dissention. Jane Howard, in her book *Families,* looked for the characteristic traits of such families and found the following qualities.

- A distinguished member, a founder, someone to admire and emulate (not necessarily still living).
- A family historian or genealogist. Someone who keeps track of the clan, facilitates communication among members, maintains scrapbooks and other forms of family history.

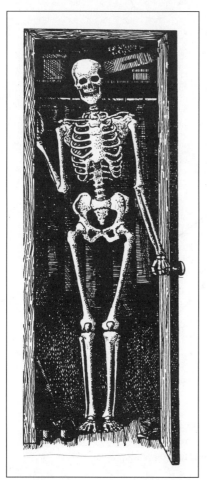

There's a skeleton in every closet!

- A basic sense of humor that permeates the entire family.
- Parents and children devoted to outside pursuits as well as each other.
- Hospitable homes with friends and relatives warmly received.
- Willingness to lend aid and support in times of need.
- At least one cherished eccentric and a general tolerance for the failings of others.
- Prized rituals, both traditional (such as holiday customs) and unique celebrations (invented by the family).
- Affectionate touching, hugs, and comforting.
- A "sense of place"—if not a home then a collection of belongings that symbolize home.
- Children are included in the talk and laughter.
- Elders are honored.

(*Thanks to the Crinklaw Family for the information on this page.)

Ever wonder about all that "removed" terminology when it comes to cousins? This chart should help. Photocopy it and post it near the memorabilia table at your next reunion.

Cousin Relationship Chart

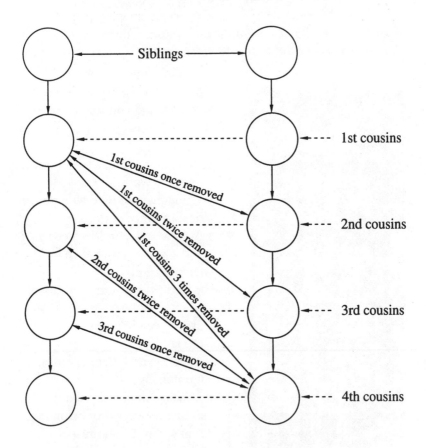

Children of siblings are 1st cousins
Children of 1st cousins are 2nd cousins
Children of 2nd cousins are 3rd cousins, etc.
The term "removed" is used to indicate a generation apart.

About the Author

Tom Ninkovich has been collecting reunion information since 1971, and in 1982 founded Reunion Research, a company that publishes guidebooks for reunion planners and furnishes information for the reunion market.

He publishes *Fun & Games for Family Gatherings, The Directory of Reunion Sites* (annual), and will soon reissue his book on school reunion planning. He has been advising and teaching about reunion planning since 1982 and serves as a media and demographic resource on the subject.

He lives in the Sierra Nevada Mountains of California. His hobbies and interests include typography, book design, and local history. He can be contacted through Reunion Research, 3145 Geary Blvd. #14, San Francisco, CA 94118.

246

Please be on our... ...unique mailing list.

Dear Reunion Planner:

Many businesses offer special discounts and services to reunion planners. Inclusion on this mailing list will help you become better informed which, in turn, will help you create better and more rewarding reunions for your family.

You will not be inundated with mail. You will probably receive anywhere from 5 to 20 pieces of mail per year from businesses that can save you money or can offer you something special for your next reunion. **You can remove yourself from the list at any time.**

Many happy reunions to you.

Tom

Tom Ninkovich

Yes, please include me on a list of family reunion planners.

Name _____

Address _____

City _____ State _____ Zip _____

Approximately how many people attend your reunions? _____

How often do you have reunions? _____

Return this form to:
Reunion Research, 3145 Geary Blvd. #14, San Francisco, CA 94118.

LifeStories Board Game

We never thought we'd be selling a game, but this one is just right for family reunions. *LifeStories* is a fun game that gets you talking about your experiences from the past. Both young and old have such experiences—this is a great game for mixing the ages.

Remember the kids you grew up with? Your favorite family dinner? A time when you were really lucky? A special vacation? Big and small events shape our lives and are fun to share with others. Recall funny moments, important times, and cherished thoughts. Pass on family history.

LifeStories is designed to build closer relationships among players. And best of all, everyone wins! For 2 to 8 players, ages 6 to 106. Children over 10 like to play as a group; younger children enjoy the game best when played with adults. $28.95. See order form on page 249.

Directory of Reunion Sites. This annual publication lists reunion sites and accommodations, nationwide. Find out which places cater specifically to family reunions. $3 if purchased alone. Free with any other purchase. No shipping charge. See order form on page 249.

The Book Store

Fun & Games for Family Gatherings by Adrienne Anderson. This book gives 235+ ideas for activities at family reunions. Skits, games, puzzles, songs, ways to mix the ages, rainy day activities; you-name-it, it's here. *Every family reunion planner should have this book.* $12.95.

Family Associations: Organization and Management by Christine Rose, tells you why and how to go about forming a family association. Includes sample by-laws. New 2nd edition. $12.95.

Find Anyone Fast by father/daughter private investigators Richard Johnson and Debra Johnson Knox. A wonderful book by the leading authorities on the subject of finding people. Completely revised, new version. Includes chapters on using the Internet and how to find women. $16.95.

We have **envelope stickers** that will definitely get more people to attend your next reunion. Attach to anything you mail out. **They come 10 per card.** Burgundy ink on glossy white paper. Peel-and-stick. Minimum order is 5 cards = $5; 10 cards = $8; 20 cards = $12; 50 cards = $20; 100 cards = $50. No additional shipping charge.

(actual size)

ORDER FORM

IMPORTANT: If this book is more than 3 years old (see front), write for an updated price before ordering.

Name _____

Address _____

City _____ State _____ Zip _____

ITEM	PRICE	AMOUNT
Family Reunion Handbook	$14.95	$_____
Fun & Games for Family Gatherings ..	12.95	_____
Family Associations: Organization		
and Management	12.95	_____
Find Anyone Fast	16.95	_____
Directory of Reunion Sites (no shipping charge)	_____	_____
LifeStories, board game (p. 247) ...	28.95	_____
Stickers for envelopes ..(no shipping charge)..	_____	_____
Shipping for one item	2.50	_____
Shipping for each additional item ..	1.50	_____
Sub total		_____
*For Priority Mail add $2 <u>more</u> per item		_____
California residents add current sales tax .		_____
Grand total		_____

Note: We will ship to multiple addresses at no additional charge. Please enclose an address list. If you are buying the book as a gift, we will enclose a gift card if you like. Please show how to make out the card.

*Books will be shipped Book Rate unless Priority is paid for.

Unconditional guarantee: If you are not satisfied with any item for any reason, please return it within 10 days for a full refund.

Make checks payable to: "Reunion Research"
Reunion Research, 3145 Geary Blvd. #14, San Francisco, CA 94118

◆ If you are returning this form for a purchase, check here ❒ to be put on our mailing list (read about our mailing list on page 246). You will *not* be put on the mailing list unless the above box is checked.

CUSTOMIZED CROSSWORD PUZZLES

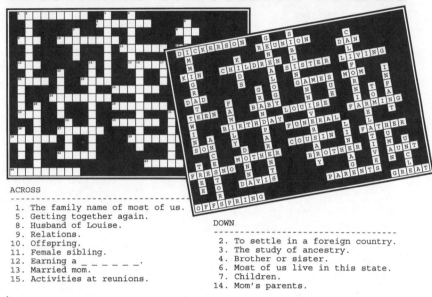

ACROSS
----
1. The family name of most of us.
5. Getting together again.
8. Husband of Louise.
9. Relations.
10. Offspring.
11. Female sibling.
12. Earning a _ _ _ _ _ _.
13. Married mom.
15. Activities at reunions.

DOWN
----
2. To settle in a foreign country.
3. The study of ancestry.
4. Brother or sister.
6. Most of us live in this state.
7. Children.
14. Mom's parents.

A crossword puzzle will really dress up your next newsletter or mailer. Or pass it around at your next reunion—maybe have a contest to see who finishes it first.

Here's how it works:

Send us a list of 50 words relating to your family (please print or type). OR send us a shorter list and we will fill it out to 50 words using common family-oriented words such as "mother," "cousin," "kin," "ancestor," etc.

The puzzle is randomly generated by computer, so some words may not be used (usually only 4–6 are left out). However, you can designate up to 5 words to be used for sure. These words will *not* be left out. Either circle or underline these words on your list. (Remember to print or type the list.)

Then make up a clue for each word. Clues are easier to create than you might think. Short ones are better. Limit of 50 characters per clue (including spaces between words).

We will send you back a blank puzzle, a list of clues, and or course, the solution. Then just paste it into your next newsletter or mailer. Or pass it around at your next reunion.

> **All this for only $19.95. Allow 4 weeks for delivery.**
> **Add $10 for rush orders.**

Send your list of words (50 or as many as you can think of that pertain to your family), a clue for each word, and the check to:

Reunion Research, 3145 Geary Blvd. #14, San Francisco, CA 94118.

Make checks out to "Reunion Research."

IMPORTANT: Include your deadline and phone number.

Index

The Directory
of Reunion Sites

The Best
Places in the U.S.
to have a reunion

- Hotels

- Motels

- CVBs

- Resorts

- C of Cs

- Condos

- Cruises

Dear Reunion Planner:

This unique little booklet should be of great help in finding the right location for your next reunion. These places all have special offers for reunion planners. Call or write them to find out exactly what they are. And please mention that you saw their ad in *The Directory of Reunion Sites*.

Below is an explanation of the terms found in the ads:

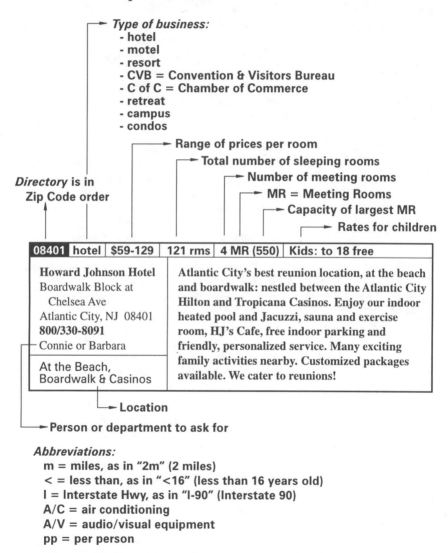

Type of business:
- hotel
- motel
- resort
- CVB = Convention & Visitors Bureau
- C of C = Chamber of Commerce
- retreat
- campus
- condos

Directory is in Zip Code order

→ Range of prices per room
→ Total number of sleeping rooms
→ Number of meeting rooms
→ MR = Meeting Rooms
→ Capacity of largest MR
→ Rates for children

| 08401 | hotel | $59-129 | 121 rms | 4 MR (550) | Kids: to 18 free |

Howard Johnson Hotel
Boardwalk Block at
　Chelsea Ave
Atlantic City, NJ 08401
800/330-8091
Connie or Barbara

At the Beach,
Boardwalk & Casinos

Atlantic City's best reunion location, at the beach and boardwalk: nestled between the Atlantic City Hilton and Tropicana Casinos. Enjoy our indoor heated pool and Jacuzzi, sauna and exercise room, HJ's Cafe, free indoor parking and friendly, personalized service. Many exciting family activities nearby. Customized packages available. We cater to reunions!

→ Location
→ Person or department to ask for

Abbreviations:
　m = miles, as in "2m" (2 miles)
　< = less than, as in "<16" (less than 16 years old)
　I = Interstate Hwy, as in "I-90" (Interstate 90)
　A/C = air conditioning
　A/V = audio/visual equipment
　pp = per person

Published annually by:
Reunion Research, 3145 Geary Blvd. #14, San Francisco, CA 94118.

| 04614 | cruises | $90-125 | 135 cabins | Free brochure package |

Maine Windjammer Association PO Box 1144P Blue Hill, ME 04614 **800/807-WIND** Sailing from Camden, Rockport & Rockland	From May to October, our 10 historic ships offer sailing adventures along the coast of Maine. Tradi- tional 6-day packages promise total relaxation, varied ports-of-call, and a beachside lobsterbake. Shorter cruises available. Vessels accommodate 20-40 guests, perfect for groups and family reunions. Let the fresh sea breeze, stars, snug harbors and delicious Downeast cooking whisk you away to a simpler world.

| 05155 | resort | $59-220 | 290 rms | 5 MR (300) | Kids: Special Deals |

Stratton Mountain Resort RR1, Box 145 Stratton Mountain, VT 05155 **800/250-4412** In the southern Green Mountains of Vermont	Vermont's premier 4-season resort, located on 4,000 acres. Skiing, 27-hole golf course, golf school, tennis school, sports center, Kids Kamp, gondola rides, adventure center. Village with shopping, restaurants. Meeting and banquet facilities. Special events year-round. Hotels and condominiums.

| 06905 | hotel | $69-159 | 445 rms | 28 MR (1000) | Kids: Free in parents rm |

Tara Stamford Hotel 2701 Summer St. Stamford, CT 06905 **203/359-1300** 1/2m to Downtown, 30m to NYC, 35m to NYC Airports	Five story full-service hotel with spacious guest rooms. Club level, with its own lounge and a variety of suites. 45 minutes from New York City by car or Metro-North commuter railroad. Easy accessibility to I-95 and the Merritt Parkway. Walking distance to a variety of shops, restaurants, movie theatres, and park. Restaurant and lounge in lobby. Free parking for 550 cars.

| 08401 | hotel | $59-129 | 121 rms | 4 MR (550) | Kids: to 18 free |

Howard Johnson Hotel Boardwalk Block at Chelsea Ave Atlantic City, NJ 08401 **800/330-8091** Connie or Barbara At the Beach, Boardwalk & Casinos	Atlantic City's best reunion location, at the beach and boardwalk: nestled between the Atlantic City Hilton and Tropicana Casinos. Enjoy our indoor heated pool and Jacuzzi, sauna and exercise room, HJ's Cafe, free indoor parking and friendly, personalized service. Many exciting family activities nearby. Customized packages available. We cater to reunions!

| 08540 | hotel | $89-159 | 348 rms | 12 MR (1000) | Kids: <17 free w/ adult |

Hyatt Regency Princeton 102 Carnegie Center Princeton, NJ 08540 **609/987-1234** 40m S. of Newark Airport 40m E. of Philadelphia	Full service hotel featuring a beautiful atrium, keyless security guest room entry, individual voicemail, complimentary in-room iron/ironing board, hair dryer, coffee maker, fully equipped health facility, outdoor tennis & basketball courts, indoor/outdoor pool. Free parking. Near historic Princeton Univ, Sesame Place, Great Adventure, shopping, golf & canoeing.

| 18360 | CVB | $60-125 | 10,000 rms | Free Reunion Planning Brochure |

Pocono Mountains CVB
1004 Main St
Stroudsburg, PA 18360
800/722-9199
Ask for Ellen

http://www.poconos.org
I-80, 2m W of E PA border

2400 acres of mountains, lakes and rivers. Fall foliage, golf & tennis resorts, skiing, family recreation packages. Enjoy white water rafting, NASCAR racing, hiking, biking and entertainment. Free site planning assistance & tours. 4 season resort destination at a convenient travel location for all compass points. Pennsylvania!—Memories last a lifetime.

| 12564 | resort | $70-82 | 85 rms | 10 MR (250) | Kids: see below |

Holiday Hills
   Conference Center
2 Lakeside Dr.
Pawling, NY 12564
914/855-1550

Kids: 2-5, 33% adult rate;
6-12, 50% adult rate

Nestled in the foothills of the Berkshires, 70 miles north of Manhattan is Holiday Hills, an extraordinary 500-acre year-round conference center. Accommodations for 175 people in comfortable rooms with private bath, excellent meeting facilities and scenic lakeside dining provide the perfect setting for your next conference or reunion.

| 23451 | hotel | $50-196 | 107 rms | 3 MR (100) | Kids: Free under 18 |

Dunes Motor Inn
921 Atlantic Ave
Virginia Beach, VA 23451
800/634-0709
888/566-5630
Sara Blackwelder

Totally renovated in 1997. 100% oceanfront hotel has 2 sundecks w/ spas, outdoor heated pool, gym, game room, on-site restaurant, free parking. Each rm contains 2 dble beds, microwave, fridge, coffeemaker. King rms available. Williamsburg/ Busch Gardens only 40 m; Internatnl airport 30 min. Golf, tennis & waterpark only minutes away.

| 24210 | CVB | $30-150 | 465 rms | Arts, History, and More! |

Abingdon CVB
335 Cummings St.
Abingdon, VA 24210
800/435-3440

Interstate 81,
   exit 17

Add history, culture, and romance to your reunion! Chartered in 1778, Abingdon is a Virginia Historic Landmark. Home to the Barter Theatre, State Theatre of Virginia; the William King Regional Arts Center; The Virginia Creeper National Recreation Trail; and much more! Unique and picturesque facilities for reunions. Call and let us help plan your next reunion!

| 24477 | resort | $60-125 | 37 rms | 1 MR (30) | Kids: 5 & under free |

Shenandoah Acres Resort
PO Box 300-FR
Stuarts Draft, VA 24477
800/654-1714
Cottage Office

12m from I-81 & I-64
   in Staunton, VA

300-acre family resort at the foot of the Blue Ridge Mtns. Sand-bottom swimming lake, game room, horseback riding, mini-golf, tennis, bike rentals, hiking, ball fields. Outdoor BBQ area w/ pavilion. All rooms A/C, many w/ kitchen & fireplace. Campground & camp cabins. Open all year. Skiing, antiques, historical sites, caverns. Blue Ridge Parkway & Skyline Drive nearby.

24540 | hotel | $48-90 | 152 rms | 8 MR (150) | Kids: <18 free in parent's rm

Stratford Inn
2500 Riverside Dr
Danville, VA 24540
800/DANVILLE
804/793-2500
Lynn Ross

S Central VA
near NC border

Tastefully decorated rooms and suites. Beautiful outdoor pool and spa. Famous restaurant w/ AAA three diamond rating. Exquisite catering in our Ballroom or off-premises. In the heart of Danville, VA, one hour from Triad International Airport, NC, and Raleigh/Durham Airport, NC. At the intersection of Rt. 29 & 58. Convenient to many points of interest.

26003 | resort | $69-145 | 212 rms | 15 MR (350) | Kids: 0-3 free; 4-12 half

Oglebay Resort
Rt. 88 North
Wheeling, WV 26003
800/972-1991
Mindy L. Matheny

4m to downtown,
62m to airport

Unique 1700-acre year-round resort with excellent accommodations and recreational activities. Oglebay is the largest tourist attraction in West Virginia and has been the site of numerous reunions! Choose from 212 guest rooms or one of 48 cottages. On Property: fishing, swimming, 4 golf courses, pedal boating, 7 retail shops, 2 museums, 30-acre zoo, Waddington Gardens and much more!

27835 | CVB | Gateway to Eastern North Carolina

Greenville-Pitt Co. CVB
525 S. Evans St
Greenville, NC 27835
800/537-5564
Contact: Andrew Schmidt

Coastal NC

The Greenville-Pitt County Convention and Visitors Bureau offers a variety of complimentary services designed to make the reunion planner's job easier. Services include accommodation arrangements, meeting and banquet space arrangements, attendance promotion, tour and events coordination, registration assistance and printed name badges.

29502 | CVB | $39 up | Free Florence Visitor's Guide

Florence CVB
PO Box 3093
Florence, SC 29502
800/325-9005

Located at the I-95 & I-20 interchange, halfway between New York and Miami. Historic sites, museums, mini-tours available, shopping, golf, softball, hockey, bowling and tennis. Civic Center with first class meeting facilities.
FLORENCE, SOUTH CAROLINA, IS YOUR REUNION DESTINATION!

30303 | hotel | $89-129 | 1068 rms | 39 MR (2100) | Kids: to 18 free

The Westin Peachtree Plaza
210 Peachtree St NW
Atlanta, GA 30303
404/589-7737
Craig Hendrick

12m to airport
30m to Stone Mtn.

Landmark hotel in heart of downtown w/ spectacular city views. Tallest hotel in Western Hemisphere. Rooftop revolving restaurant, bar and view. 1 block from Hard Rock Cafe, Planet Hollywood, MARTA Station. 5 blocks to Underground Atlanta, World of Coca-Cola Museum, Centennial Olympic Park, Georgia Dome, CNN. Easy drive to Stone Mtn, M.L. King Memorial, Six Flags, Turner Stadium.

30303	hotel	$59-99	238 rms	2 MR (125)	Kids: 12 & under stay free

Super 8 Hotel & Conference Center 111 Cone St. Atlanta, GA 30303 Toll Free: 888/524-2400	238 deluxe single and double rooms, 4500 sq. ft. of meeting/banquet space including a ballroom on the top level of the property. Walking distance to tourist attractions, dining, shopping, entertainment, including Hard Rock Cafe and All Star Cafe. Parking available.

32055	motel	$30-45	100 rms	1 MR (35)	Kids: under 18 free

Knights Inn Rt 13, Box 201 US 90 & I-75 Lake City, FL 32055 904/752-7720	Free golf green fees, 27 hole course. Free local calls. Free cable TV including HBO. Pool and shuffle board. Picnic area and barbeque grill. Large parking area for RVs, motor homes and big trucks. Free continental breakfast.
170m to Orlando	

32118	hotel	241 rms	6 MR (450)	Kids: to 18 free w/ parents

Treasure Island Inn 2025 S. Atlantic Ave Daytona Beach, FL 32118 800/543-5070 Belinda Damm www.daytonahotels.com	Eleven story beachfront hotel. 241 rooms and hospitality suites, many w/ kitchens. Oceanfront meeting rooms. Large pool deck. 2 swimming pools, 2 whirlpools, multi-tiered sun deck. Free Family Recreation Program. 2 restaurants, lounge, gift shop, game room. Coupon book worth $1000 at local businesses. Free parking. Special reunion recreation/theme parties available.
Direct oceanfront	

32301	CVB	$30-150	Attractions for the whole family.

Tallahassee Area CVB 200 W. College Ave Tallahassee, FL 32301 800/628-2866 Ask for Convention Sales	Tallahassee is Florida's "Capital" city. Shaping Tallahassee's character are antebellum homes, historic churches, enchanting gardens, nature trails, historic museums, petting zoos and nearby beaches. Often described as "the other Florida," Tallahassee is truly a Florida to explore. Contact our Convention Sales department for details on services offered and upcoming special events.
www.co.leon.fl.us/ visitors/index	

32407	resort	1054 rms	Kids: Under 12 stay and play free

Paradise Found Resorts & Hotels 11127 Front Beach Rd. Panama City, FL 32407 800/807-2232	Full-service resorts and hotels to fill any need. All beach properties are oceanfront. Reunion Specialists on-site. Banquet facilities and 5,500 square feet of meeting space. Located on "The World's Most Beautiful Beaches" in Panama City Beach, Florida. Enjoy hospitality "Southern Style." *See display ad.*

| 33040 | hotel | $79-149 | 222 rms | 3 MR (570) | Kids: <16 free |

Holiday Inn
3841 N. Roosevelt Blvd
Key West, FL 33040
800/292-7706
Ask for Sales Dept.

Affordable luxury hotel, located at the "gateway" of Key West Florida. 222 newly refurbished, tropically appointed rooms overlooking lush gardens or the Gulf of Mexico. 3 miles from downtown shopping district. On-site beach, water sports shop, and tennis. 6212 sq. ft. of flexible reunion space (small to large). One mile to airport and golf course. Our staff is dedicated to making your reunion a great success.

| 33312 | hotel | $35-69 | 300 rms | 5 MR (250) | Kids: To 12 free; 13+ adult |

Ramada Inn
2275 State Road 84
Ft. Lauderdale, FL 33312
800/447-7901 ext 500
Ask for Sales Dept.

3m to airport &
beaches

The friendliest place for reunions! In the center of all South Florida attractions. 300 spacious air conditioned rooms with cable TV, FREE Showtime, FREE tennis on two courts, two heated pools, volleyball, golf available, 3000 sq. ft. banquet facilities, restaurant, lounge, game room. Minutes from beaches, Las Olas Blvd, great shopping and all pro sports. FREE airport shuttle, FREE parking.

| 35203 | hotel | $75-95 | 147 units | 7 MR (200) | Kids: <17 free w/ parents |

The Tutwiler Hotel
2021 Park Place N.
Birmingham, AL 35203
205/322-2100 ext 1227
Victoria Cabines

4m to airport

Birmingham's historic Four-Star, Four-Diamond hotel centrally located downtown across from Lynn Park. Nearby attractions include Birmingham Museum of Art, Civil Rights Institute, Alabama Sports Hall of Fame, VisionLand, McWane Center & much more. Restaurant on-site, free airport transportation, roll-aways $15 each. The perfect spot for a special, unique reunion.

| 37395 | resort | $34-95 | 52 cottages | 2 MR (75) |

Watts Bar Resort
6767 Watts Bar Hwy.
Watts Bar Dam, TN 37395
800/365-9598

16m W of I-75, btw.
Knox. & Chatt.

Family oriented, with clean, comfortable cottages. A/C, heat, TV, linens, many w/ kitchens, on scenic Watts Bar Lake. Full-service restaurant, children's menu. Swimming & wading pools, hiking trails, tennis courts, shuffleboard, playground. Gift shop. Guest & transient dockage w/ power. Tackle shop w/ live bait, licenses, fishing boat, pontoon & canoe rentals. *www.wattsbarresort.com*

| 38551 | resort | $36 up | Kids: under 5 free |

Cedar Hill Resort
2371 Cedar Hill Rd
Celina, TN 38551
800/872-8393
931/243-3201

N Central TN

On beautiful Dale Hollow Lake with 620 miles of shoreline to explore. This complete resort in the Cumberland Mtns, offers 31 cottages, 6 motel rooms, 20 houseboats, a swimming pool, a restaurant and marina. Houseboats hold maximum of 12. Excellent fishing, scuba diving and water skiing. Calm waters, no mosquitos, average 82° summer water temperature. Send for 4-color brochure.

40004	CVB	500 rms	Planning assistance available.

Bardstown-Nelson Co. Tourist & Convention Commission 107 E. Stephen Foster Bardstown, KY 40004 **800/638-4877**	Bardstown...where family, heritage and tradition abound. One of America's top 100 towns offers a variety of unique reunion sites, family attractions and southern hospitality. Visit My Old Kentucky Home, Kentucky Railway Museum, and Stephen Foster The Musical or dine on an elegant Dinner Train, tour world famous distilleries and enjoy unique shopping.
35m S. of Louisville	

40004	hotel	$55-69	102 rms	5 MR (300)	Kids: <19 free w/ parents

Holiday Inn Hwy 31E & Bluegrass Pkwy PO Box 520 Bardstown, KY 40004 **502/348-9253** Ask for "Sales"	Our 102 room hotel features affordable accommodations, award winning service, banquet rooms, fitness facility, beautiful outdoor pool & playground, par-3 9-hole golf course, driving range, and miniature golf. Historic Bardstown, one of America's top 100 small towns, is located in central Kentucky and is within 1 hour's drive of many popular family attractions. Packages available.
35m S. of Louisville	

44446	CVB	$45-120	Free planning guide available.

Trumbull County CVB 650 Youngstwn-Warren Rd Niles, OH 44446 **800/672-9555** Contact Jim Mahon	Nestled in the heart of the Old Connecticut Western Reserve, Trumbull County offers a variety of reunion destinations: golf resort, bed/breakfast inns, and major chain properties. Visit Ohio's 2nd largest Amish community, National McKinley Presidential Memorial, basket factory, twenty-three golf courses, and so much more. Call TODAY!!
1/2 way btw Cleveland & Pittsburgh	

44446	hotel	$45-90	100 rms	1 MR (200)	Kids: to 16 free

Park Inn International 1225 Youngstwn-Warren Rd Niles, OH 44446 **330/652-1761** 330/652-8287 Fax	On the Strip—full of activities! Centrally located to serve Warren-Niles-Youngstown. Kitchenettes available. Complimentary continental breakfast. Outdoor pool. Surrounded by attractions, dining & shopping. A/V equip. for rent. RV parking. Children's activities nearby. 180 holes of golf within 15 miles. Rollaways $7 extra. 45 min. to Sea World & Geauga Lake.
10m N of Youngstown, 5m to I-80	

46360	CVB	$35-120	1200 rms	Free Reunion Planner

LaPorte Co. CVB 1503 S. Meer Rd Michigan City, IN 46360 **800/634-2650** Contact Linda Jones	The perfect location to meet in the Midwest! We're on the southern shore of Lake Michigan along the Indiana Dunes National Lakeshore. Charter fishing, riverboat casino, 135-store upscale outlet mall, historic driving tour, and a variety of museums featuring military history, vintage automobiles, and old lighthouses. Let us help you plan your next reunion.
1 hr E of Chicago on I-94 & I-80/90	

| 60173 | CVB | $60s-80s | 10,000 rms | Chicago's Northwest Suburbs |

Greater Woodfield CVB
1375 E Woodfield Rd
Suite 100
Schaumburg, IL 60173
800/847-4849
Ask for reunion specialist

35m NW of Chicago
10m to O'Hare Airport

Ideal suburban location—host to hundreds of veterans and family reunions annually. 45 hotels from first class to economy to resorts. Rates discounted on many weekends and holidays. Superb shopping at outlet malls and Woodfield Shopping Center—one of the world's largest. Hundreds of nearby attractions, Medieval Times, riverboat gaming, museums galore and more!

| 60532 | CVB | $59-99 | Chicago's Affordable Alternative |

Lisle Illinois CVB
4746 Main St.
Lisle, IL 60532
800/733-9811

Lisle is conveniently located equidistant between downtown Chicago, O'Hare and Midway Airports. At the intersection of I-88, I-355, and I-294, we are in the heart of Chicagoland. Four first class hotels with excellent rates. A wide variety of restaurants and attractions.

| 61036 | CVB | Let us do the ground work for you. |

Galena/Jo Daviess Co.
Conv. & Visitors Bureau
720 Park Avenue
Galena, IL 61036
88-GALENA-2
815/777-3557
Susan Michnevitz

NW corner of IL

Head for our hills! Unique blend of history, family fun, scenery, shopping. Camping, RV hookups, B&Bs, hotels, motels, resorts. Golf (miniature too), water park, museums, alpine slide, parks w/ BBQ grills & pavilions, historical sites. Call for free Visitor's Guide & group package details. Let us help arrange your best reunion yet!!!

| 61085 | resort | $custom pkgs. | 2 MR (150) | Near historic Galena |

Maple Lane
Country Resort
3114 S. Rush Creek Rd.
Stockton, IL 61085
815/947-3773
Rose V. Stout

NW corner of IL,
Jo Daviess County

Unique scenic country farmland estate. Pool, gazebo, picnic tables, games. Nearby golf, skiing, state parks, antiques, gambling, historic sites, shopping, restaurants. Tour working farm, cheese factory, petting zoo, herb farm, chocolate factory. Horseback riding, hayrides, family fun nights, craft classes, Kookie Camp, murder mystery dinners. Sleeping capacity 50, plus tents/campers. Homecooked meals. Open all year.

| 61101 | CVB | $49-110 | 3000 rms | Free reunion planning kit |

Rockford Area CVB
211 N. Main St.
Rockford, IL 61101
800/521-0849
Ask for Vickie Fogel

60 min W of O'Hare

Illinois' second largest city, on I-90 & I-39 in north central Illinois. A friendly, hassle-free destination with affordable prices that won't blow you away! World-class attractions, too: Anderson Japanese Gardens, Magic Waters, Time Mueseum, Aldeen Golf Course ....plus 7,000 acres of parks and forest preserves. Free parking. O'Hare shuttles.
See display ad.

62220	motel	$29-59	145 rms	3 MR (70)	Kids: to 12 free

Executive Inn
1234 Centreville Ave
Belleville, IL 62220
888/845-1234
Sandy Preston

Southeast corner of
158 & 15

All A/C. Indoor-outdoor pools, full fitness center, picnic areas, lounge & restaurant, guest laundromat, free meeting room & one complimentary room with 10 rooms paid. Roll-away = $5. Next door to convention center. Belleville historic area, apple & strawberry orchards, Lady of Snow Shrine. Cable TV. HBO.
15 miles to St. Louis Arch and Downtown.

64801	CVB	$30-80	1700 rms	Free meeting planner's guide

Joplin CVB
222 W. 3rd St.
Joplin, MO 64801
800/657-2534
Ask for Teresa Gilliam

I-44 & Hwy. 71

Centrally located; Joplin offers an array of indoor and outdoor activities, suitable for all ages. Groups can gather in one of 19 City Parks. Enjoy a round of golf, canoe and fish the streams, walk the trails, shop for antiques, or walk the mall. Visit the Precious Moments Chapel, George Washington Carver's National Monument, Lowell Davis' Red Oak II.

65615	hotels	Branson Missouri Wholesale Reunion Packages

**Branson America's
Showplace**
PO Box 2290
Branson, MO 65615
800-627-4596
Ask for Reunion Sales

Edgewood Receptive Service has been serving the Ozarks for over 25 years, offering negotiated wholesale reunion packages. Our friendly and professional staff can accommodate all your reunion needs. Accommodations only, meals only, ticketing only. Complete customized packages and motorcoach transportation.

65616	hotel	$49-79	210 rms	5 MR (150)	Kids: to 13 free

Branson Towers Hotel
236 Shephard of the
Hills Expressway
Branson, MO 65616
800/683-1122
John Johnson

35m to Airport,
Near all attractions

Full catering and meeting space available at reasonable costs. Oversized rooms w/ 2 queen beds. Indoor pool and spa, complimentary continental breakfast & coffee 24-hrs per day. Whippersnapper Restaurant on property. Gift shop, game room, guest laundry. Reunions get great rates and suite upgrades. Nightly ice cream social in the Grand Piano Lobby.

67202	hotel	$49-69	262 rms	11 MR (1200)	Kids: to 18 free

**The Broadview
A Grand Heritage Hotel**
400 W. Douglas
Wichita, KS 67202
800/362-2929
Heather Hartman

Historic hotel built in 1922. Features 262 sleeping rooms and 25,000 sq. ft. of meeting space. Centrally located downtown. Within walking distance of museums, shopping, baseball stadium, ice skating, and river walks along the Arkansas River. Dog track, aviation museum and zoo close by. Complimentary airport shuttle. Call for more information.

75234	hotel	$59-89	380 rms	10 MR (500)	Kids: to 18 free w/ parents

Holiday Inn Select
2645 LBJ Fwy.
Dallas, TX 75234
972/243-3363
Teddi Davis

9m to DFW Airport
5-30m to all major attractions

Full-service hotel. Indoor/outdoor heated pool. Terrific location for families. Convenient to Galleria, Texas Stadium, Six Flags, Sandy Lake, West End, Downtown, and other area attractions. Free Health Club, parking, and cable TV. Restaurant and Pizza Hut. Children under 12 eat free with parents. Full conference and banquet facilities. Call or write for our free Reunion Planning Guide.

77024	hotel	$49-99	173 rms	5 MR (150)	Kids: Free

Radisson Suite Hotel
10655 Katy Fwy.
Houston, TX 77024
713/461-6000

Next to
Town & Country Mall

Deluxe 2-room suites sleep up to six. Rooms include full American breakfast buffet, refrigerator and bottled water, microwave and popcorn, coffeemaker, hairdryer and 2 TVs. Exercise room and outdoor pool. Nightly hors d'oeuvres in Lobby Lounge with live music. Convenient access to major attractions, dining and shopping. Hospitality suites. Specially designed reunion packages available.

77056	hotel	$ seasonal	449 rms	29 MR (360)

Doubletree Hotel
2001 Post Oak Blvd
Houston, TX 77056
800/222-8733
713/961-9300
Sales Department

Post Oak-Galleria area

Affordable accommodations for the perfect reunion. 24-hour room service, iron, ironing board, hairdryers and coffee makers in all rooms. Outdoor pool, sauna, exercise room and seasonal pool bar. Attractions include Galleria shopping, Astro World, Water World, LB Johnson Space Center and Museum of Fine Arts.

77090	hotel	$49-129	250 rms	4 MR (75)	Kids: <16 free

Lexington Hotel
16410 N. Fwy. 45
Houston, TX 77090
281/821-1000

Affordable all-suite property featuring spacious studios, one- and two-bedroom suites. Located two miles from IAH Airport, the Lexington Suites also has a heated swimming pool, complimentary breakfast, and easy access to every major freeway. Area attractions include fine cuisine, night life, shopping, Splashtown USA, and Sam Houston Raceway Park.

78216	hotels	$49-119	9 locations/meeting facilities available

The Drury Hotels
of San Antonio
91 NE Loop 410
San Antonio, TX 78216
210/341-0774
210/341-8244 fax
Ask for Irene Lodge

Locations are in "Central" San Antonio. All hotels offer free continental breakfast, free local calls, free airport shuttle (airport locations only), outdoor swimming pools, free cable TV with one premium movie channel. Suites and auto rentals available at most locations. 100% satisfaction guaranteed. Children under 18 stay free in parents' room. Close proximity to fine restaurants and shopping malls.

78627 | CVB | $40-80 | 295 rms | Free Reunion Planner

Georgetown CVB PO Box 409 Georgetown, TX 78627 **800/436-8696** www.georgetown.org juliemus@gte.net 25m N of Austin	Halfway between Dallas and San Antonio on Interstate 35, Georgetown is the gateway to the Hill Country. Our charming community is a relaxing getaway for the whole family. Families can enjoy a picnic under old Cyprus trees in San Gabriel Park or a catered meal at one of our meeting facilities. Ask about free games to rent for all ages.

79761 | CVB | $30-85 | 1900 rms | Reunion information available

Odessa CVB 700 N. Grant #200 Odessa, TX 79761 **800/780-HOST** 915/333-7871 Between El Paso & Ft. Worth on I-20	Odessa, Texas. A city of contrasts! Professional hockey, Water Wonderland, great shopping, entertainment, and one-of-a-kind museums such as the Confederate Air Force Museum and the Presidential Museum. Major hotel chains with ample convention space. Easily accessible via Midland International Airport. Serviced by Interstate 20 and Highway 385. RV hookups available for any size group.

80424 | resort | $90-250 | Hotel rooms, condominiums, & townhouses

The Village at
   Breckenridge,
   A Wyndam Resort
PO Box 8329
Breckenridge, CO 80424
800/332-0424 Call Jim Born
 	
75m W of Denver
	The best location in Breckenridge, on Main Street adjacent to the mountains. Activities for both young and old include: horseback riding, golf, biking, hiking, fishing, jeep tours to ghost towns, historic train rides, gold panning, alpine slides, campfire cook-outs and more. Film, art and music festivals occur throughout the summer months. Never a dull moment!

80446 | resort | $59-149 | 342 rms | 16 MR (300) | Kids: 17 & under free

Inn at Silver Creek PO Box 4222 Silver Creek, CO 80446 **800/926-4386** (press 2) Ask for Charles 90 min NW of Denver on Hwy 40	Under one roof, our hotel offers a variety of affordable family accommodations featuring kitchenettes, fireplaces, patios, newly remodeled athletic club w/ heated outdoor pool, sundeck, 4 hot tubs, sauna, weight room, tennis courts, restaurant and bar, giftshop. Centrally located between Rocky Mountain National Park and Winter Park Resort. Lots of activities!! Call Today!

80482 | condos | $70-400 | 115 units | 2 MR (50) | The Perfect Location

Beaver Village Condos PO Box 349 50 Village Dr Winter Park, CO 80482 **800/824-8438** Ask for Group Dept. 3 blks frm Downtown Winter Park	Home away from home in a secluded forest property. Deluxe 1, 2, and 3 bedroom condominiums with fully equipped kitchens and fireplaces. Clubhouse with heated indoor pool, sauna, 3 hot tubs, and meeting room with catering kitchen. Only 1.5 miles to Winter Park Resort for summer and winter fun.

80482	resort	$69-559	130 rms	5 MR (150)	Kids: free in unit w/ adults

Iron Horse Resort PO Box 1286 Winter Park, CO 80482 **800/621-8190** Group Sales	Winter Park's only ski-in/ski-out resort & conference center. Iron Horse features condominium accommodations w/ full hotel services. Fully equipped units from studios to 2 bdrm 3 bath suites. Restaurant & lounge, outdoor swimming pool, 4 hot tubs, exercise rm, secluded group picnic area, free local shuttle. A luxury resort at affordable prices. Special seasonal group value packages.
Winter Park's premier resort & conf. center	

80482	condos	290 rms	1 MR (55)	Kids: Free w/ paying adult

Winter Park Adventures PO Box 66 Winter Park, CO 80482 **800/832-7830**	Reunion specialists offering 30 properties, varied amenities and price ranges. Summer activities include Rocky Mountain National Park, golfing, mountain biking, river rafting, horseback riding, fishing, hiking, alpine slide, rodeos, boating and more. Winters offer world class downhill skiing, snowmobiling, ice skating, sleigh rides. Call for package details.
70m NW of Denver	

80903	CVB	$25-300	9700 rms	Free Visitor Guide

Colorado Springs CVB 104 S. Cascade Ave #104 Colorado Springs, CO 80903 **800/888-4748 Ext 138**	Located at the foot of famous Pikes Peak, Colorado Springs offers magnificent mountain scenery and a delightful, seasonal climate. Excellent accommodations are available for every taste and budget. Unique, exciting attractions and recreational opportunities offer every visitor an unforgettable adventure....from the Garden of the Gods and Air Force Academy to gaming in Cripple Creek.
See our display ad.	

87110	hotel	$59-99	173 rms	4 MR (225)	Kids: To 17 free

Best Western Winrock Inn 18 Winrock Center NE Albuquerque, NM 87110 **800/866-5252** Julie Hasty	Located in Uptown Entertainment District. Hotel w/ beautiful lagoon w/ ducks & fish. Adjacent to mall, movie theaters, & many restaurants. Free full hot breakfast buffet included in rate. Outdoor heated pool. Banquet rms w/ catering. Lots of attractions nearby: fairgrounds, Atomic Museum, Sandia Tramway, golf courses, Old Town, zoo, aquarium. Free parking. 1 comp guest room per 15 paid.
8m fm airport on I-40	

87710	C of C	Free 4-color visitors guide.

Angel Fire Chamber of Commerce PO Box 547 Angel Fire, NM 87710 **800/446-8117**	A premier family ski and golf resort area high in the Sangre de Cristo mountains of northern New Mexico. Hotels, condos, houses for rent. Meeting rooms, picnic areas, catered parties. Mountain biking, horseback riding, hiking, fishing & golf. In winter: skiing, snowmobiling, sleigh rides and more. www.angelfirenm.com E-mail: chambr@angelfirenm.com
25m E of Taos, NM, on Hwy 434	

90602	hotel	$69-89	202 rms	8 MR (350)	Kids: to 18 free w/ parents

Whittier Hilton
7320 Greenleaf Ave
Whittier, CA 90206
562/945-8511
Tatiana Paton

Off I-605, between I-10 and I-5

Centrally located between all major Los Angeles airports and freeways, the AAA, 3 Diamond rated Whittier Hilton provides an ideal hub for business and leisure travelers visiting Los Angeles and Orange Counties. 150 unique shops, restaurants and theaters. Pool, spa and fitness center. 30 minutes from Disneyland and Knotts Berry Farm. 30 minutes from downtown Los Angeles.

92101	hotel	$89-150	280 rms	23 MR (950)	Kids: to 12 free

U.S. Grant Hotel
326 Broadway
San Diego, CA 92101
800/237-5029
Ask for Group Sales

Located in Downtown San Diego

Historic hotel across frm Horton Plaza (outdoor mall w/ 135+ stores). Walking distance to GasLamp Quarters w/ 75+ restaurants, Seaport Village, San Diego Bay & Children's Museum. Minutes to world famous Zoo and SeaWorld. Complimentary hospitality suite & airport transp. 2 restaurants, Bruegger's Bagels & Chandler's Gift Shop. Recipient of Mobil Four Star & AAA Four Diamond awards.

92106	hotel	$72-115	237 rms	3 MR (160)	Kids: <19 free w/ adult

Holiday Inn San Diego Bayside
4875 N. Harbor Dr.
San Diego, CA 92106
800/662-8899
Ask for Sales Dept.

See our display ad.

Beautiful bayside location offering renovated and spacious guest rooms w/ refrigerators, coffee, hair-dryers, pay-per-view movies and free HBO. Amenities include a large heated pool and spa, tropical courtyard w/ billiards and ping-pong, a 9-hole putting course and exercise room. Reunions receive a complimentary hospitality suite. Water-view banquet rms & poolside courtyard are available. Free parking.

92614	hotel	$96-112	293 rms	5 MR (150)	Kids: 12 & under free

Embassy Suites Hotel
2120 Main St
Irvine, CA 92614
714/553-8332
Melissa Gordon

1/2m to 405/55
1/2m to Airport

All-suite hotel. Private bedrooms. Complimentary full cooked-to-order breakfast. Complimentary beverages for 2 hours nightly. Refrigerator, 2 TVs, free cable/movie channel, coffee maker, hair dryer, ironing board/iron. Indoor pool, whirlpool, sauna/fitness center. Meeting space capacity to 150. Restaurant/catering.

93463	resort	$335/415	73 rms	6 MR (150)	Kids: <2 free; 3-5 $40; 6+ $65

The Alisal Guest Ranch and Resort
1054 Alisal Rd
Solvang, CA 93463
800/425-4725, Ext 264
Dianne Calderon, DOS

40m N of Santa Barbara, 35m to S.B. Airport

Resort-bungalows with wood burning fireplaces. Modified American Plan includes breakfast/dinner. Activities available: golf (2, 18-hole championship courses), tennis, horseback riding, fishing and boating on private lake, children's programs. Round-up Vacation Package (RUV) includes all activities for 2 during certain times of the year. *E-mail:* sales@alisal.com *Internet:* www.alisal.com

95112 | hotel | $89-229 | 515 units | 14 MR (600) | Kids: Under 18 free

Hyatt San Jose
1740 N. First St.
San Jose, CA 95112
408/793-3976
Michael Robasciotti

1m from San Jose Airport

A full-service hotel on 18 acres in the heart of Silicon Valley. Lush landscaped gardens w/ gazebos, ponds, outdoor swimming pool w/ Jacuzzi. Just 1 mile from San Jose International Airport. 21,000 sq. ft. of banquet space. An ideal environment for your next family or class reunion. Newly renovated guestrooms. Complete amenity package includes computer, fax, printer, and Net accessibility. Groups to 1000. Free parking.

95354 | CVB | $35-120 | 1500 rms | Come visit Castle Air Museum

Modesto Convention & Visitors Bureau
1114 "J" St
Modesto, CA 95354
800/266-4282
Phyllis Rabusin

Central Valley of Calif.

Have the best of ALL worlds! Meet in a warm & welcoming city in the center of California! Enjoy attractions from Hershey's Chocolate to Yosemite Nat'l. Park and San Francisco. Pan for gold in the nearby Gold Country, tour the St. Stan's Brewery and Delicato Vineyards. Visit nearby Castle Air Museum. Free reunion services. Great hotel packages!

95451 | resort | $25-150 | 8 cabins | 1 MR (75) | Kids: under 5 free

Edgewater Resort
6420 Soda Bay Rd
Kelseyville, CA 95451
800/396-6224
Sandra West

2.5 hr N of San Francisco
2 hr W of Sacramento

Guaranteed the best full-service campground on the 100-mile shoreline of Clear Lake. 8 cabins, 61 RV/camping sites. Group BBQ patio, commercial kitchen & clubhouse. Pool, beach, pier, dock, boat launch/rentals, laundry, pets OK. Activities: lawn or pool volleyball, horseshoes, ping-pong, game-room, unlimited watersports & fishing. Nearby golf and hiking. Ask about Reunion Specials.

96740 | resort | $68-100 | 530 rms | 12 MR (1200) | Kids: <18 free

Kona Surf Resort and Country Club
78-128 Ehukai St
Kailua-Kona, HI 96740
800/932-9466
www.ilhawaii.net/konasurf
Ask for "Sales"

16m to Airport

530 rm oceanfront hotel, considered one of the best-valued resorts on the Big Island. Next to Keauhou Bay, near Kailua-Kona. Salt water & fresh water swimming pools, 36-hole golf course, tennis, volleyball, shuffleboard, free Polynesian shows. Rooms are large, have magnificent views, free coffee & refrigerators. In Honolulu, see sister property, Hawaiian Waikiki Beach Hotel.

97528 | CVB | $35-125 | Group Rates—Great Fun—Good Company

Grants Pass V&CB
PO Box 1787
Grants Pass, OR 97528
541/476-5510
Convention Sales

SW Oregon

1200 rooms to choose from. We maintain a close relationship with local lodging, restaurants, and attractions. Located in the middle of an outdoor recreation "mecca" with tons of activities for every member of your group. Grants Pass, Oregon, is "Where the Rogue River runs."

Other Hotels and Agencies that Offer Reunion Accommodations.

Listed in Zip Code order.

Best Western Black Swan Inn, Route 20, Lee, MA 01238, **800/876-7926**

Radisson Hotel, 11 Beaver St, Milford, MA 01757, **508/478-7010**

Hilton at Dedham Place, 25 Allied Dr, Dedham, MA 02026, **617/329-7900**

Heritage Inn Conference Resort, Heritage Rd, Southbury, CT 06488

Town House Motel, 351 Franklin St, Hightstown, NJ 08520, **800/922-0622, x405**

Ramada Inn, 195 Route 18 South, E. Brunswick, NJ 08816, **908/828-6900**

Hofstra University, 111 Student Center, Hempstead, NY 11550, **516/463-5067**

Gavin's Golden Hill Resort, PO Box 6, E Durham, NY 12423, **800/272-4591**

Watson Homestead Retreat, 9620 Dry Run Rd, Painted Post, NY 14870, **800/962-8040**

Lehigh Valley CVB, 2200 Avenue A, Bethlehem, PA 18017, **800/747-0561**

Pocono Mountains CVB, 1004 Main St, Stroudsburg, PA 18360, **800/722-9199**

Wyndam Bristol Hotel, 2430 Pennsylvania Ave NW, Wash DC 20037, **202/955-6400**

Hyatt Dulles, 2300 Dulles Corner Blvd, Herndon, VA 22071, **703/713-1234**

Quality Inn/Shenandoah Valley, PO Box 100, New Market, VA 22844, **540/740-3141**

Atlanta's DeKalb CVB, 750 Commerce Dr #200, Decatur, GA 30030, **800/999-6055, x7581**

Days Inn, 60 S. Beachview Dr, Jekyll Island, GA 31527, **888/635-3003**

Marina Hotel & Conf. Center, 530 N Palmetto Ave, Sanford, FL 32771, **800/290-1910**

The Ritz Plaza, 1701 Collins Ave, Miami Beach, FL 33139, **305/534-3500**

The Shore Club, 1901 Collins Ave, Miami Beach, FL 33139, **800/327-8330**

Ramada Resort, 6701 Collins Ave, Miami Beach, FL 33141, **305/865-8511**

Embassy Suites, 3974 NW South River Dr, Miami, FL 33142, **800/772-3787, x370**

Marriott Hotel, 6650 N. Andrews Ave, Ft. Lauderdale, FL 33309, **954/771-0440, x6621**

Embassy Suites, 1100 SE 17th St, Ft Lauderdale, FL 33316, **800/854-6146**

Holiday Inn, 6600 S. Tamiami Trl., Sarasota, FL 34231, **941/924-4900**

Hampton Inn, 5995 Cattleridge Rd, Sarasota, FL 34232, **941/371-1900**

Fountain Park Resort Hotel, 5150 West U.S. 192, Kissimmee, FL 34746, **800/672-9601**

The Ohio State Park Resorts, Rt 2, PO Box 7, Cambridge, OH 43725, **800/990-9020**

Holiday Inn Lakeside, 1111 Lakeside Ave, Cleveland, OH 44114, **216/241-5100**

Oak Cove Resort, 58881 46th St, Lawrence, MI 49064, **616/674-8228**

Hotel Fort Des Moines, 1000 Walnut, Des Moines, IA 50309, **800/532-1466**

Racine Marriott Hotel, 7111 Washington Ave, Racine, WI 53406, **414/886-6100**

Nelson's Resort, 7632 Nelson Rd, Crane Lake, MN 55725, **800/433-0743**

Hotel Alex Johnson, 523 6th St, Rapid City, SD 57701, **800/888-ALEX (2539)**

Days Inn O'Hare S., 3801 N Mannheim Rd, Schiller Park, IL 60176, **847/678-0670**

Hampton Inn, 1087 E. Diehl Rd, Naperville, IL 60563, **630/505-1400, 630/505-1416**

Executive Inn, 1234 Centreville Ave, Belleville, IL 62220, **888/845-1234**

Mt. Vernon CVB, 200 Potomac Blvd, Mt. Vernon, IL 62864, **800/252-5464**

Van Buren C of C, PO Box 356, Van Buren, MO 63965, **800/692-7582**

Thousand Hills Golf Resort, 245 S. Wildwood Dr, Branson, MO 65616, **800/697-9472**

Best Western Inn of the Ozarks, PO Box 431, Eureka Springs, AR 72632, **800/552-3785**

Marriott Hotel, 3233 Northwest Expwy, Oklahoma City, OK 73112, **405/879-7014**

La Grange Area C of C, 171 S. Main, La Grange, TX 78945, **800/LAGRANG**

Wildwood Suites, PO Box 565, 120 Sawmill Rd, Breckenridge, CO 80424, **800/866-0300**

B/W Le Baron Hotel, 314 W Bijou St, Colo. Springs, CO 80905, **800/477-8610, x448**

Hampton Inn, Gold Dust & Scottsdale Rd, Scottsdale, AZ 85253, **602/443-3233**

Ramada Plaza Hotel, 1600 South 52, Tempe, AZ 85281, **800/346-3049, 602/967-6600**

Best Western Executive Inn, 333 W Drachman, Tucson, AZ 85705, **800/255-3371**

Carlsbad C of C, PO Box 910, Carlsbad, NM 88221, **800/221-1224**

Quality Hotel, 5249 W Century Blvd, Los Angeles, CA 90045, **310/645-2200, x1321**

Carson Hilton Inn, 2 Civic Plaza Dr, Carson, CA 90745, **310/830-9200, x107**

La Quinta Resort and Club, 49-499 Eisenhower Dr, La Quinta, CA 92253, **800/598-3828**

Riverside CVB, 3443 Orange St, Riverside, CA 92501, **909/222-4700**

Radisson Miyako Hotel, 1625 Post St, San Francisco, CA 94115, **800/533-4557**

Cupertino Inn, 10889 N. DeAnza Blvd, Cupertino, CA 95014, **800/222-4828**

Bell Haven Resort, 3415 White Oak Way, Kelseyville, CA 95451, **707/279-4329**

Rocky Point Resort, 3894 Lakeshore Blvd, Lakeport, CA 95453, **707/263-4673**

Sandy Bar Ranch, PO Box 347, Ishi Pishi Rd, Orleans, CA 95556, **916/627-3379**

Inn by the Lake, 3300 Lake Tahoe Blvd, S. Lake Tahoe, CA 96150, **800/877-1466**

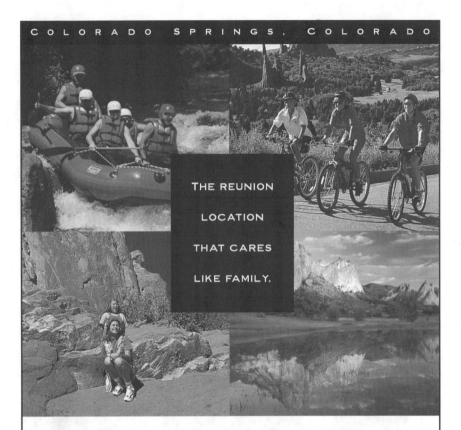